COMPLETE

PRELIMINARY
for Schools

Student's Book
without answers

GW00683617

B1

WITH ONLINE PRACTICE

Emma Heyderman and
Peter May

Cambridge University Press
www.cambridge.org/elt

Cambridge Assessment English
www.cambridgeenglish.org

Information on this title: www.cambridge.org/9781108539050

© Cambridge University Press and UCLES 2019

First published 2019

20 19 18 17 16 15 14 13 12 11 10 9 8 7 6 5 4 3 2 1

Printed in the United Kingdom by Latimer Trend

A catalogue record for this publication is available from the British Library

ISBN 978-1-108-53905-0 Student's Book without answers with Online Practice

Contents

Map of the units

Unit title	Reading	Writing	Listening
1 My life and home	**Part 5:** 'Sonia's home' – living on a boat Reading for understanding of vocabulary	**Part 1:** An email Planning a reply	**Part 2:** Listening for specific information Two candidates doing Speaking Part 1
2 At school	**Part 6:** 'On their way to school' – an unusual school journey in China Reading for detailed understanding of words and sentences	A post about what you used to do at primary school **Part 2:** An article on what makes a great school Using a mind map to plan an answer	Emily talking about her experiences as an exchange student **Part 1:** Seven short texts about daily life Two candidates doing Speaking Part 3
Vocabulary and grammar review Units 1 and 2			
3 Having fun	**Part 3:** 'Ariana's hobby – sand sculptures' Reading for detailed understanding	**Part 2:** A story about a day out Planning paragraphs	**Part 4:** Ryan Parilla – an Instagram photographer Talking about a skiing holiday Two candidates doing Speaking Part 2
4 On holiday	**Part 1:** Identifying text purpose	**Part 1:** An email Suggesting where to go in a city and what to do	Discussing a quiz **Part 3:** 'A bushcraft skills course for young people' A family discussing their next holiday
Vocabulary and grammar review Units 3 and 4			
5 Different feelings	**Part 4:** 'How I dealt with stress' Identifying the topic of a paragraph Identifying linking words (*this, then, do, also, however,* etc.)	**Part 2:** A story Using adjectives to describe feeling	**Part 2:** Listening for facts, opinions or feelings Two candidates doing Speaking Part 4
6 That's entertainment!	**Part 2:** 'Turn off the TV and go out!' Selecting events from an entertainment guide	**Part 2:** An article about a celebration in your country Using the correct style for an article	Eliza and Bella planning a night out **Part 1:** Seven short texts about daily life Two candidates doing Speaking Part 3
Vocabulary and grammar review Units 5 and 6			
7 Getting around	**Part 1:** Identifying text purpose	**Part 1:** An email Useful email expressions	**Part 4:** Olivia talks about extremely heavy snow while travelling in Italy Identifying distracting information Mia and Owen discuss getting to the station on time Two candidates doing Speaking Part 2
8 Influencers	Famous families **Part 6:** An article about Hannah Alper, a famous *influencer*	**Part 2:** An article about a person you admire Using correct spelling and punctuation	**Part 3:** 'How to become famous on YouTube' Completing notes Carter and Will discuss presenters for a YouTube channel Three candidates doing Speaking Part 1
Vocabulary and grammar review Units 7 and 8			
9 Stay fit and healthy	**Part 3:** 'Teenager Julia Ryan talks about sleep' Identifying opinion and attitude	**Part 2:** A story about feeling nervous Using a range of past tenses to explain what happened	**Part 2:** People talking in six different situations Identifying the situation and what you need to listen for Two candidates doing Speaking Part 4
10 Looks amazing!	**Part 2:** 'Our top picks at the Street Food market' Selecting places to eat	**Part 2:** An article	**Part 1:** Seven short texts about daily life Listening carefully for information Two candidates doing Speaking Part 2
Vocabulary and grammar review Units 9 and 10			
11 The natural world	'Scientists use robot chick to study penguins' **Part 5:** 'A school expedition abroad'	**Part 1:** An email Checking your work for mistakes	**Part 4:** Looking for the Iberian lynx Identifying expressions with similar or different meanings Two candidates doing Speaking Part 4
12 Express yourself!	**Part 4:** 'Can you live without technology for a week?' Matching sentences to paragraphs	**Part 2:** A story Using a range of tenses and reported speech	Raising money for charity **Part 3:** A competition to design a new app Two candidates doing Speaking Part 1
Vocabulary and grammar review Units 11 and 12			

Speaking	Pronunciation	Vocabulary	Grammar
Part 1: Saying your name, how old you are, where you live and study	-s endings /s/, /z/ and /ɪz/	House and home Countable and uncountable nouns	Prepositions of time Frequency adverbs Present simple and present continuous State verbs *a few, a bit of, many, much, a lot of* and *lots of* Prepositions of place
Part 3: Discussing a new lunchtime club for students Agreeing and disagreeing Making a decision	-ed endings /d/, /t/ and /ɪd/	A typical school day *fail, pass, take, lose, miss, study* and *teach* *do, earn, have, make, spend* and *take*	Past simple Past simple and past continuous *used to* *So do I* and *Nor/Neither do I*
Part 2: Describing a picture Explaining what you can see and where things are	-ing endings /ŋ/	Leisure activities Prepositions of place Phrasal verbs People's hobbies	Verbs followed by *to* or -ing
Part 3: Discussing where to go in a capital city Making suggestions and giving reasons	Weak forms in comparative structures	Holiday activities *travel, journey* and *trip* Buildings and places	Comparative and superlative adjectives *a bit, a little, slightly, much, far, a lot* *not as ... as ...* *big* and *enormous* (gradable and non-gradable adjectives)
Part 4: Describing personal experiences Asking other people what they think	Modal verbs: weak and strong forms	Feelings Adjectives and prepositions Adjectives with -ed and -ing Adjectives of emotion and their opposites	*can, could, might, may* (ability and possibility) *should, shouldn't, ought to, must, mustn't, have to* and *don't have to* (advice, obligation and prohibition)
Part 3: Discussing plans for a festival Moving on to a new subject	Contrastive stress	Television programmes Going out *been/gone, meet, get to know, know* and *find out*	Present perfect *just, already* and *yet* *since* and *for* Present perfect or past simple?
Part 2: Describing what people are doing in photos Adding new points, and correcting yourself Describing things you don't know the name of	Word stress in compound nouns	Weather Compound words	*extremely, fairly, quite, rather, really* and *very* *too* and *enough* The future: *will, going to*, present continuous and present simple Prepositions of movement
Part 1: Answering general questions Talking about your daily routine and what you like	Conditional sentences: Contracted words	Phrasal verbs Describing people Adjective prefixes and suffixes Adjective order	Zero, first and second conditionals *When, if, unless* + present, future
Part 4: Discussing sport, fitness and health Showing agreement and polite disagreement	Word stress: agreeing and disagreeing	Illnesses and accidents Sports *go, play* and *do*	*which, that, who, whose, when* and *where* clauses (defining and non-defining) Past perfect
Part 2: Describing everyday objects in photos Explaining what things are made of or used for	Connected speech: linking sounds	*course, dish, food, meal* and *plate* Shops and services	Commands and instructions *Have something done*
Part 4: Discussing ways to help the environment Giving examples	Word stress in longer nouns	The natural world Noun suffixes	The passive: present and past simple Comparative and superlative adverbs
Part 1: General questions Talking about habits and routines	Intonation in direct and indirect questions	Collocations: using your phone *ask, ask for, speak, talk, say* and *tell* Negative prefixes	Reported speech and reported commands Reported questions Indirect questions

Introduction

Who this book is for

Complete Preliminary for Schools is a stimulating and thorough preparation course for school-aged learners who wish to take the **B1 Preliminary for Schools exam** from **Cambridge Assessment English**. It helps them to develop the necessary reading, writing, listening and speaking skills for the exam as well as teaching essential grammar and vocabulary. For those who are not planning to take the exam in the near future, the book provides skills and language based around engaging topics, all highly relevant for school-aged learners moving towards a B1 level of English.

What the Student's Book contains:

- **12 units for classroom study**. Each unit contains:
  - an authentic exam task taken from each of the four papers (Reading, Speaking, Writing and Listening) in the **B1 Preliminary for Schools exam**.
  - essential information on what each part of the exam involves, and the best way to approach each task. Exam advice boxes before exam tasks explain how to do this.
  - a wide range of enjoyable speaking activities designed to increase learners' fluency and ability to express themselves.
  - a step-by-step approach to doing Preliminary for Schools Writing tasks.
  - grammar activities and exercises for the grammar learners need to know for the exam. When you are doing grammar exercises, you will sometimes see this symbol ⊙. These exercises are based on research from the **Cambridge Learner Corpus** and they deal with the areas which often cause problems for students in the exam.
  - vocabulary activities and exercises for the vocabulary you need to know for the exam. When you see this symbol ⊙ by a vocabulary exercise, the exercise focuses on words which Preliminary for Schools candidates often confuse or use wrongly in the exam.
- **Six unit reviews**. These contain exercises which revise the grammar and vocabulary in each unit.
- **Speaking and Writing reference sections**. These explain the possible tasks students may have to do in the Speaking and Writing papers, and they give you examples and models together with additional exercises and advice on how best to approach these Speaking and Writing exam tasks.
- A **Grammar reference section** which clearly explains, unit by unit, all the main areas of grammar which you will need to know for the **B1 Preliminary for Schools exam**. There are also practice exercises for all grammar points.

Also available:

- **Downloadable audio online** containing all the listening material for the 12 units of the Student's Book plus material for the Speaking Bank. The listening material is indicated by coloured icons 🎧 02 in the Student's Book.
- A **Teacher's Book** containing:
  - **Step-by-step guidance** for teaching the activities in the Student's Book.
  - A number of suggestions for **alternative treatments** of activities in the Student's Book and suggestions for **extension activities**.
  - **Photocopiable recording scripts** from the Student's Book listening material.
  - **Complete answer keys** including recording scripts for all the listening material.
  - **12 photocopiable word lists** (one for each unit) containing vocabulary found in the units. Each vocabulary item in the word list is accompanied by a definition supplied by the corpus-informed *Cambridge Learner's Dictionary*.
  - **Access to extra photocopiable materials online** to practise and extend language abilities outside the requirements of the **B1 Preliminary for Schools exam**.
- A Student's **Workbook** containing:
  - 12 units for homework and self-study. Each unit contains further exam-style exercises to practise the reading, writing and listening skills needed in the **B1 Preliminary for Schools exam**. In addition, they provide further practice of grammar and vocabulary, which also use information about common Preliminary for Schools candidate errors from the Cambridge Learner Corpus ⊙.
- A **'Vocabulary Extra'** section, which contains twelve pages of further revision and practice of the essential Preliminary for Schools exam vocabulary contained in the Student's Book units.
- **Downloadable audio online** containing all the listening material for the Workbook.
- A **Test Generator** containing:
  - A **Grammar and Vocabulary Test** at standard and plus levels of each of the 12 units in the Student's Book.
  - Three **Term Tests** including grammar, vocabulary and PET Writing, Speaking, Listening and Reading exam tasks.
  - An **End of Year Test** including grammar and vocabulary from all 12 units, with PET Writing, Speaking, Listening and Reading exam tasks.

B1 Preliminary for Schools content and overview

Part/Timing	Content	Exam focus
1 **Reading** 45 minutes	**Part 1** Five very short texts: signs and messages, postcards, notes, emails, labels, etc. followed by five three-option multiple choice questions. **Part 2** Five descriptions of people to match to eight short texts. **Part 3** Longer text with five four-option multiple choice questions. **Part 4** Gapped text where five sentences have been removed Candidates must select the five correct sentences from a list of eight. **Part 5** Four-option multiple choice cloze text with six gaps. Candidates select the word which best fits each gap. **Part 6** An open cloze text consisting of a text with six gaps. Candidates think of a word which best suits each gap.	**Parts 1–4** and **Part 6**: Candidates are expected to read for the main message, global meaning, specific information, detailed comprehension, understanding of attitude, opinion and writer purpose and inference. **Part 5**: Candidates are expected to show understanding of vocabulary and grammar in a short text, and the lexico-structural patterns in the text.
2 **Writing** 45 minutes	**Part 1** An informal email. Candidates write an email of about 100 words in response to a text. **Part 2** An article or story. There is a choice of two questions. Candidates are provided with a clear context and topic. Candidates write about 100 words.	Candidates are mainly assessed on their ability to use and control a range of Preliminary-level language. Coherent organisation, spelling and punctuation are also assessed.
3 **Listening** approximately 30 minutes	**Part 1** Short monologues or dialogues with seven three-option multiple choice questions with pictures. **Part 2** Six short unrelated dialogues with six three-option multiple choice questions. **Part 3** Longer monologue. Candidates complete six sentences with information from the recording. **Part 4** Longer monologue or interview. Six three-option multiple choice questions.	Candidates are expected to identify the attitudes and opinions of speakers, and listen to identify gist, key information, specific information and detailed meaning, and to identify, understand and interpret meaning.
4 **Speaking** 12 minutes	**Part 1** A short conversation with the interlocutor. The interlocutor asks the candidates questions in turn, using standardised questions. **Part 2** An individual long turn for each candidate. A colour photograph is given to each candidate in turn and they talk about it for about a minute. Each photo has a different topic. **Part 3** A two-way conversation between candidates (visual stimulus with spoken instructions). The interlocutor sets up the activity. **Part 4** A discussion on topics related to the collaborative task in Part 3. The interlocutor asks the candidates the questions.	Candidates are expected to be able to ask and understand questions and make appropriate responses, and to talk freely on topics of personal interest.

1 My life and home

Starting off

1 **Work in pairs and answer the questions.**

- The pictures show four bedrooms. Tell each other what you can see in the photos.
- Which room is most like yours? Which is the most different? Give reasons.
- What changes would you like to make to your room?
- When you go away, what do you miss about your room?

Listening Part 2

1 **Work in pairs. Tell your partner about these things.**

- the building where you live
- the street where your home is
- a place where you would like to live

- Before you listen, quickly read the first line of each question and underline the key words.

- Don't choose an answer until you have heard the whole text for that question.

Exam advice

2 You will hear people talking in six different situations. With your partner, look at questions 1–6. Who will you hear? What is the situation in each conversation?

1 two friends, a flat they would like to live in

1 You will hear two friends talking about the kind of flat they would like to live in.
They agree that it should
  A be on one of the higher floors.
  B have at least three bedrooms.
  C be close to public transport.

2 You will hear a boy telling his friend about changing school. What does he say about it?
  A He finds the lessons hard.
  B He still misses his old school friends.
  C He thinks his new classmates are unfriendly.

3 You will hear a girl talking about a trip to the beach. What did she like best about it?
  A swimming in the sea
  B going on a free boat trip
  C playing volleyball

4 You will hear two friends talking about the town where they live. They agree that
  A there's too much traffic.
  B some parts of it are dangerous.
  C it's smaller than they would like.

5 You will hear a boy talking to a friend about a shop. What does the boy think about the shop?
  A There aren't enough assistants.
  B The prices there are reasonable.
  C It sells a wide variety of items.

6 You will hear two friends talking about their homes. The girl says her room would be better if
  A it was quieter.
  B it was a lot bigger.
  C it was sometimes warmer.

3 For each question, choose the correct answer. Listen again and check your answers.

02

4 Think of the three best and worst things about the place where you live. Use the ideas below, or your own. Work in small groups and compare ideas.
• how big or small it is
• interesting places to visit
• the people who live there
• traffic and public transport
• how safe it is
• things for young people to do

Prepositions of time

▶ **Page 116 Grammar reference**
Prepositions of time

5 Exam candidates often make mistakes with prepositions of time. Choose the correct option in *italics*.
  1 I sometimes leave work *in* / *on* the evening.
  2 *On* / *In* summer, you must come to Poland.
  3 I'll see you *on* / *at* 4 o'clock.
  4 We usually go to the beach *at* / *in* the morning.
  5 I go shopping *in* / *on* Saturday.

6 Complete the table with phrases from the box. Think of more phrases to add to the table.

5 o'clock 2020 bedtime half past four July 25 May my birthday Sundays the afternoon the holidays ~~the weekend~~ weekdays winter

at (with times of the day and *the weekend*)	*in* (with parts of the day, years, months and seasons)	*on* (with days and dates)
the weekend		

7 When do people do the things in the pictures? When do you do them? Use prepositions of time.

Some people go by bus very early in the morning. I get the bus at 8.15.

Grammar

Frequency adverbs

▶ **Page 116 Grammar reference:**
Frequency adverbs

1 Read about daily habits in Julian's town. How similar is it to life where you live?

On weekdays, most people get up between seven and eight o'clock and they sometimes have cereal for breakfast. They have lunch at around one o'clock most days. Dinnertime is usually at about six. People don't usually go to bed late. They often go to bed at ten.

2 Work in pairs.

1 Do frequency adverbs like *often*, *sometimes* and *usually* go before or after the main verbs (like *go* or *have*)?

2 Which is correct: frequency adverb + *be*, or *be* + frequency adverb?

3 Where do we usually put longer frequency expressions like *every day* or *most days*?

3 Complete the sentences with the words in brackets.

1 I listen to music on the radio. (occasionally)

I occasionally listen to music on the radio.

2 I check my phone for messages. (every two hours)

3 I'm late for school. (never)

4 I write emails to friends. (sometimes)

5 I don't have lunch at home. (always)

6 I'm sleepy in the morning. (almost every day)

7 I go out on Monday nights. (hardly ever)

8 I stay in bed late. (most weekends)

4 Make sentences 1–8 from Exercise 3 true for you. Change the frequency adverbs, if necessary. Then work in pairs and compare your sentences.

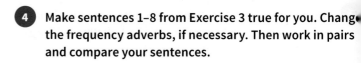

I rarely listen to music on the radio.

Really? I listen to music on the radio all the time.

5 Work in pairs. How often do you do the things in the pictures? Use expressions like *every day*, *once a week* and *twice a month*.

I text my best friend every day.

I tidy my room once a month!

Reading Part 5

1 Work in small groups. Look at the pictures on page 11.

- Tell each other about the homes in the pictures.
- Which would you like to have a holiday in? Which would you like to live in all the time?
- Do you know of other unusual places to live?

> • Look at the words before and after each gap.
>
> • Don't look at the gaps yet. Read the text to get a general idea of the type of text, its topic and the main points.
>
> • Try each of A, B, C and D in the gap. Which has the right meaning <u>and</u> fits the grammar of the sentence?

Exam advice

2 Read the article without filling in the gaps. Answer the questions.

1 What kind of text is it? (e.g. a story, an article …)

2 Which photo matches the text?

3 Which <u>four</u> of these points are in the text?

- Sonia goes to lots of places and does exciting things.
- She doesn't meet people of her own age.
- Her education takes place on the boat.
- Living on a boat has some disadvantages.
- She doesn't usually feel afraid when she's on the boat.

3 Read the article below and for each question, choose the correct answer. Use the questions in *italics* to help you.

Sonia's Home

Most teenagers live in flats or houses, but right now Sonia Ruiz is waking up somewhere in the Pacific Ocean because her home is a 20-metre boat. She has **(1)** .... over half her life sailing with her mother and father, who are both scientists.

Sonia's unusual **(2)** .... of life means she regularly sees whales and gets to swim with dolphins, and she has **(3)** .... friends all over the world. She does her schoolwork online and her studies are going well.

Life on board, though, is sometimes uncomfortable. Space is limited, so there are no wide-screen TVs or soft sofas. Bad **(4)** .... that lasts for days is common, **(5)** .... in winter. Storms at sea can be frightening, although modern boat equipment usually helps sailors **(6)** .... them.

Sonia loves her boat and she nearly always feels safe on it. She contacts friends by using social media and whenever they get together, they have great fun in the sea and on the beach.

1 *Which word do we use with a period of time?*
   A passed   **B** used   **C** taken   **D** spent

2 *Which noun often goes with 'of life'?*
   A path   **B** way   **C** road   **D** track

3 *Which verb often goes with 'friends'?*
   A added   **B** formed   **C** caught   **D** made

4 *Which noun often goes with 'bad'?*
   A climate   **B** forecast   **C** weather
   D temperature

5 *Which adverb means 'especially'?*
   A particularly   **B** extremely
   C completely   **D** absolutely

6 *Which verb means 'keep away from'?*
   A prevent   **B** control   **C** avoid   **D** remove

4 Work in small groups. Which of these would you like? Which wouldn't you like? Give reasons.

- often going to different places
- rarely seeing friends
- never going to school
- making new friends around the world
- having very little space at home
- living close to nature all the time

5 Do you think it's good for a teenager to live like Sonia? Why / Why not?

1

Grammar

Present simple and present continuous

▶ **Page 117 Grammar reference**
Present simple and present continuous

▶ **Page 118 Grammar reference**
State verbs

1 Match the extracts from the article (1–5) with the uses of the present simple and present continuous (a–e).

1 Most teenagers **live** in flats or houses.   *e*
2 Sonia Ruiz **is waking up** somewhere.
3 She regularly **sees** whales.
4 Her studies **are going** well.
5 Sonia **loves** her boat.

a something that happens regularly
b something in progress, but not at the present moment
c verbs not normally used in the continuous
d something happening at the present moment
e something that is generally true

2 Complete the email with the present simple or present continuous form of the verbs in brackets.

Hi David,

I **(1)** ......*'m writing*...... (write) to you from our hotel, right next to the sea! I **(2)** .... (sit) in my bedroom right now, which **(3)** .... (have) a big window, and I **(4)** .... (look) out across the waves at a little island. I **(5)** .... (love) it here, and in the evening I sometimes **(6)** .... (stay) here and watch the sun go down.

Every day, we **(7)** .... (go) for a walk along the cliffs. The weather **(8)** .... (get) hotter every day. It was 35°C yesterday! But we always **(9)** .... (leave) the house early in the morning while that cool wind from out at sea **(10)** .... (blow). I **(11)** .... (have) a really good time here, and I **(12)** .... (not want) to go home!

Bye for now,

Molly

3 Make questions using the present simple or the present continuous. Add or change words if necessary.

1 what / 'habit' / mean?
2 the school bus / stop / in your street?
3 who / watches / the most / TV / in your house?
4 you / prefer / to get up / early or late?
5 everyone / talk / to / their partners / at the moment?
6 what colour clothes / you / wear / today?
7 who / sit / behind / us / in this lesson?
8 what / you / sometimes / forget / to do / in the morning?

4 Work in pairs. Ask and answer the questions from Exercise 3.

> What does 'habit' mean?

> It means something you often do.

5 Do the task below.

- Use the present continuous to write three questions about what your partner is doing, thinking or feeling now, e.g. *Are you feeling good?*
- Use the present simple to write three questions about what your partner likes, wants or prefers, e.g. *Do you prefer weekdays or weekends?*
- Ask and answer the questions.

6 **/P/** /s/, /z/ and /ɪz/

Try saying these words. Which ones end with /s/? Which end with /z/? Which end with /ɪz/?

belongs catches changes chooses does finishes forgets gets goes likes lives loves passes plays practises prefers sees speaks studies thinks uses walks wants washes wears works

7 Work in pairs. Think of a friend or family member. Tell your partner these things about them.

- facts, e.g. *She lives in … , she belongs to …*
- things he or she often does, e.g. *He often plays …*
- something your friend is doing around now, e.g. *She's learning Spanish.*
- what you think your friend is doing right now, e.g. *He's walking home.*

8 Now ask your partner more questions about the friend or family member.

> Where does she go to school?

> Is he doing English lessons this year?

Vocabulary

House and home

1 Which of these does your home have?

> a balcony   a bathroom   a bedroom   a dining room
> a garage   a garden   a hall   a kitchen
> a living room   stairs

2 Look at the pictures. Where can you find the things from the box?

> armchair   bath   blankets   chest of drawers   cooker
> cupboards   cushions   dishwasher   duvet   fridge
> microwave   mirror   pillow   rug   sink   sofa   taps
> toilet   towels   wardrobe   washing machine

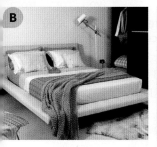

Countable and uncountable nouns

▶ **Page 118 Grammar reference**
Countable and uncountable nouns

3 Choose the correct option in *italics*. Check with the extract from the *Cambridge Learner's Dictionary*.

I am looking for new *furniture / furnitures* for my room.

> **furniture** *noun* [U]
> objects such as chairs, tables and beds that you put into a room or building.
> **Common Learner Error**
> We cannot make *furniture* plural. Do not say 'furnitures'.

4 Look at the extract again. What tells you the noun *furniture* is uncountable? What letter do you think there is for a countable noun?

5 Think about the kitchen in your home. Write down three countable and three uncountable things you can find there. Tell your partner.

Grammar

a few, a bit of, many, much, a lot of and *lots of*

▶ **Page 118 Grammar reference**
a few, a bit of, many, much, a lot of, lots of

1 Look at what Gina says about her free time. Then complete the rules with *countable* or *uncountable*.

> I don't have much time to watch TV. There aren't many programmes I like and I usually have a lot of homework in the evenings. After that, I often like to do a bit of exercise. Sometimes my friend comes to my house. We talk a lot and we play a few video games. That's lots of fun!

Rules

1 For small numbers with .... nouns we use *a few*.

2 For small amounts with .... nouns we use *a bit of*.

3 With .... nouns in questions and negative sentences we use *much*.

4 With .... nouns in questions and negative sentences we use *many*.

5 We use *a lot of* or *lots of* for large amounts or numbers. We use them with *countable or uncountable nouns*.

6 If there is no *noun*, we use *a lot* instead of *a lot of*.

2 Choose the correct option in *italics*.

1 I put *a bit of / a few* make-up on, but not *many / much*.

2 It doesn't take *many / much* time to wash those clothes and it only takes *a lot of / a few* hours to dry them.

3 I've got *a bit of / a few* video games but I can't buy any more because they cost *much / a lot of* money.

4 Those new light bulbs don't use *many / a lot of* electricity, so *lots of / much* people are buying them.

5 I don't use *much / many* shampoo, just *a bit of / a few* drops. My hair always goes dry if I use *a lot / a lot of*.

6 There isn't *much / a lot* space in my bedroom so I don't keep *a bit of / many* things there.

3 Work in pairs. Ask your partner what he or she likes doing at home. Use expressions from Exercise 1. Which answer most surprises you?

> Do you watch much TV?

> I watch a few programmes. But I spend a lot of time at home playing the piano.

Speaking Part 1

Prepositions of place

▶ **Page 119 Grammar reference**
Prepositions of place

▶ **page 152 Speaking bank**
Speaking Part 1

1 Exam candidates often make mistakes with prepositions like *at*, *in* and *on*. Choose the correct option in *italics*.

1 Sometimes we play *on / at* his house.
2 He sometimes goes running *at / in* the park.
3 We usually stay *in / at* home playing computer games.
4 There's a window *on / in* the left of my bed.
5 I normally spend my day *in / at* the beach.
6 I have some photos *in / on* the wall.

2 Work in pairs. Tell each other about your apartment or house. Describe each room and what's in it. Draw a picture of your partner's home. Show it to your partner.

3 Complete the gaps with *at*, *in* and *on*.

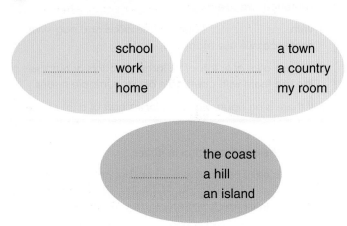

.... school
work
home

.... a town
a country
my room

.... the coast
a hill
an island

4 Put the words in order to make questions. Then match the questions with the answers.

1 your / what's / name?
   What's your name?
2 old / you / are / how?
3 live / where / you / do?
4 at / English / do / study / school / you?
5 it / you / like / do?

a In Ancona, a town on the coast, in Italy.
b Yes, because I enjoy talking to people in English.
c I'm 13. I'll be 14 next month.
d Matteo Bianchi.
e Yes, I have English lessons every day.

5 Work in pairs. Ask and answer the questions from Exercise 4. Use the correct prepositions in your answers.

6 Complete the dialogue with the correct form of the verbs in brackets and prepositions of place and time.

Matteo: How old (1) ....*are you*.... (you / be), Alba?
Alba: I'm 15. My birthday was (2) .... March.
Matteo: And where (3) .... (you / come) from?
Alba: I live (4) .... Manresa, a town about 60 kilometres from Barcelona.
Matteo: Who (5) .... (you / live) with?
Alba: With my parents and my little brother Miquel, who's still (6) .... primary school.
Matteo: How (7) .... (you / go) to school?
Alba: I usually go by bus, but (8) .... spring and summer I sometimes walk.
Matteo: What (9) .... (you / enjoy) doing in your free time?
Alba: Well, I really like seeing my friends (10) .... the evenings and (11) .... weekends, but I often stay (12) .... home and read.

7 Listen and check.
 03

- In the Speaking exam, be friendly and polite when you meet the examiners and the other candidate.
- Speak clearly and loudly enough for the examiners and your partner to hear you.
- Give longer answers by adding details such as places and times of day.

Exam advice

8 Work in new pairs. Ask and answer the questions from Exercise 6.

Writing Part 1

▶ page 145 Writing bank
An email

 1 Work in pairs. Look at the exam task and answer the questions.

1 Who has written to you?

Alex, your English-speaking friend.

2 What do you have to read?

3 What kind of text must you write?

4 What news does Alex tell you first? How do you feel about this?

5 What does Alex ask you next? What information must you give?

6 What does Alex ask you in the third sentence?

7 What does Alex ask you last?

Read this email from your English-speaking friend Alex, and the notes you have made.

To:

From: Alex

Hi,

Many thanks for inviting me to come and stay with you for a couple of weeks. I asked my mum and dad and they said yes! —— *Brilliant!*

Which month would be best for me to come? —— *Say when and why.*

We've never really talked about your home. What's it like? —— *Describe it.*

I'll start planning my trip today. What should I bring with me? —— *Suggest ...*

See you soon!

Alex

Write your **email** to Alex, using **all the notes**.

• You <u>must</u> answer this question in the exam.

• Read the instructions and the email that's included in the question. Who do you have to write to? Which points must you include?

• Note down ideas and plan your reply. How many paragraphs will you need?

Exam advice

2 Read Frankie's reply and answer the questions.

1 How many main paragraphs does Frankie use?

2 Which paragraph deals with each of the notes?

3 How many sentences does Frankie write about each of the notes?

4 In Frankie's email, find prepositions of place, prepositions of time and frequency adverbs.

From: Frankie

To: Alex

Hi Alex,

I'm so happy you can spend a fortnight at my place. I'm really looking forward to it!

Summer is lovely here. I usually spend August on the coast, so July would be the perfect time.

I live in a three-bedroom flat on the fifth floor, in a quiet neighbourhood. It's comfortable, with modern furniture, big windows and a large balcony where I sometimes have barbecues at weekends.

It hardly ever rains in July, so I'd recommend bringing just light clothes, plus your swimming costume. There's lots to do here and I'm sure we'll have a fantastic time.

See you in the summer!

Frankie

3 Plan your own reply to Alex. Use each of the notes as a heading and write your own ideas below them.

Brilliant!	Say when and why	Describe	Suggest
It's great that ...			

4 Write your email in about 100 words.

• Begin and end in a friendly way.

• Use paragraphs, one for each of the notes.

• Write at least one sentence about each of the notes.

• Try to use frequency adverbs and prepositions of place and time.

5 Check your partner's email. Has your partner:

• organised the email like Frankie's?

• written about all four notes on Alex's email?

• written about 100 words?

2 At school

Starting off

A typical school day

1 Work in pairs. Put the activities from the box in order to make a typical school day. Add your own ideas.

> do homework   go home   have a break
> have lunch at school   make notes
> pay attention   set off for school   work in groups

1 set off for school

2 Work in pairs. Look at the photos and answer the questions.

- What can you see in each photo?
- How do you think they are connected with different types of school?

Reading Part 6

1 Match the sentences (1–4) with the photos (A–D). Do not complete the gaps for now.

1 At **Brooklyn Free School**, there (1) .... no exams, homework or marks. The students make (2) .... rules.

2 In the **School of the Future** in the USA, the students don't have (3) .... buy books. They use a computer (4) .... is connected to the internet.

3 **Ørestad Gymnasium** in Denmark is a school (5) .... classroom walls. More than 1,000 students study in open-learning zones where teachers walk around helping (6) ....

4 If (7) .... live on a huge continent like Australia, your nearest school might be hours away. Students who live too far (8) .... a school study at the **School of the Air** and receive their lessons over the internet.

2 What type of word is missing in each gap (1–8) in Exercise 1 (a verb, a preposition, etc.)?

3 Read the sentences from Exercise 1 again and write one word in each gap.

4 Look at the photo. Where do you think these children are going to school?

5 For each question, write the correct answer.
Write **one** word for each gap.

ON THEIR WAY TO SCHOOL

The children **(0)** ....of........ Gulu, which is a small village in China, used to have **(1)** .... unusual journey to school. Their village **(2)** .... located in a deep valley surrounded by mountains and it took them five hours to get to their school. The pupils had to climb up a mountain along a path that was **(3)** .... narrow in places that they were in danger of falling into the valley below.

Their teacher, Shen Qijun, ran this school **(4)** .... over 26 years. Although his students enjoyed school, only two of **(5)** .... went to university. Everything changed when a newspaper wrote a report and this journey to school became famous. The local government decided **(6)** .... close the school because the journey was too dangerous. People sent money and the families could afford to send their children to the town below the mountain to attend school there.

Exam advice

- Without filling in any of gaps 1–6, quickly read the text to find out what it's about.
- For each gap, look at the sentence and decide what kind of word (e.g. a preposition) is missing.
- Read the sentence again and think of the word which best fits the gap.

6 What do you like about your school? What would you like to change? Make notes on the ideas below. Add your own ideas.

> classrooms and facilities
> journey and location
> rules, homework and exams
> teachers and subjects   timetable

7 Work in groups. Tell each other your ideas.

> I'd like to have new desks in the classroom. These ones are too small!

> I would like to walk or cycle to school. I don't like going by bus every day.

Vocabulary
fail, pass, take, lose, miss, study and *teach*

1 Exam candidates often make mistakes with *fail*, *pass*, *take*, *lose*, *miss*, *study* and *teach*. Complete the sentences with words from the boxes.

> **fail   pass   take**

1 We have to ....*take*.......... an exam at the end of this course. (= do an official test)

2 I hope I .... the exam and get a good mark. (= be successful in an exam)

3 I'm studying a lot because I don't want to .... my exam. (= not be successful in an exam)

> **lose   miss**

4 I don't want to .... my class. (= not go to something or arrive too late to get on a bus, a train, etc.)

5 I often .... my keys. (= not be able to find something or someone)

> **learn   study   teach**

6 I want to .... how to ride a horse. (= get new knowledge or skills)

7 My dad's going to .... me how to cook. (= give new knowledge or skills)

8 My brother would like to .... biology at university. (= go to classes, read books, etc. to try to understand new ideas and facts)

2 Choose the correct option in *italics*.

1 How often do you *take* / *make* exams?

2 Do you ever *miss* / *lose* your books, homework or school bag?

3 What subject(s) does your favourite teacher *teach* / *learn* you?

4 Would you like to *take* / *learn* a new sport, a new language or a musical instrument?

5 Is it sometimes OK to *miss* / *lose* school?

6 Do you know what degree you'd like to *learn* / *study* at university?

3 Write follow-up questions for each question in Exercise 2.

1 Do you like exams? Do you study a lot for them?

4 Work in pairs. Ask and answer the questions from Exercise 2, and your extra questions.

Grammar
Past simple

▶ **Page 120 Grammar reference** Past simple

1 Work in pairs. Last year, Emily went to Mexico City to be an exchange student. What differences do you think she found between her life in Canada and her life in Mexico?

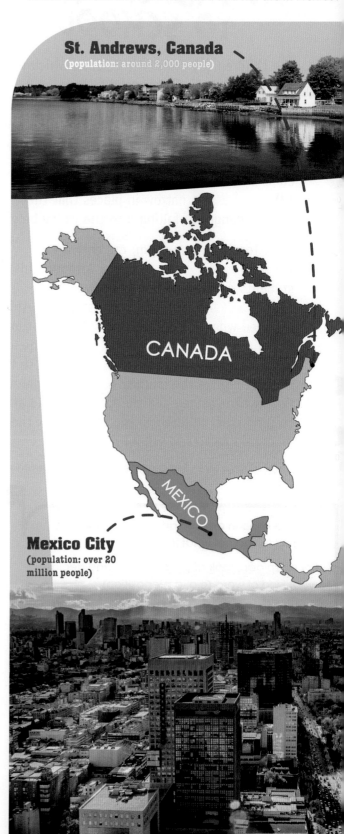

St. Andrews, Canada (population: around 2,000 people)

CANADA

MEXICO

Mexico City (population: over 20 million people)

2 Listen to Emily talking about what was different. Make notes on these topics.
04
- the school uniform
- the city
- shops and entertainment

3 Work in pairs. Write the interviewer's questions, using *you* and the past simple.

1 Where / go / last year? *Where did you go last year?*
2 Where / stay?
3 Why / choose / Mexico City?
4 Speak / Spanish / before / go?
5 How / feel / when / first / arrive?
6 Like / the city?
7 What subjects / study?
8 Enjoy / the experience?

4 Listen again and complete Emily's answers.
04
1 I ....*went*........ to Mexico.
2 I .... with Alicia and her family in Mexico City.
3 I .... to improve my Spanish.
4 Yes, I did. I .... French and Spanish at school in Canada.
5 When I ...., I .... scared.
6 I .... it a lot.
7 I .... maths, chemistry, biology, Spanish and lots of other subjects.
8 Oh yes, I did. I'm really glad I .... there.

5 Look again at Emily's answers. <u>Underline</u> the regular past simple forms. Ⓒircle the irregular past simple forms.

6 **/P/** /d/, /t/ and /ɪd/
05
Listen to the sentences. How do we pronounce these regular past simple *-ed* endings? Choose the correct option.

1 I stay<u>ed</u> with Alicia and her family.   /d/   /t/   /ɪd/
2 I want<u>ed</u> to improve my Spanish.   /d/   /t/   /ɪd/
3 I lik<u>ed</u> the city a lot.   /d/   /t/   /ɪd/

7 Complete the table with the past simple form of the verbs from the box. Then listen and check.
06

arrive   decide   help   invite   like   live   need
~~stay~~   study   want   wash   watch

/d/	/t/	/ɪd/
stayed		

8 Work in pairs. Student A, ask the questions from Exercise 3. Student B, read Emily's answers from Exercise 4. Then change. Try to say the regular past simple endings correctly.

9 Exam candidates often make spelling mistakes with the past simple. <u>Underline</u> and correct one spelling mistake in each sentence.

1 My friends and I plaied football in the playground.
2 In the first lesson our English teacher teached us some new words for sports.
3 When I moved to a new school, I studyed very hard.
4 Last weekend, I founded a very good restaurant in my town.
5 When I arived at school, my friends weren't there.
6 My friend Sara bringed her dog to school one day.
7 I'm reading a book that my teacher recommend to me.
8 We puted all our things in the car and we set off on holiday.

10 Complete Amelia's review with the past simple form of the verbs in brackets.

How was your experience as an exchange student?

It **(1)** ....*was*........ (be) an incredible experience.
I **(2)** .... (spend) four months in a high school in Beijing. I **(3)** .... (choose) China's capital city because I **(4)** .... (want) to go somewhere very different. Wellington, the capital of New Zealand, has a population of 200,000, while Beijing has a population of over 20 million!
Before I **(5)** .... (leave) home, I **(6)** .... (be) worried about the new language and culture. I remember that I **(7)** .... (feel) very nervous when I **(8)** .... (say) goodbye to my family. My host family in China **(9)** .... (look after) me really well. I **(10)** .... (eat) all kinds of new food, I **(11)** .... (see) some wonderful places and of course I **(12)** .... (make) a lot of new friends.
I would definitely recommend the experience to other students.

11 Work in pairs. Think of a place you went to. Ask and answer the questions.

- Where did you go?
- Why did you go there?
- How did you feel?
- What did you think of the place?

Where did you go?

I visited Madeira.

At school **19**

Grammar

Past simple and past continuous

▶ **Page 120 Grammar reference**
Past continuous

1 Look at the picture. What happened to Emily when she was walking to school?

2 Listen and check. What do you think happened next?
07

3 Listen to the rest of Emily's story. Were you right?
08

4 Look at the extracts from Emily's story. Answer the questions.

1 *Suddenly a woman <u>appeared</u> from nowhere and she <u>started</u> screaming at the dogs. The dogs <u>ran</u> off.*
Did the three actions happen at the same time? What happened last?

2 *The sun (was shining) and I (was feeling) good.*
Do we know when the sun started shining?
Do we know if the sun stopped shining?

3 *I (was walking) to school with Alicia when we <u>saw</u> a group of dogs.*
Did Emily and Alicia see the dogs before they started walking to school?

5 Complete the rules with *past simple* or *past continuous*.

Rules

- We use the (1) ...*past simple*.... to talk about actions or situations in the past (often one action happened after the other).

- We use the (2) .... to talk about an activity that was already happening at a moment in the past. We don't say if this activity finished or not.

- We often use the (3) .... and the (4) .... together to show that an action happened in the middle of an activity.

- We can use *when, as* or *while* to introduce the activity in the (5) ....

When/As/While *I was walking to school, I saw a group of dogs.*

- We generally use *when* to introduce the action in the (6) ....

*I was walking to school with Alicia **when** we saw a group of dogs.*

6 Alicia goes to Canada to stay with Emily. Complete Emily's blog with the past simple or past continuous form of the verbs in brackets.

One morning, Alicia (1) ....*woke up*........ (wake up) early for school and she (2) .... (go) downstairs. I (3) .... (talk) loudly to my dad in the kitchen. We (4) .... (stop) talking and I (5) .... (say), 'Look outside! There's 20 cm of snow on the ground. We'll have to ski to school!' Alicia (6) .... (feel) excited and nervous at the same time. Snow in Mexico City is very rare and she (7) .... (not know) how to ski. I (8) .... (help) her to put on the skis. As we (9) .... (set off) for school, one of the neighbours (10) .... (shout), 'Everything is closed. No school today!'

We (11) .... (take off) our skis and we (12) .... (start) playing in the snow.

7 Listen and check.
09

8 Work in pairs. Choose a title below (or use your own) and prepare a story about an unusual day at school, like Emily's day. Use the past simple and past continuous.

> Bad weather stops classes!
> I become teacher for a day!
> Famous visitor arrives at school!
> No electricity all day!

9 Work in groups. Tell each other about the unusual day.

Listening Part 1

1 Read the questions and <u>underline</u> the key words.

1 <u>What</u> do the <u>students</u> need to <u>bring tomorrow</u>?

A **B** **C**

2 What time does the girl's school start?

A **B** **C**

3 Where does the boy live?

A **B** **C**

4 Where did the boy find his football boots?

A **B** **C**

5 What did the girl eat before she came home?

A **B** **C**

6 What are the two friends going to buy Paul for his birthday?

A **B** **C**

7 What is the weather forecast for tomorrow?

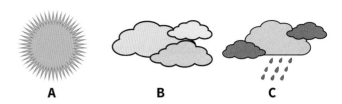

A **B** **C**

2 Work in pairs. Look at the pictures for questions 1–7 in Exercise 1. What can you see in each one?

- Before you hear each recording, underline the key words in each question (nouns, verbs and question words) so that you know exactly what to listen for.

- The first time you listen, try to choose the correct answer. Then, as you listen again, check your answers.

Exam advice

3 Listen and make notes of the important words you hear next to the pictures. Then listen again and for each question, choose the correct answer.

Grammar
used to

▶ **Page 121 Grammar reference**
   used to

1 Read Marina's post. Which words does Marina use to talk about things that happened regularly in the past but don't happen now?

What was your primary school like? Did you use to have the same teacher for all your subjects, for example?
Yeah! We used to have the same teacher for everything and we rarely got homework. We used to have little tests but nothing serious. I always used to have lunch at school. After lunch, we didn't use to have proper lessons, our teacher used to take us to a big room to play games. At the end of the day, my mum or dad used to collect me from school.
Marina, Bologna, Italy

2 Answer the questions.

1 Does *used to* change when we change the subject pronoun (*I/you/he/she*, etc.)?

2 What happens to *used to* in a negative sentence and in a question?

3 What verb form generally follows *used to*?

3 Write a post saying what you used to do or have at primary school.

In primary school, I used to draw a lot.
I didn't use to . . .

At school **21**

2

Vocabulary

do, earn, have, make, spend and *take*

1 Complete the questions with *do, earn, have, make, spend* or *take*.

In which school subject(s) …

1 can you ....*have*.......... fun?
2 can you ....friends?
3 do you need to ....a good memory?
4 do you ....most of your time learning facts?
5 does it ....a long time to do homework?
6 do you often ....mistakes?

Which school subject(s) …

7 would you like to ....as a degree at university?
8 can help you ....money?

2 Work in pairs. Ask and answer the questions from Exercise 1.

Speaking Part 3

▶ **page 159 Speaking bank** Part 3

1 Tanya and Gareth's teachers would like to introduce one of these new subjects. Listen and answer the questions.

> bicycle repair
> creative writing
> communication skills
> computer programming
> home economics
> money matters

1 Which subject(s) does Tanya suggest?
2 Which does Gareth suggest?
3 Which subject do they both choose?

So (do) I and *Nor/Neither (do) I*

▶ **page 121 Grammar reference** *So (do) I* and *Nor/Neither (do) I*

2 Underline the words that Tanya and Gareth use to agree. When do we use *nor*? When do we use *so*?

1 **Gareth:** I'm not sure about that one.
  Tanya: Nor am I.
2 **Tanya:** I still think communication skills is the best option.
  Gareth: So do I. Let's go for that.

3 Complete the sentences. Listen and check.

1 <u>Shall we</u> ....with creative writing?
2 <u>How</u> ....communication skills?
3 <u>Good</u> .... Let's talk about another subject.
4 <u>I don't</u> .... Some of us don't have bikes.
5 <u>I'm not</u> ....about that one.
6 ....<u>go for that</u>.

4 Match the underlined phrases from Exercise 4 with these uses.

- Suggesting: *Shall we*
- Agreeing:
- Disagreeing:
- Deciding:

> - Listen carefully to the examiner's instructions. Then look at the pictures.
> - Talk about the different things in the pictures by making suggestions and replying politely to your partner's suggestions.
>
> **Exam advice**

5 Work in pairs. Read the instructions for the Speaking Part 3 task. Do the task. Talk for about two minutes.

> A teacher would like to organise a new lunchtime club for students to practise their English. Here are some activities they could do.
>
> Talk together about the different activities the students could do at the club and say which will be the most popular with their classmates.

Writing Part 2

▶ **Page 148 Writing bank**
An article

1 Read the task below and answer the questions.

1 What do you need to write?
2 What information do you need to include?

You see this advert for a writing competition.

> **Articles wanted!**
> *What makes a great school?*
> *Is it the people who work there, the facilities or something else?*
> *What sort of clubs and activities should a great school offer?*
> The best article will win a laptop.

Write your article.

2 Make a list of things that make a great school.

teachers, facilities . . .

3 Complete the mind map with your ideas from Exercise 2. Add reasons. You may need to add some more shapes and lines to the map.

4 Read Charlotte's answer below. Does she have any of your ideas from Exercise 3?

What makes a great school?

In my opinion, in a great school, the students enjoy being there because the teachers teach well and they learn new things every day.

The classrooms are large and bright and there is enough space for everyone. When we were at primary school, we didn't use to start class until 9 o'clock. I believe that a later start to the day is better.

I also feel that a great school needs a wide variety of school clubs. In some schools, students can do interesting things like making films, blogs and music, while in my school, we can only choose between football and basketball.

5 Look at the questions. Can you answer 'yes' to all of them for Charlotte's answer?

1 Does the article include all the information for the task?
2 Is the answer written in paragraphs?
3 Are the ideas connected with words *like* and, *because* and *while*?

> • Read the instructions and the text in the task. Decide what information you need to include.
>
> • Think about the topic and your reader. Note down some ideas and decide how many paragraphs you will write.
>
> • Make a plan for each paragraph. Then write your article.

Exam advice

6 Write your article in about 100 words. Use your ideas from Exercise 3.

7 When you are ready, use the questions from Exercise 5 to check your writing. If you can answer 'yes' to all the questions, it is probably a good answer.

1 Vocabulary and grammar review

Grammar

1 Complete the email with *at*, *in* or *on* in each gap.

Hi everybody,

Well, here I am **(1)** *in* New Zealand, staying with a very friendly family **(2)** .... the town of Westport. It's quite a big house and my bedroom is **(3)** .... the second floor. I like it because there are lots of cupboards to put my things **(4)** .... and the bed is much bigger than the one **(5)** .... my room **(6)** .... home!

(7) .... the evenings and **(8)** .... weekends, the family sometimes take me out, though most of the time we just stay **(9)** .... and watch TV. I usually go to bed quite early, sleep well and get up **(10)** .... about 7.30 **(11)** .... the morning.

I'm enjoying myself a lot here, but I'm looking forward to being home again **(12)** .... August 15th.

Write soon!

Aiden

2 Choose the correct option in *italics*.

1 I have a big family and there's always a lot of *housework* / *houseworks* to do.
2 We've got *a few* / *a bit of* time before the film starts. Let's get a drink.
3 It's very dark and cold here in winter so I don't go out *a lot* / *a lot of*.
4 The living room is very big but there's not *many* / *much* furniture in it.
5 Max usually spends a lot of *time* / *times* in his room.
6 I haven't got *much* / *many* work today, so I'll go out.
7 Paula isn't very well, but I think she can eat *a few* / *a bit of* food now.
8 My parents sometimes invite *a bit of* / *a few* people to have dinner with us.

3 <u>Underline</u> and correct one mistake in each sentence.

1 We don't <u>eat always</u> in the dining room.
   We don't always eat in the dining room.
2 Hello, I call to ask if you want to go out tonight.
3 Why do you stand here in the rain at this time of night?
4 I'm tired usually in the morning.
5 I'm never believing anything my brother tells me.
6 I every day make my own bed.
7 How do you often have a bath?
8 I get normally home at about half past five.

Vocabulary

4 Label the pictures with words from Unit 1.

1 armchair

2 s _ _ _

3 f _ _ _ _ _

4 c _ _ _ _ _

5 d _ _ _ _ _ _ _ _

6 m _ _ _ _ _ _ _ _

7 d _ _ _ _

8 c _ _ _ _ o _ d _ _ _ _ _ _

9 w _ _ _ _ _ _ _

10 w _ _ _ _ _ _ m _ _ _ _ _ _

Vocabulary

1 Choose the correct option in *italics*.

1 I was late for school because I *lost* / ~~missed~~ the bus.

2 Our teacher says that you can learn from *making* / *doing* mistakes.

3 My grandfather taught me to be positive. I *learned* / *studied* a lot from him.

4 The physics test was very easy so I think I'll *pass* / *fail* it.

5 Sam went on a school trip yesterday and he *got* / *had* a lot of fun.

6 When Helen changed schools, she soon *did* / *made* a lot of new friends.

7 I'm nervous because we're *taking* / *passing* a difficult exam today.

8 When my brother leaves school, he'd like to *do* / *make* engineering at university.

Grammar

2 Underline one mistake with a verb in each sentence.

1 A TV company <u>choosed</u> my school to make a film because it is the oldest in the city.

2 I think I lefted my school bag at your house last night.

3 The teacher was kind. She teached the students well.

4 I woke up very early because I was planing to go to the lake.

5 My dad only payed €75 for his mobile phone.

6 While my sister was riding her bike, she felt and injured her leg.

7 When I was younger, I prefered to take the bus to go to school.

8 I met Holly a very long time ago. We were studing at the same school in London.

3 Complete the sentences with the past simple or past continuous form of the verbs in brackets.

1 Anita ....*fell*........ (fall) asleep when she ....*was doing*.... (do) her homework.

2 When I got to my classroom, some of my friends .... (chat) and one of them .... (write) on the board.

3 Yesterday, when we .... (have) lunch, the phone .... (ring).

4 While I .... (buy) some milk in the supermarket, I .... (see) a famous TV actor.

5 At first I .... (think) chemistry .... (be) difficult but now I love it.

6 My rabbit .... (escape) as I .... (clean) its cage.

7 When my best friend .... (jump) off the table, it .... (break).

8 On Monday we .... (read) an article in English and then we .... (write) a short text about it.

9 Last weekend I .... (stay) at my cousins' house. I really .... (enjoy) myself.

10 I .... (feel) tired after the long walk so I .... (go) to bed.

4 Complete the sentences with the words from the box. There are three extra words you do not need.

> give gave use used
> used didn't wasn't weren't

1 When my mum was younger, she .... to play basketball at school.

2 At primary school, I didn't .... to have lunch at school.

3 When Mr Marsden was our teacher, he used to .... us a lot of homework.

4 Before Eva bought an alarm clock, she .... to be late for school.

5 My grandparents .... use to watch TV because they didn't have one.

3 Having fun

Starting off

1 Complete the leisure activities with the verbs from the box. Which activities can you see in the photos?

> diving ~~doing~~ going playing
> posting riding seeing taking

1 ......*doing*...... sports
2 .... photos
3 .... dancing
4 .... a bike or a horse
5 .... computer games
6 .... friends
7 .... messages on social media sites
8 .... in the sea

2 Work in pairs. What's the best way to spend your free time? Put the leisure activities in order.

3 Work in small groups.

- Which other leisure activities do young people enjoy in your country? Why?
- Are these activities difficult to learn? Why? / Why not?
- How much time a week do you spend doing your favourite leisure activity?

Listening Part 4

1 Work in pairs.

- Look at the photo of a boy skateboarding, and the photo of a building. Do you think they are interesting?
- How old do you think the photographer is?

2 You will hear a radio interview about a young photographer called Ryan Parrilla. Look at questions 1–6. What kind of information (a reason, a place, a person, a thing or an action) do you think you need to listen for?

- Before you listen, look at each question and decide what kind of information you need.

- Listen for details about this kind of information and choose the best answer.

Exam advice

3 For each question, choose the correct answer. Then listen again and check.

13

1 Why did Ryan put his photos on Instagram?
  A A firm he worked for said it would make him famous.
  B It meant he could communicate with people in many countries.
  C Most new photographers use Instagram at first.

2 Ryan most likes to take photos of
  A people and places in New York.
  B wildlife on the coast.
  C famous people he sees in the city.

3 Ryan believes that he has taken his best photos
  A when unexpected things happened.
  B after making careful preparations.
  C very early in the morning.

4 Ryan first took photos with
  A his father's camera.
  B his own camera.
  C his sister's phone.

5 When Ryan was twelve he used to
  A play lots of computer games.
  B read about top photographers.
  C have lessons at home with a teacher.

6 What does Ryan think young photographers should do?
  A Wait until they are older to try to become successful at photography.
  B Find out what type of photography is in fashion.
  C Do the kind of photography that they particularly enjoy.

4 Work in groups.
- What kind of photos do you like taking?
- What kind of photos do you like looking at?
- Is there a hobby you would like to turn into a job?

@ryanparrilla

Vocabulary
Prepositions of place

1 Listen to Kirsty talking on the phone. Draw these objects on the picture. Check on page 163.

14

- Kirsty's racket
- her tennis balls
- her trainers
- her T-shirt

2 Write sentences describing where the objects from Exercise 1 are. Use the prepositions from the box.

above	behind	in front of	inside
next to	on	on the right	
opposite	under		

Kirsty's racket is in front of the wardrobe. It's on the floor.

Reading Part 3

1 Work in pairs. Look at the photos. What do you think they show? Do you like them?

2 Read the text quickly. What is the writer's purpose?

1 to explain how to become an expert at making sand sculptures
2 to describe a sand sculpture that she made
3 to give some advice about making sand sculptures
4 to encourage more people to make sand sculptures

3 Read the text again and answer the questions.

1 Why did Ariana decide to start making sand sculptures?
2 What did Ariana realise when she started making her first sculpture?
3 How did Ariana feel when her first sand sculpture failed?
4 In the final paragraph, what does Ariana say annoys her?

- Quickly read the text to get the general idea of what it is about.

- For each question, decide what the text says about it before you look at options A–D.

- Choose the option that is most similar to what the text says.

Exam advice

4 Read the text and the questions below. For each question choose the correct answer.

1 Ariana decided to start making sand sculptures
   A because she's always been good at other kinds of a...
   B because she saw some sculptures that her friends had made.
   C because wanted to do a new outdoor activity with her friends.
   D after being impressed by some near her house.

2 What did Ariana realise when she started making her first sculpture?
   A She wasn't very patient.
   B She thought it would be easier.
   C She knew straight away it wouldn't be a success.
   D She disliked people watching her make the sand sculpture.

3 How did Ariana feel when her first sculpture failed?
   A She felt like giving up her new hobby.
   B She was embarrassed because of how it looked.
   C She regretted that she ignored some useful advice.
   D She was angry with herself for wasting four hours.

4 In the final paragraph, what does Ariana say annoys he...
   A people damaging her sculptures
   B the sea covering her sculptures
   C the weather destroying her sculptures
   D people believing it is only a hobby for children

ARIANA'S HOBBY
SAND SCULPTURES

I live on the coast of Portugal where there are lots of beautiful sandy beaches and warm sunny days. It's the perfect location for my favourite hobby – making sand sculptures. I'd never actually thought of making sand sculptures before until my friends and I discovered some fantastic ones that were all along the shore near where I live. I couldn't believe that such beautiful model buildings, incredible creatures, and some amazingly realistic faces of famous people were all made out of sand. From that moment, I knew that this was something I just had to do, even though I'd never considered myself to be an artist or very creative.

In fact, anyone can create a sand sculpture, but it's much harder than it looks as I soon discovered. The first sand sculpture I ever tried making was a two-metre long dolphin. I was making brilliant progress on it until quite suddenly the

head started to break off! I tried everything to try and fix it, so it would s... in one piece, but it was hopeless. Soon the whole thing was a big pile... sand on the beach. Some people sunbathing nearby seemed to think... was extremely funny, but that just made me want to keep trying even... more. I wished I'd listened to an expert on YouTube who recommends digging up wet sand and to use it to build the sand sculptures because sticks together better. So, I did that for my next sculpture of a camel. An... I managed to complete it in four hours, though they don't always take that long to make.

I've heard people say that making sand castles is for kids, not adults, but that doesn't bother me at all. Many people don't understand that even lightly touching a sand sculpture can make a whole section fall off, which can take ages to rebuild and I get upset when that sometimes happens. Of course, heavy rain can do some damage, but not as much as you might think. As long as you build far enough up the beach, the waves won't wash a sand sculpture away either. So, when you're next at the seaside, make one yourself – you'll get a great sense of achievement!

5 Work in pairs.

- Would you like to build sand sculptures? If so, what kind?
- Which of the activities below do you enjoy doing?
- Which would you <u>not</u> like to do? Why?

> flying a kite   sailing   sunbathing
> swimming in the sea   windsurfing

Grammar

Verbs followed by *to* or *-ing*

▶ **Page 122 Grammar reference**
Verbs followed by *to* or *-ing*

Rules

- We can use *-ing* or *to* (+ the infinitive) after verbs such as *start, begin, like, love, hate, prefer* and *continue* with little difference in meaning.

  *Its head **started breaking** off.*
  *Its head **started to break** off.*

- With other verbs, only one form is possible.

1 Look at the <u>underlined</u> verbs. Which are followed by a verb ending in *-ing*? Which are followed by *to*? Complete the table.

1 Some people sunbathing nearby <u>seemed</u> to think this was extremely funny.
2 … that just made me want to <u>keep</u> trying.
3 I wished I'd listened to an expert on YouTube who <u>recommends</u> digging up wet sand.
4 I <u>managed</u> to complete it in four hours.

verb + *-ing*	verb + *to*
keep	seem

2 Add these verbs to the table.   Can you add more verbs?

> afford   agree   decide   enjoy   fancy   feel like
> finish   hope   learn   mind   miss   practise
> promise   want   would like

3 Some verbs can be followed by *-ing* or *to*, but with a change of meaning. Look at sentences 1–4.

Which two are about:
- something the speaker has to do?
- a memory of something in the past?

1 I <u>remember</u> just chatting to her.
2 I must <u>remember</u> to get a map.
3 Don't let me <u>forget</u> to take my sunglasses.
4 I'll never <u>forget</u> flying over that beach.

4 Some of the sentences have a mistake. <u>Underline</u> the mistakes and correct them.

1 I forgot <u>asking</u> you about your family. *to ask*
2 I hope see you soon!
3 I really enjoyed to help at a pop concert.
4 I remember moving into our new house.
5 Do you fancy to come out with us?
6 We hope to go to the same island again next year.
7 When we finished to eat I went home.

5 Complete the questions with the correct form of the verbs in brackets.

1 Where do you fancy ....*going*.... (go) this evening?
2 What kind of music do you enjoy .... (listen) to at home?
3 What are you planning .... (do) at the weekend?
4 Do you remember .... (go) away on holiday when you were younger?
5 Do you ever forget .... (bring) anything to your lessons?
6 What would you like .... (do) tomorrow?

6 **/P/** *-ing* endings /ŋ/
Listen and check the sentences from Exercise 5. Then answer the questions.

1 How do we pronounce *-ing*? Is there a /g/ sound?
2 Is this part of the word stressed?

7 Work in pairs. Ask and answer the questions from Exercise 5.

8 Tell your partner about the things below.

Something you …   I'm learning to play the drums.

1 are learning to do.
2 can't afford to buy.
3 decided to do last week.
4 must remember to do tomorrow.
5 will finish doing soon.
6 shouldn't forget to do next weekend.
7 are planning to do on Sunday.
8 really love doing.

Vocabulary
Phrasal verbs

▶ **Page 123 Grammar reference**
Phrasal verbs

phrasal verb:
a phrase which consists of a verb plus a preposition or adverb or both. The meaning of this phrase is different from the meaning of its separate parts: ***look after*** (= be responsible for), ***hang on*** (= wait) and ***run out of*** (= use all of) are all phrasal verbs.

1 Complete these example sentences with the three phrasal verbs in the dictionary extract.

1 Can you .... a moment? I'm nearly ready.
2 If you .... money, I'll lend you some.
3 Could you .... my phone while I go for a swim?

2 Match the phrasal verbs in the article to meanings 1–10.

CHOOSE YOUR HOBBY

Which kind of hobby would be good for you? If you find group activities exciting and you'd like to join in, why not put your name down for something like white-water rafting or rock climbing? Or, if you love animals, you could take up horse riding. It can be a bit expensive, though, so before you sign up for 20 or 30 lessons, you need to be sure you won't give up a couple of weeks later! Cycling may be cheaper, and of course you can set off along the road whenever you like and go on riding all day if you want. Or how about a creative hobby such as painting, photography or playing a musical instrument? That's something you can look forward to doing whenever you have a spare moment, and once you find out which you like best you'll probably never go off it.

1 take part in an activity with other people *join in*
2 start doing a hobby
3 register to do something
4 arrange to do an organised activity
5 start a journey
6 stop doing something before you have completed it
7 continue
8 feel happy about something that is going to happen
9 stop liking
10 get information about something

3 Which *two* of the phrasal verbs have three words? Which phrasal verb is separated by other words?

4 Work in pairs. Complete the dialogue with the correct form of phrasal verbs from Exercise 2.

Chris: Hi, Ava. Are you and Megan going away on holiday soon?

Ava: Yes, on Saturday. We want to (1) ......*set off*...... very early in the morning.

Chris: Are you going to the coast?

Ava: No, we (2) .... beach holidays a long time ago. There are always too many people. We've decided to (3) .... skiing instead. We're off to the Alps.

Chris: Do you know how to ski?

Ava: Er, not really. That's why I'm going to (4) .... my name .... for lessons.

Chris: I tried skiing once but I found it really difficult. After three days I (5) .... and went home!

Ava: Well, the lessons (6) .... until the afternoon, every day, so I hope I can improve quickly. I'm really (7) .... trying, anyway!

Chris: Yes, I'm sure you'll have a great time.

5 Listen and check.

🎧 16

6 Work in pairs. Tell your partner about an activity, sport or subject you found difficult at first.

• When did you take it up?
• Did you ever feel like giving up?
• Do you look forward to playing/doing it now?
• Do you want to go on doing it?

Vocabulary

People's hobbies

1 **Work in small groups.**

1 Match the hobbies in box A with the pictures.

2 Match the hobbies with the people and equipment in box B.

chess: picture 7, chess player, board, pieces.

A

> chess   camping   cooking   cycling   music   painting   photography

B

> backpack   bike   board   brush   camera   camper   chess player
> cook   cooker   cyclist   helmet   instrument   musician   oven
> paint   painter   photographer   pieces   tent

2 **Work in pairs. Which other words go with the hobbies?**

chess: indoor game, black and white squares, queen, move

3 **Choose a hobby from Exercise 1 and describe it to your partner. Do not say the hobby. Your partner has to guess what it is. Then swap roles.**

You're outdoors. You have to find somewhere safe and dry. You put up your tent, light a fire to cook your food or use a little gas stove. You sleep in a sleeping bag . . .

Speaking Part 2

▶ **page 154 Speaking bank**

1 **Work in groups. Look at the photos.**

- What are these activities called?
- What do you know about each activity?
- Which activity do you think is most fun? Why?

2 **Listen to Rosa describing one of the photos. Which photo is it? Tick (✓) the things she talks about.**

activities	☐	people	☐
clothes	☐	place	☐
colours	☐	time of day	☐
equipment	☐	weather	☐
objects	☐		

3 **Listen again. Complete the sentences.**

1 In the photo I ......*can see*........ some boys.
2 The boy at the front .... a red cap.
3 It .... a very quiet road.
4 .... there are some buildings.
5 .... they're in a city.
6 There also .... some traffic lights behind them.
7 The weather .... cloudy.

4 **Answer the questions.**

1 Why do we say *looks like* in Question 3, but *looks* (without *like*) in Question 7?
2 Which prepositions of place does Rosa use in sentences 1–7?

> - Listen carefully to the instructions and then study your photo.
> - Talk about everything you can see (the place, people, objects, colours, clothes and weather).
> - Use prepositions of place (e.g. *next to, opposite*) to say where things are.

Exam advice

5 **Work in pairs. Using expressions from Exercise 3, take turns to describe one of the other photos for one minute.**

6 **Discuss the questions with your partner.**

- Did you both speak for at least a minute?
- Did you follow the Exam advice?
- Can you think of ways you could improve the description?

7 **Work in pairs. Look around your classroom and describe these to your partner.**

- a part of the room (where it is and what size it is)
- three objects in the room (where they are and what they look like)
- another pair of students (where they are, what they are wearing and what they are doing)

8 **Think of a photo that you really like (e.g. of you, your family or your friends). Describe it to your partner and say why it is special to you.**

Writing Part 2 (A story)

▶ **page 150 Writing bank**
A story

1 In Writing Part 2, you can choose to write a story. Look at this task and answer the questions.

1 Do the instructions give you the first line?
2 Should you write in the first person *(I)* or the third person *(he/she/it)*?

- Your English teacher has asked you to write a story.
- Your story must begin with this sentence:
  I had a really great day out.

2 The story below has three paragraphs. Decide which paragraph:

a describes the main events *2*
b sets the scene for the action
c describes the writer's feelings after the main event
d tells us how the writer felt during the action
e introduces the story (saying who did what, where and when)

3 Plan your own story for the task from Exercise 1. Make notes before you write. Use the ideas below.

- Use your imagination to invent a completely new story.
- Write about something that has happened to you, or someone you know.
- Use an idea from a film, TV programme or book, but change it a bit.
- Discuss your ideas with a partner, and ask them for suggestions.
- Plan your story in two or three paragraphs.

- Read the instructions. If you are given the first sentence, don't forget to use it.
- If there's a name or pronoun (e.g. *I* or *she*) in the first sentence, use it in your story.

Exam advice

4 Write your story in about 100 words.

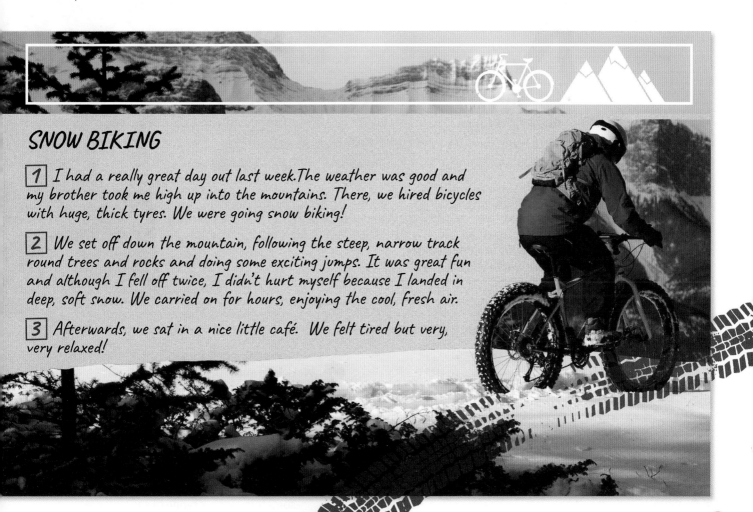

SNOW BIKING

1 I had a really great day out last week. The weather was good and my brother took me high up into the mountains. There, we hired bicycles with huge, thick tyres. We were going snow biking!

2 We set off down the mountain, following the steep, narrow track round trees and rocks and doing some exciting jumps. It was great fun and although I fell off twice, I didn't hurt myself because I landed in deep, soft snow. We carried on for hours, enjoying the cool, fresh air.

3 Afterwards, we sat in a nice little café. We felt tired but very, very relaxed!

Starting off
Holiday activities

1 Work in pairs. Look at the photos of some popular holiday destinations. Where would you like to go? Why? Use the words in the box.

> buy gifts / souvenirs   go sightseeing
> hire a bike   go snorkelling   hang out with friends
> look around a market   take photos

> I'd like to go to Amsterdam and hire a bike because I love cycling. What about you?

> I'd prefer to go to Bali to go snorkelling.

2 Listen to Joe asking Sonia about her last holiday. Where did she go? What did she do? Compare answers in pairs.

3 Work in groups. Discuss the questions.

When you go on holiday, do you prefer to …

1 go somewhere in your own country or go abroad?
2 do lots of different activities or hang out by the pool or beach?
3 go on a tour with a guide or make your own plans?
4 send different messages to your friends or post something for everyone to see?

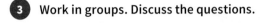

Reading Part 1

1 Look at this first question from Reading Part 1. What do you have to do in this part?

Boat trip

Due to bad weather, this has been put off until the same time tomorrow morning. Lunch will still be provided.

The notice for the boat trip is telling customers

A   the refreshments have changed.

B   the time has changed.

C   the day has changed.

2 Look at the text in Exercise 1 again. What kind of text is it? What information does it have?

3 Read the text and <u>underline</u> the key words. Then find words in each option (A, B and C) which have a similar meaning.

4 Now choose the correct letter: A, B or C.

- With each text, think about what kind of text it is.
- Underline the key words in each option. Then look for words and phrases in the options and the text that have similar meanings.

Exam advice

5 Look at the text in each question (2–5). What does it say? For each question, choose the correct answer.

2

Hi Dan, I had loads of fun today! My friends and I went sailing today before playing tennis. Then we had a barbecue on the beach and ate the fresh fish we'd caught. Back soon, Vicki

A   After playing tennis, Vicki went on a boat trip.

B   Vicki ate dinner on the beach before going sailing.

C   During her boat trip, Vicki went fishing.

3

From: Dave

To: Rob

Subject: Snowboard

Can I still borrow your snowboard for the trip? Pete says he can lend me his but I think yours is better. Let me know.

A   Pete's snowboard is not as good as Rob's.

B   Dave would rather borrow Pete's snowboard.

C   Rob would prefer to lend his snowboard to Pete.

4

Pool Rules

Please shower before entering
Diving is only permitted in the deep end
No food or drink in the pool area

A   Eating and drinking is not allowed next to the pool.

B   After swimming, please use the showers provided.

C   Diving is forbidden in all parts of the pool.

5

Mum,
Please wake me up at 7 tomorrow morning. I don't want to miss the bus for the trip and I'll need to make some sandwiches.
Claire

Claire is asking her mum to

A   make her some sandwiches for her trip.

B   make sure she is awake by a certain time.

C   drive her to the bus stop.

6 Work in groups. Choose one of the holiday destinations in the photos on page 34. Plan a holiday together.

- Where are you going? In which season and how long for?
- What are you going to see and do there?
- Where will you stay? Where will you eat?

7 Present your holiday to the class. Listen carefully to each presentation. Decide on the best idea.

4

Vocabulary
travel, *journey* and *trip*

1 Exam candidates often make mistakes with *travel*, *journey* and *trip*. Choose the correct options in *italics*.

1 My parents often go on business *journeys / trips*.

2 I'd love to win a *trip / journey* to Australia staying in a five-star hotel.

3 Last summer, we *tripped / travelled* around my country.

4 I've just got back from holiday. It was a wonderful *travel / trip*.

5 I'm really afraid of flying so I often get very nervous about the *travel / journey*.

2 Look at this extract from the *Cambridge Learner's Dictionary* and check your answers from Exercise 1.

> **travel, journey or trip?**
> The noun **travel** is a general word which means the activity of travelling.
> *Air travel has become much cheaper.*
>
> **travel** verb to make a journey
> *I spent a year travelling around Asia.*
>
> Use **journey** to talk about when you travel from one place to another.
> *He fell asleep during the train journey.*
> *Did you have a good journey?*
> ~~Did you have a good travel?~~
>
> A **trip** is a journey in which you visit a place for a short time and come back again.
> *a business trip*
> *a 3-day trip to Spain*

3 Work in groups. Ask and answer questions to find someone who …

- would like to travel around the world.
- went on a trip abroad last summer.
- often gets bored on long journeys.
- prefers trains to cars.
- doesn't like travelling.

> Would you like to travel around the world?

> Yes, I would.

> Where would you like to go?

Grammar
Comparative and superlative adjectives

▶ **Page 124 Grammar reference**
Comparative and superlative adjectives

1 Work in pairs. Read these facts. Decide if they are true or false. Then check your answers on page 164.

a The population of Canada is <u>larger than</u> the population of Tokyo.

b <u>The longest</u> country in the world is Brazil.

c Rain is <u>more common</u> in Rome <u>than</u> in Paris.

2 Sentences a–c above compare things. Complete the rules with the correct sentence letter.

> **Rules**
>
> 1 We generally use **comparative adjectives** (e.g. *larger than*) to say that something has more size, height, etc. than another: sentences ......A...... and ....
>
> 2 We generally use **superlative adjectives** (e.g. *the longest*) to say that within its group, something has the most size, height, etc.: sentence ....

3 Exam candidates often make mistakes with comparative and superlative adjectives. Complete the table.

	adjective	comparative	superlative
regular	deep	(1) .... than	the deepest
	safe	(2) .... than	the safest
	noisy	(3) .... than	the (6) ....
	big	(4) .... than	the (7) ....
	beautiful	more beautiful than	the (8) ....
irregular	good	better than	the (9) ....
	bad	(5) .... than	the (10) ....
	far	farther / further than	the farthest / the furthest
more/less		more	the (11) ....
		less	the (12) ....

4 <u>Underline</u> and correct the mistake in each sentence.

1 I don't like living in the countryside even if it is more safe than the city.

2 That's the worse joke I have ever heard in all my life.

3 In the centre is the bigest market in Europe.

4 Portugal is the hotest country I have ever visited.

5 This town is more quiet than the town I used to live in.

6 My best friend is taler than me and better looking too!

5 Work in pairs. Look at the sentences from Exercise 4 again. What are the spelling rules for regular comparative and superlative adjectives?

6 Complete the sentences with the comparative or superlative form of the adjective in brackets. Then choose the correct option (A, B or C).

THE BIGGEST...
THE FASTEST...

1 North America is ....*bigger*........ (big) than

  A Asia   B Africa   C South America

2 What is ....*the largest*.... (large) country in the world?

  A Russia   B Canada   C China

3 What is .... (dangerous) creature in the world?

  A the snake   B the mosquito   C the shark

4 An African elephant is .... (light) than a

  A a blue whale   B brown bear   C giraffe

5 A howler monkey is .... (noisy) than

  A a parrot   B a lion   C a lion and a parrot

6 What is .... (slow) fish in the world?

  A the seahorse   B the tuna   C the shark

7 Great White Sharks are .... (fast) than

  A tunas   B killer whales   C dolphins

8 Where is .... (busy) train station in the world?

  A New York   B London   C Tokyo

9 Y40 Deep Joy is .... (deep) diving pool in the world. It's in

  A Italy   B Sydney   C Argentina

10 Antarctica is .... (dry) than

  A Australia   B Europe   C any other place in the world

7 Listen to Abby and Lucas discussing the quiz and check your answers.

19

8 **/P/ Weak forms in comparative structures**

20 Listen to the extracts. Are the underlined syllables stressed or not stressed?

- I wouldn't like to share my home with a howler monkey. They're much loud<u>er th</u><u>an</u> parrots or lions.

- Great White Sharks can swim at 40 kilometres per hour, so they're fast<u>er th</u><u>an</u> dolphins, which can swim at 30 kilometres per hour.

a bit, a little, slightly, much, far, a lot

▶ **Page 125 Grammar reference**
a bit, a little, slightly, much, far, a lot

9 How different are these places and animals? Use the comparative form of the adjectives in brackets to write sentences. Use *a bit*, *a little*, *slightly*, *much*, *far* or *a lot*.

1 Mount Everest, in the Himalayas, is around 8,850 metres high. K2, also in the Himalayas, is around 8,611 metres high. (high)

Mount Everest is slightly higher than K2.

2 An African elephant's brain weighs over 5 kg. A human adult's brain weighs about 1.3 kg. (heavy)
An African elephant's brain is ....

3 Arica in Chile gets 0.76 mm of rain per year. Death Valley in Arizona, USA, gets less than 50 mm per year. (dry)
Arica is ....

4 84 million people travel through Atlanta International Airport, USA each year. 67 million people travel through London's Heathrow Airport. (busy)
Atlanta International Airport is ....

5 Cherrapunji in India gets 11,777 mm of rain every year. Tutendo in Colombia receives 11,770 mm per year (wet)
Cherrapunji is ....

6 Cheetahs can run at 120 kilometres an hour. Elephants can run at about 20 kilometres an hour. (fast)
Cheetahs can ....

(not) as … as

▶ **Page 125 Grammar reference**
(not) as … as

10 Read part of a blog about Shanghai, in China. Then answer the questions.

> One of my favourite cities in the world is Shanghai, in China. It isn't the capital, that's Beijing. Shanghai is <u>not as polluted as</u> Beijing, even though Shanghai is bigger and more people live there. It's an international city. It's <u>as international as</u> many other large cities in the world like New York or London, so it has a lot to offer.

1 What expression do we use to say things are the same?
2 What word do we add to say things are different?
3 Does the form of the adjective change?

11 Write down an example of each thing from the box.

> your favourite activity   your favourite animal
> your favourite celebrity   your favourite city

12 Work in pairs. Compare your favourite things from Exercise 11. Say which you think is better.

What's your favourite animal?

I love cats.

I don't. I think dogs are much better than cats because cats aren't as friendly as dogs.

Vocabulary
Buildings and places

1 Work in pairs. Look at the photos. What can you see? Use some of the words from the box.

> art gallery book shop bridge cinema
> department store factory fountain library
> market monument shopping centre sports centre
> stadium town hall youth club

> I think the stadium is in Barcelona. And you?

2 Which of the things from Exercise 1 do you have in your town or city? Which do you like most?

3 Write the opposite of each adjective.

> cheap clean dangerous dull empty
> interesting low near old quiet ugly wide

1 crowded	5 dirty	9 safe
2 narrow	6 beautiful	10 expensive
3 high	7 lively	11 noisy
4 modern	8 boring	12 far

4 Work in groups. Ask and answer questions about where you do these activities. Remember to say why.

> get fit get some peace and quiet go shopping
> have a good time stay dry when it's raining take photos

> We often go to the market, but we rarely go to the shopping centre because it's too crowded and noisy.

Grammar
big and *enormous*

▶ **Page 125 Grammar reference**
Gradable and non-gradable adjectives

1 Match descriptions 1–3 with photos A–D. Then answer the questions.

1 The Statue of Liberty was a gift from France in 1886 and, at 93 metres, it's quite <u>tall</u>. Visitors need to climb 354 stairs to get to the top.

2 The Mall of the Emirates is very <u>large</u>. Apart from shops and restaurants, there's a games centre, a cinema and a theatre, two hotels and you can also go skiing.

3 The Camp Nou (or 'New Ground') football stadium is absolutely <u>enormous</u>. 99,354 people can watch football there, so it is the biggest stadium in Europe.

- Which of the <u>underlined</u> adjectives can we use with *very*, *extremely* and *quite*? (These are called **gradable** adjectives.)
- Which of the adjectives can we use with *absolutely* or *totally*? (These are called **non-gradable** adjectives.)

2 Write the gradable adjectives for these non-gradable adjectives. Sometimes, more than one answer is possible.

1	enormous *big*	5	terrible
2	tiny	6	exhausting
3	boiling	7	fascinating
4	freezing	8	fantastic

3 Exam candidates often make mistakes with non-gradable adjectives. Choose the correct options in *italics*.

1 It's a(n) *very / absolutely* wonderful place.

2 It was an *extremely / absolutely* good movie. You should see it.

3 That dog is *very / absolutely* enormous.

4 The weather is *absolutely / quite* hot.

5 This food is *very / absolutely* nice.

4 Listen to Ani answering these questions. Make notes on her answers.

1 Where do you come from?

2 What do you like about living there?

3 What would you change about where you live?

5 Work in pairs. Ask and answer the questions from Exercise 4. Try to use *very*, *quite*, *extremely* and *absolutely* with gradable and non-gradable adjectives.

Listening Part 3

1 Work in groups. What can you see in the photos? Would you like to do a bushcraft course? Why? / Why not?

> **Bushcraft** describes the skills we need to stay alive in the wild, for example how to look for drinking water or build a fire.

2 Read these notes about a bushcraft skills course for young people. Decide what information you think is missing from each space (*number, date, noun,* etc.).

BUSHCRAFT SKILLS
COURSE FOR YOUNG PEOPLE

SATURDAY MORNING
- meet your guide outside the **(1)** ....
- learn how to use equipment
- make a **(2)** .... to sleep in
- prepare food for lunch, e.g. a **(3)** .... you have caught

SATURDAY AFTERNOON
- look for wild foods

OTHER EXAMPLE ACTIVITIES INCLUDE HOW TO
- make drinking water
- follow the stars
- predict the weather with **(4)** ....

FURTHER INFORMATION:
Email address: **(5)** .... @bushcraftskills.com
Phone number: **(6)** ....

> - Before you listen, read the notes carefully and think about what kind of words are missing.
> - Write down the answers exactly as you hear them.

Exam advice

3 You will hear a woman talking to a group of young people about the bushcraft courses she organises. For each question, write the correct answer in the gap. Write one or two words, or a number.

4 Listen again and check.

5 Work in groups.
- How could these skills help you in your everyday life?
- What other skills should young people learn?

Writing Part 1

▶ **Page 145 Writing bank**
An email

1 Read this Writing Part 1 task.
1 What do you need to write?
2 What information should you include?

Read this email from your English-speaking friend Stevie, and the notes you have made.

> **From:** Stevie
>
> As part of a school project, I have to write about a city which people often visit. I'd like to write about a city in your country. Can you suggest one? — *What about ...?*
>
> Which time of year is the most popular with tourists? — *Tell Stevie.*
>
> I don't know much about your city. What's it like? — *Describe it.*
>
> What can tourists do there? — *Tell Stevie.*
>
> See you soon,
> Stevie

Write your email to Stevie, using **all** the notes.

2 Read Bandile's answer. Which city is he writing about?

> Dear Stevie,
>
> Why don't you write about my city? Johannesburg is the largest city in South Africa and the most visited city in Africa. One of the best things about my city is the weather because the sun even shines in winter. Tourists mainly come in our summer which is between December and February so the city gets really crowded then.
>
> There is so much for visitors to do in Johannesburg. For something unusual, go on the graffiti walking tour and then visit 27 Boxes – a shopping centre made of enormous boxes. And when you get hungry, try the food market. The choice of food is absolutely amazing.
>
> Bye for now,
> Bandile

3 Read Bandile's email again.

1 Does the email answer all the parts of the question?

2 Is the answer well organised?

3 Does the email open and close in a suitable way?

4 Are the ideas connected with words like *and*, *because* and *which*?

5 Is there a variety of vocabulary and grammar (tenses, adjectives, etc.)?

6 Is the email about 100 words?

4 Write your own answer to the task from Exercise 1 in about 100 words. You can use the <u>underlined</u> expressions from Bandile's email.

5 Work in groups. Read each other's emails to find out if you can answer 'yes' to all the questions from Exercise 3.

• In preparation for the exam, it is useful to write rough drafts. Your teacher and other students can then help you to improve your work before you write your final draft.

• In the real exam, you won't have time to write a rough draft. Just make notes before you start writing.

Exam advice

6 Write the final draft of your email.

Speaking Part 3

▶ Page 159 Speaking bank

1 Listen to a family talking about their next holiday. Which type of holiday do they choose?

2 Work in pairs. Answer these questions about the conversation.

1 Does each member of the family take turns to speak?

2 Does each member make a suggestion and then give reasons for their suggestion?

---

3 Complete the sentences. Then listen again and check.

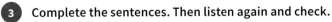

1 Why .... we all go to Paris for our next holiday? ......S......

2 I'd .... to go somewhere quieter. ....

3 It's one of the .... beautiful places in the world. ....

4 Not camping again, please! We got .... wet last time. ....

5 What .... trying a new sport like surfing or snorkelling? ....

6 Let's .... that! ....

7 There's so .... to do. ....

4 Decide which sentences from Exercise 3 are suggestions (S) and reasons (R).

• Don't talk for a long time without letting your partner speak.

• Give reasons for your suggestions and ask the other candidate to give reasons for theirs.

Exam advice

5 Do this task with a partner. Talk for about two minutes.

A family would like to visit the capital city in their country for a day.

Here are some things they could do there.

Talk together about the different things they could do, and say which would be the most enjoyable.

3 Vocabulary and grammar review

Vocabulary

1 **Choose the correct preposition in *italics*.**

1 In class, I sit *behind / between* two friends, so the three of us are all on the front row.

2 I live *next to / near* my school and I can walk there in ten minutes.

3 I live on the third floor and my cousins live right *below / above* us on the fourth floor.

4 At the cinema I couldn't see much when a tall man sat down *in front of / opposite* me.

5 You can either cross the river on the bridge or take the tunnel *under / in* it.

6 We ran *between / inside* a shop when the rain started.

2 **Match the beginnings of sentences 1–8 with endings a–h.**

1 I'm going to put my name ......c......
2 We're all really looking ....
3 People who like art often take ....
4 I need to find ....
5 I'm sure that you can deal ....
6 In the next game, you can join ....
7 It's a long walk, so I need to set ....
8 If I spend too much, I'll run ....

a up painting as a hobby.
b with any problems like that.
c down for swimming lessons.
d off very early in the morning.
e forward to surfing tomorrow.
f out of money soon.
g in and play for our team.
h out some information for my homework.

3 **Choose the correct option (A, B or C).**

1 While I'm away, a neighbour is ... our cat.
   A looking for
   B looking after
   C looking at

2 My brother has a wonderful ... of old coins.
   A collection
   B collecting
   C collect

3 My brother is a very good .... He makes some lovely meals.
   A cook
   B cooker
   C cooking

4 I want to learn the piano, or another musical …
   A object.
   B equipment.
   C instrument.

5 The bus … for children is much lower than for adults.
   A fee
   B fare
   C value

6 It's more fun to take … in a game than just watch it.
   A team
   B part
   C practice

Grammar

4 **Complete the email with the *-ing* or the infinitive form of the verb in brackets.**

Hi Louis,

I'm planning **(1)** to go (go) away on holiday next week, but there are still so many things I need **(2)** .... (do) before I leave! I want **(3)** .... (take) some new clothes with me, but I can't afford **(4)** .... (buy) expensive things. Actually I don't feel like **(5)** .... (spend) anything at all, so now I've decided **(6)** .... (borrow) some clothes from my sister. I'm sure she won't mind! I'm also hoping **(7)** .... (see) my friends here before I go, so I've suggested **(8)** .... (spend) Sunday afternoon together. And when I'm away, I must remember **(9)** .... (send) you photos. I forgot **(10)** .... (do) that last summer, but I promise I will this time!

See you on Friday

Aria

Vocabulary

1 Complete Clara's email with adjectives in the correct form. The first letter is given and there is one space for each other letter in the word.

Hi George,

I live in Bilbao, which is a very large city in Spain. In fact, it is the **(1)** *biggest* city in the area. Bilbao is **(2)** g _ _ _ _ – I love it! It's located on the north coast and it can be quite rainy. April is by far the **(3)** w _ _ _ _ _ _ month but January is the **(4)** c _ _ _ _ _ _ month. Last January was **(5)** f _ _ _ _ _ _ _, temperatures fell to -20C! As for the city itself, Bilbao is absolutely fascinating. I love shopping and there are many places to go in the city centre. My friends love the shopping centre. It's always fun and **(6)** l _ _ _ _ _ . I prefer El Corte Inglés, it's a **(7)** h _ _ _ department store. Tourists usually visit the Guggenheim Museum, but I think it's a bit **(8)** b _ _ _ _ _. Why don't you come and visit me?

Hope to hear from you soon.

Lots of love,

Clara

2 Choose the correct option in *italics*.

1 At 250 metres below the sea, Jericho is the world's *highest / lowest / widest* city.

2 Gustave Eiffel was responsible for building the Eiffel Tower and the Statue of Liberty. The Statue of Liberty is slightly older *then / as / than* the Eiffel Tower.

3 One of the most popular tourist attractions in the world is Istanbul's Grand Bazaar which is a(n) *absolutely / very / far* large market.

4 The pool at San Alfonso del Mar, Chile is *more / far / very* larger than any other swimming pool in the world.

5 Steve Fossett was the first person to *travel / trip / journey* around the world in a hot-air balloon. He took just under 15 days.

6 The world's largest *bookshop / department store / library* is in Washington DC in the USA. It has over 38 million books that only people working for the government can borrow.

Grammar

3 Exam candidates often make mistakes with comparative adjectives. Underline and correct the mistakes in the sentences.

1 My city is much ~~more better~~ *better* than any other city in the world.

2 It is more easy for you to walk to my house.

3 That's the worse restaurant we've ever been to.

4 I like living in the city much more that the countryside.

5 Those days on holiday were the happier days of my life.

6 Hotels are more cheaper here than the hotels in the city.

4 Read the article about a holiday and think of the word which best fits each gap. Write only one word in each gap.

Last August, we set off for our summer holiday in Turkey. I thought the journey was going to be really terrible but it wasn't as **(1)** *bad* as I'd expected. The hotel was brilliant. It was nearer to the beach **(2)** .... the hotel we stayed in last year and the food was absolutely delicious. In fact the restaurant in our hotel was the **(3)** .... popular restaurant in town. We tried lots of new sports. Of all the activities, I liked going snorkelling **(4)** .... It really was an amazing experience. The weather was boiling. I have never visited a place as hot **(5)** .... this. I don't think I'll ever forget that holiday. That beach has to be one of the most beautiful places **(6)** .... the world.

5 Different feelings

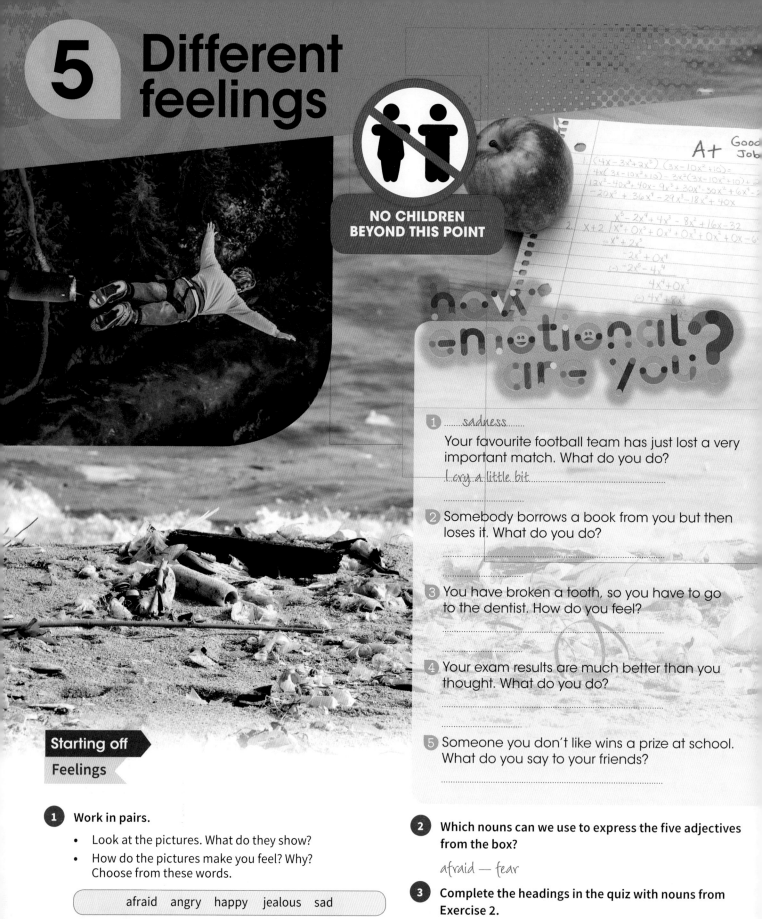

NO CHILDREN BEYOND THIS POINT

A+ Good Job

how emotional are you?

1 ......sadness......
Your favourite football team has just lost a very important match. What do you do?
~~I cry a little bit~~

2 Somebody borrows a book from you but then loses it. What do you do?

3 You have broken a tooth, so you have to go to the dentist. How do you feel?

4 Your exam results are much better than you thought. What do you do?

5 Someone you don't like wins a prize at school. What do you say to your friends?

Starting off

Feelings

1 Work in pairs.
- Look at the pictures. What do they show?
- How do the pictures make you feel? Why? Choose from these words.

> afraid   angry   happy   jealous   sad

> The first picture makes me feel happy.

2 Which nouns can we use to express the five adjectives from the box?

afraid — fear

3 Complete the headings in the quiz with nouns from Exercise 2.

4 Do the quiz. Make notes on your answers.

5 Work in groups. Compare your answers from Exercise 4.

Listening Part 2

1 Match the feelings from the box with definitions 1–6.

> bored confident disappointed
> embarrassed ~~grateful~~ nervous

1 feeling or showing thanks *grateful*
2 unhappy because something wasn't as good as you hoped, or didn't happen
3 worried about something that will or might happen
4 sure that you can do something well
5 feeling ashamed or shy
6 unhappy because something isn't interesting or you've got nothing to do

2 Look at the exam task below. <u>Underline</u> the key words in questions 1–6.

> • Read each question to understand what the situation is. Decide what you have to listen for (e.g. a feeling or an opinion).
> • You can change your mind about an answer when you listen again.
>
> **Exam advice**

3 Listen to people talking in six different situations. For each question, choose the correct answer.

24

1 You will hear a <u>young woman</u> talking about taking part in a <u>singing contest</u>.
   <u>After</u> she finished singing, <u>she felt</u>
   A confident about winning the competition.
   B disappointed with her scores.
   C embarrassed by her performance.

2 You will hear two friends talking about camping.
   The girl advises the boy to
   A pack plenty of food.
   B take some warm clothes.
   C camp close to a lake.

3 You will hear a boy talking to his friend about a literature exam.
   How does he feel?
   A nervous about taking it
   B bored of revising
   C happy with his friend's advice

4 You will hear a girl telling a friend about studying abroad.
   Who did she have most fun with?
   A other students on the course
   B people in the town centre
   C the family she stayed with

5 You will hear a boy telling his friend about how he travels to school.
   Why has he decided to go by bike?
   A to save some money
   B to get more exercise
   C to help reduce pollution

6 You will hear a girl talking to a friend about going shopping.
   Who annoyed her yesterday?
   A people who worked in the shop
   B other customers in the shop
   C pedestrians outside the shop

4 Listen again and check.

24

5 Work in pairs. What annoys you? Why?

> People who don't say 'please' or 'thank you' really annoy me!

Grammar

can, *could*, *might* and *may*

▶ **Page 126 Grammar reference**
Modal verbs: *can, could, might,* and *may* (ability and possibility)

1 Look at the <u>underlined</u> modal verbs for ability and possibility. Then answer the questions.

> So, do you think you'll try again in next year's contest?
>
> Yes, if I <u>can</u>. I <u>might not</u> win, but I think I <u>could</u> do better than this year.

1 Which modal verb is negative?
2 Where does *not* go?
3 What is the short form of *cannot* and *could not*?
4 What form of the verb goes after a modal verb?

2 Exam candidates often make mistakes with modal verbs. <u>Underline</u> and correct one mistake in each sentence.

1 We can to go to the cinema next weekend.
2 I know it may seems strange.
3 Sorry but tomorrow I'm not can go.
4 What we could do?
5 We can doing a lot of sports here.
6 It's could be quite boring for you.
7 We could met at 8 o'clock near the cinema.

3 Read the message. Then complete the rules with the <u>underlined</u> words.

> Hi Kylie, I'm sorry I <u>couldn't</u> meet you yesterday and I don't think I <u>can</u> go out on Thursday, either. I <u>may</u> be busy all evening on Friday, too, so Saturday <u>might</u> be better. There's a new film on at the cinema. I don't know much about it but it's got our favourite actor in it, so it <u>could</u> be really good! Let me know what you think. Lauren

1 We use .... to talk about ability in the present and .... to talk about ability in the past.

2 We use .... , ... or .... for possibility in the present or future, with no real difference in meaning.

4 Choose the correct option in *italics*.

> Hi Lauren, thanks for your message. I **(1)** *might not / couldn't* reply to you earlier because I was in class. I **(2)** *may / can* see you're very busy at the moment, so perhaps it **(3)** *can / might* be better to meet another weekend. It's a shame we **(4)** *can't / may not* see each other more often. You're my best friend and I know I **(5)** *might / can* always tell you anything. I **(6)** *could / couldn't* phone you in the next few days if you like. Love, Kylie

5 Work in pairs.

1 Student A: think of a place, then say what you can and can't do there.
Student B: guess what the place is.

> You can eat ice cream, you can't arrive late, you can't talk during the film ...

> The cinema!

2 Tell your partner about things you *could*, *may*, *might* or *might not* do next weekend.

> I could go to the park, but I may just stay in and watch TV.

Speaking Part 4

▶ **Page 161 Speaking bank**

1 Work in groups.

1 How do teenagers in your country usually chat to each other? e.g. *by phone, online messaging*

2 What do they most often talk about? e.g. *friends, sport*

2 Listen to Rafael from Mexico and Lian from China talking about chatting to people. Complete the questions.

1 .... do you most enjoy chatting .... ?

2 .... do you .... chat?

3 .... can you chat .... people?

4 .... do you most like chatting .... ?

3 Listen again. Complete the questions they use to ask for each other's opinion.

1 How .... you?

2 .... you?

3 What .... you?

4 Do you .... ?

5 What do you .... ?

> • Take turns with your partner and try to speak for about the same length of time.
>
> • Make the discussion longer by asking your partner for more information or about their opinions.

Exam advice

4 Work in pairs.

• Student A: ask your partner the questions from Exercise 2.

• Student B: answer the questions, using questions from Exercise 3 to take turns.

Grammar

Modals for advice, obligation and prohibition

▶ **Page 126 Grammar reference**
Modal verbs: *should, shouldn't, ought to, must, mustn't, have to, don't have to* (obligation and prohibition)

1 Look at the people in pictures A and B. <u>Underline</u> the modals used in the advice.

You ought to get a new T-shirt.

You shouldn't go out tonight.

2 Read the rules. Then match pictures C–F with sentences 1–4.

1 You must wear this for the wedding.   F
2 You have to be 14 to go on this.
3 You mustn't make such a mess!
4 You don't have to pay.

> **Rules**
>
> • Use *have to* when a rule or a law says it's necessary to do something.
>
> • Use *don't have to* when it's not necessary to do something.
>
> • Use *must* when the speaker thinks it's necessary to do something.
>
> • Use *mustn't* when you're not allowed to do something.

3 Complete the sentences using *must, mustn't, have to* or *don't have to.*

1 It's still early.
   We ....*don't have to*............ go home yet.

2 You look tired.
   You .... take a break.

3 It's a secret.
   You .... tell her what I said.

4 Great, it's a holiday!
   I .... get up early!

5 No, you can't drive the car. You .... be 18!

4 Read these comments by students about school rules. Choose the correct option in *italics.*

1 'We *shouldn't /* (*mustn't*) use dictionaries during exams.'

2 'It's a rule that we *ought to / have to* wear a uniform.'

3 'We *don't have to / mustn't* go to school on Saturdays.'

4 'Our teachers say we *must / ought to* always switch off our phones in class.'

5 'We *shouldn't / don't have to* make any noise in lessons.'

5 Work in pairs. Use modal verbs to say which sentences from Exercise 4 are true for your school.

> We can use dictionaries in some exams.

> We can't in my school. We mustn't use them in any exams.

/p/ Modal verbs: weak and strong forms

6 Listen and repeat the sentences.

a I can buy another one.
b I can't afford that one.
c I could meet you at 5.30.
d I couldn't live without my phone!
e I should get up earlier on Sundays.
f I shouldn't go to bed so late.

7 Listen again and answer the questions.

1 In which sentences is it easier to hear the modal verb? Do these sentences also contain *not*?
2 How is *not* written? Is it easy to hear this?
3 Which sentences have a weak form of the modal verb, which is not so easy to hear? Do these sentences also contain *not*?

8 Work in pairs.

Tell your partner about something you …
1 have to do at home.
2 mustn't do at school.
3 don't have to do at weekends.
4 must do this week.
5 shouldn't do but sometimes do.
6 ought to do but probably won't do.

> I have to tidy my room every week.

Vocabulary

Adjectives and prepositions

1 Work in pairs. How do you feel when you have to do things other people tell you? Give examples.

> I feel annoyed with my parents when they tell me to eat things I don't want to.

2 In the examples above, *with* follows *annoyed*. In these sentences written by exam candidates, underline the preposition which comes after the adjective.

1 My father was very angry with me.
2 I never get tired of watching this film.
3 He was very sorry about what happened.

3 Complete the table with the prepositions *about*, *of* and *with*. Then think of more adjectives for each preposition and add them to the table.

afraid, ashamed, jealous, bored, fond	(1) ....
angry, disappointed, pleased, satisfied	(2) ....
sad, nervous, crazy, sure, depressed	(3) ....

Note: some adjectives can be followed by different prepositions with no change of meaning (*Ivy was getting bored of/with the book. It was a red car, I'm sure of/about that*). Others take one preposition for someone (*She's angry with Luca*), but another for something (*She's angry about the late train*).

4 Complete the questions with the correct prepositions. T ask your partner the questions.

1 Is there anything in the news you feel sad .... ?

2 Is there anyone you sometimes get angry .... ?

3 When you were small, what were you afraid .... ?

4 What do you sometimes get bored .... ?

5 Is there anything you feel nervous .... ?

Adjectives with -ed and -ing

▶ **Page 127 Grammar reference**
Adjectives with -ed and -ing endings

1 Quickly read the story. Do not complete the gaps at the moment.

1 Why did Leo ask the airline to help?
2 What happened in the end?

2 Look at this sentence. What -ing adjective does it use? How does the spelling change from the word in brackets?

For many people the flight from Europe to Australia is long and boring. (bore)

3 The sentence could be changed like this. What -ed adjective does it use? When do we use the -ing adjective and when do we use the -ed adjective?

Many people feel <u>bored</u> on the long flight from Europe to Australia.

4 Complete the text with the correct form of the adjectives in brackets. Use -ing if it describes something, or -ed if it tells us how someone feels.

5 Work in pairs.

Talk about the last time you were …
• surprised.
• tired.
• disappointed.

Now ask your partner to describe situations that were:
• exciting.
• interesting.
• embarrassing.

6 Write three pairs of sentences using the adjectives from gaps 2, 8 and 10 in the text.

It's relaxing to listen to music.
I always feel relaxed when I play my favourite song.

LOVE in the AIR

For many people, the flight from Europe to Australia is long and **(1)** ......*boring*...... (bore). But it wasn't for Abbie and Leo Davies – because that's where they first met.

'Abbie was sitting next to me,' said Leo. 'I felt **(2)** .... (relax) talking to her and we got on really well. We chatted all the way to Sydney and it was **(3)** .... (surprise) how quickly the time went.'

But they forgot to get each other's phone number, so after the flight Leo contacted the airline. 'To be honest, it was a bit **(4)** .... (embarrass) because the staff were quite **(5)** .... (amuse) by the situation, but anyway I gave them her seat number, and waited.'

Abbie, too, was feeling sad.

'I was **(6)** .... (annoy) with myself for not getting his number,' she said, 'though I was also a bit **(7)** .... (disappoint) he didn't ask me for mine. I thought he wasn't really **(8)** .... (interest) in seeing me again. So I was **(9)** .... (amaze) when the airline phoned to ask if I wanted to call Leo. I was so **(10)** .... (excite) that I phoned him that evening, and soon we had our first date. Now we're married and we're very happy together.'

Reading Part 4

How I dealt with stress

1 Work in pairs.

1 Which of the things in the box are the most stressful?

> bullying changing school difficulty sleeping exams
> family problems moving to another city
> school work speaking in public

2 What other causes of stress are there?

3 What happens to people when they feel stressed?

2 Quickly read the article. What is the topic of each paragraph?

1: the effects of stress

- Quickly read the main text. What is each paragraph about?

- Look at the ideas before and after each gap, then look for similar ideas in A–H.

- Look for words that often link ideas, for example *this, then, do, also* and *however.*

Exam advice

3 You are going to read an article about dealing with stress. Five sentences have been removed from the article. For each question, choose the correct answer. There are three extra sentences which you do not need to use.

A One I particularly like has a 'quick tips' section you can use in stressful situations.

B It was so funny that I felt more cheerful straight away.

C That made me realise I couldn't go on feeling so stressed.

D I knew I had to finish that first.

E It recommended that everyone should laugh more often every day.

F So I took up dancing instead.

G People who do this often seem to be more miserable than everyone else.

H If it's longer, I find it hard to get back into what I was concentrating on.

4 Work in pairs.

- Do you think an 'anti-stress' app could make you feel better? Why? / Why not?

- Which of the other ideas in the article might help you relax? Why?

- What other ways can you think of to deal with stress?

1 For months I'd been unable to relax and I felt awful. I worried about things, I wasn't sleeping well and I couldn't concentrate on my school exams revision. Then my best friend told me that everyone thought I was always in a bad mood. **(1)** ....*C*...............

2 I began by making some simple changes to my routine. Each morning when I woke up, I thought about things I was looking forward to, so that I started the day in a more positive mood. I kept doing that until it became a habit. I also knew I should do more exercise, but to tell the truth I don't enjoy doing sports. **(2)** ....That really helped me to relax, particularly when I learnt to concentrate on enjoying the experience rather than let negative thoughts go through my mind.

3 I changed the way I study, too. I used to put off working as long as I could until finally I had to study for hours non-stop, often until late in the evening when I was getting really tired. Nowadays I try to do my homework straight after school and every 40 minutes or so, I take a break, usually for no more than ten minutes. **(3)** ....

4 I've also discovered some great anti-stress apps for my phone, such as Mindshift, Live Happy and Smiling Mind. Some of these are designed for teenagers, with yoga and breathing exercises to help you relax, a 'book of happy memories' that you create for yourself to look at when you're feeling down, and relaxing sounds such as the ocean. **(4)** .... Some of these apps are free.

5 Last month I read an article which said people with a good sense of humour are usually happier and more relaxed. **(5)** .... So watching cartoons or your favourite comedy series really can help you relax – and even make it easier to do your homework!

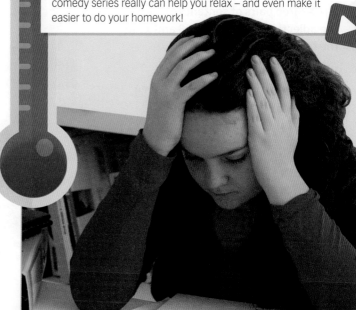

Vocabulary

Adjectives and their opposites

1 Match the adjectives in box A with their opposites in box B.

A

> ~~awful~~ funny generous miserable
> ashamed nervous dull strange

B

> cheerful spectacular ~~fantastic~~ mean
> ordinary proud relaxed serious

2 Work in pairs.

Tell your partner about something …
- strange that happened in a film you saw.
- fantastic that happened during the holidays.
- awful that happened at school.
- funny that you saw online or on TV.

Writing Part 2: A story

▶ **Page 150 Writing bank**
A story

1 Read this Writing Part 2 task and answer the questions.

> - Your English teacher has asked you to write a story.
> - Your story must begin with this sentence:
>   *Olivia read the message from her friend and smiled.*

1 Are you given a first line?
2 Should you write in the first or the third person?
3 Which are the key words?

2 Read the example answer. Then answer the questions.

1 Where and when does most of the action happen?
2 Who are the main characters and what is their relationship?
3 What is the situation?
4 What problem do the characters have?
5 How is this problem solved?
6 How does the story end?

Olivia read the message from her friend and smiled. She was excited because Ellie, who lived abroad, was coming to visit her this Friday!

Just as Olivia reached the airport to pick up Ellie, she received a call. 'There's thick fog here and my plane can't take off,' explained Ellie. 'I'm not sure what'll happen.'

'I'm really disappointed,' replied Olivia.

As Olivia waited at the airport, she became quite miserable. But then, Ellie called again. 'The sky's cleared!' she said. Three hours later Olivia was delighted when Ellie's flight had finally landed. Ellie said, 'It's fantastic to see you!'

3 Read the story again. Find four adjectives that describe how Olivia felt.

4 Read this Writing Part 2 task and answer the questions from Exercise 1.

> - Your English teacher has asked you to write a story.
> - Your story must begin with this sentence:
>   *Matthew felt excited as he waited for the train.*

5 Think about the questions from Exercise 2 and plan your story.

- Decide where and when to set your story.
- Plan the main events and think about the kind of person your main character is.
- Try to make your story interesting for your readers.

Exam advice

6 Write your story in about 100 words.

6 That's entertainment!

Reading Part 2

1 Tom and Ian are looking for something to do one afternoon. Read about what they like and dislike. Underline the key words.

Tom and Ian have a free afternoon but neither of them like crowds. They're interested in theatre and exhibitions for young people, but they don't have much money.

2 Read the entertainment guide and decide which event is the most suitable for Tom and Ian. <u>Underline</u> where you find the information. Then answer the questions.

1 Tom and Ian are interested in theatres and exhibitions. Why isn't D suitable?

2 Neither of them like crowds. Why isn't G suitable?

3 Read the guide again. Decide which event would be the most suitable for the people (2–5).

> • Underline the key words in the descriptions of people.
>
> • Read A–H to find information that matches the key words in 1–5.

Exam advice

2  Alice's parents want to take her to see something brand new and have a meal afterwards somewhere close by. They want to go by public transport but they don't want to walk too far.

3  Jack is keen on cartoons. As he'll be alone, he would like to go somewhere where he can get to know people with similar interests and also add to his collection of old books and magazines.

4  Two 14-year-old friends, Patricia and Stef would love to see a live performance in a foreign language. Whenever they go out together, they always buy something to eat during the interval.

5  Su's mum has promised to take her to see a show with music for her birthday. Su would like to see something with an enjoyable story but her mum isn't fond of rock or pop.

Starting off

Television programmes

1 Match the photos with the types of TV from the box.

> advert   cartoon   chat show   comedy series
> cooking show   quiz show   reality show
> sports   the news   wildlife documentary

2 Listen to Clare asking Nick about TV. How much does Nick watch? What are his favourite types of programme? *(27)*

3 Listen again and write down Clare's six questions. Then work in groups. Ask and answer Clare's questions. *(27)*

52

TURN OFF THE TV AND GO OUT!

A Beautiful Sunset ★★★

This band returns once again to play songs from their latest album. Expect an amazing performance from these musicians who have sold over 80 million records. Tickets are on sale for €60, the price includes a free souvenir T-shirt. Enjoy a meal in our restaurant after the show. Public transport nearby.

The Sports Palace

C Captain Rob's Adventures in 4DX ★★★

Not cheap but this animated version of a well-known film is an experience you definitely can't get at home. The picture and sound quality is fantastic, and the 4D effects are amazing. Feel the wind and the waves, as you sail with Captain Rob. Choice of restaurants nearby. Public transport within easy walking distance.

Filmworld 4DX

B Our lives, their lives

Now in its second year, this exhibition explores the lives of teenagers from all around the world through photographs and cartoons, music and interviews. Some of the interviews are with parents who are asked to compare their lives with those of their children. Free entry to this popular museum, which is rarely busy after 3 pm. Don't miss the excellent gift shop.

Jameson Museum

F Paris 1792

Paris during the French Revolution and Marco Morelli has fallen in love with a rich young woman. However, one of the family's servants is also in love with her. This is a brand-new version of the Italian opera with amazing singing and real classical music! Audiences of all ages will be entertained. Food and drink not permitted in the theatre.

Elizabeth Theatre

G Big sight

Held over three days, this comic market celebrates Japanese animation. In this huge conference centre, fans can meet other fans, buy rare comics, dress up as their favourite characters and take selfies. No admission fee. Reasonably priced food, but expect long queues for everything, even the toilets!

The Conference Centre

D The Music Teacher ★★

Based on a film, this musical is now showing on stage. An out-of-work guitarist tells some lies and gets a job as a teacher. He persuades some of his students to create a rock group so that they can take part in the Battle of the Bands competition. Afternoon and evening performances from €50. Refreshments available.

Queens Theatre

H Traditional Future

For less than €8, watch Anuang'a Fernando from Kenya as he uses traditional words from his own country, modern music and movement to perform this work of art. Anuang'a Fernando has already performed this show in Paris and Italy. Book soon – the theatre only holds 200 people. Snacks will be available. Close to public transport.

Drake Hall

E Rubbish

The Opera House has been turned into a big tent for *Rubbish.* Set on the streets in the 1940s, young artists do gymnastics, dance and theatre using rubbish like wheels, furniture and boxes. First performances this week! Under-15s must be accompanied by an adult but ask about family discounts at our restaurant. A two-minute walk from the underground.

Opera House

4 Work in pairs. Which event would you like to attend? Why?

Vocabulary
Going out

1 Look at the words in the box. Are they used to talk about a film, a play or a concert? Complete the diagram.

> acting admission audience book early
> interval live music perform refreshments
> reviews screen stage subtitles ticket

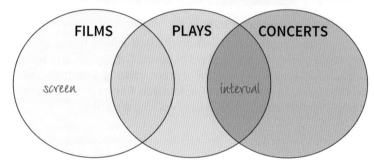

FILMS PLAYS CONCERTS

screen interval

2 Complete the questions with words from Exercise 1.

1 Do you read ....*reviews*........ before you see a film?
2 Do you ever watch films in English with ....?
3 Think of the last time you went to see a film, play or concert. Did you have to .... or could you buy tickets on the door?
4 How often do you buy .... like popcorn at the cinema?
5 Do you prefer to listen to music at home or to go out to see ....?
6 Can young people afford to go to the cinema in your town? How much is the ....?
7 Would you rather see your favourite actor on the screen or on ....?
8 Some people are fantastic actors. Are you good at ....?

3 Work in groups. Ask and answer the questions from Exercise 2. Remember to say why or why not.

Grammar
Present perfect

▶ **Page 128 Grammar reference**
Present perfect

1 Listen to Eliza and Bella planning a night out together in Madrid. What do they decide to do?

2 Listen again and complete the sentences.

1 Have you .... *The Lion King* <u>yet</u>?
2 I've <u>already</u> .... it.
3 I haven't .... the new Robin Hood film <u>yet</u>.
4 I've <u>just</u> .... how to play one of the songs.

3 How do we form the present perfect? When do we use this tense?

4 Complete the rules with *already*, *just* or *yet*.

Rules

1 Use .... to talk about things that happened a short time ago.

2 Use .... to say something has happened, often sooner than expected.

These two words normally go in the middle of the sentence, between *have* and the past participle.

3 Use .... in questions and negative sentences when we expect something to happen. It means 'until now'. This word normally goes at the end of the sentence.

5 Harry has not been in contact with Jodie for a long time and decides to send an email. Complete Harry's email using the words given in the present perfect.

> ● ● ●
>
> Hi Jodie,
>
> Sorry I haven't written to you for so long but I've had a lot of exams. I've got so much to tell you. **(1)** My sister and her boyfriend / just / get married. **(2)** My dad / not find / a new job / yet. **(3)** But he / start / a course in computing. **(4)** My mum / just / win / a prize in a photography competition. **(5)** you / see / the new Star Wars film yet? **(6)** I / already / see / it / three times. It's great! What about you? **(7)** You / finish / your exams yet?
>
> Please write soon,
>
> Harry.

1 My sister and her boyfriend have just got married.

▶ **Page 128 Grammar reference**
since and *for*

6 Exam candidates often make mistakes with *since* and *for*. Look at the sentence from Eliza and Bella's conversation and answer the questions.

We've been good friends <u>for</u> three years but we haven't been to a show together <u>since</u> last summer.

1 Which word do we use to talk about the beginning of a period of time? ....

2 Which word do we use to talk about the whole period of time? ....

7 Complete the sentences with *since* or *for*.

1 I've lived here ....I was born.

2 I've been at my school ....three years.

3 I've had these shoes..............................five months.

4 My grandparents have been married ....a very long time.

5 I've known my classmates..............................last year.

8 Work in pairs. Use *how long* to write questions about the sentences from Exercise 7.

1 How long have you lived here?

9 Work in different pairs. Ask and answer your questions in Exercise 8.

Present perfect or past simple?

▶ **Page 129 Grammar reference**
The present perfect or the past simple?

1 Read about Martin Garrix. What is he famous for?

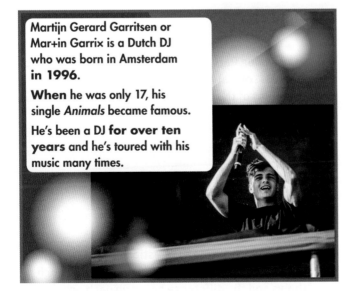

Martijn Gerard Garritsen or Mar+in Garrix is a Dutch DJ who was born in Amsterdam **in 1996.**

When he was only 17, his single *Animals* became famous.

He's been a DJ **for over ten years** and he's toured with his music many times.

2 Read about Martin Garrix again. <u>Underline</u> the verbs in the present perfect and circle the verbs in the past simple.

3 Do we normally use the time expressions in bold in Exercise 1 with the present perfect or the past simple?

4 We use some time expressions with the present perfect and others with the past simple. Complete the table with time expressions from the box.

already   at 8 o'clock in the morning
~~for ten years~~   ~~in 1996~~   last year   since 2010
this week   today   two months ago   yesterday   yet

present perfect	past simple
for ten years	in 1996

5 <u>Underline</u> the time expressions in the sentences. Then complete the sentences with the present perfect or past simple form of the verbs in brackets.

1 I ......*saw*...... (see) that show <u>three months ago</u>.

2 ....you ....(read) this month's *Surf* magazine yet?

3 I ....(not do) my homework today.

4 Our football team are playing better now. We only ....(win) twice last year.

5 You look tired. What time ....you ....(go) to bed last night?

6 How many exams ....you ....(take) since the beginning of this year?

7 Let's go to the beach! I ....(not go) for ages!

6 Work in pairs. You are going to interview another student in the class. Look at the example below and write questions on the topics in the box.

a best friend   a favourite sport
a free-time activity   a foreign language
a pet   a phone

Have you got a mobile phone? Where did you get it? How long have you had it?

7 Work in different pairs. Take turns to ask and answer your questions from Exercise 6. Add more questions.

Have you got a phone?

Yes, I have.

How long have you had it?

I've had it for six months.

Where did you get it?

My mum bought it online.

Do you like it?

Vocabulary

been/gone, meet, get to know, know and *find out*

1 Read the example sentences and answer the questions.

Paul isn't at home, he's <u>gone</u> to a friend's home. His sister Sophia has just got home. She's <u>been</u> to the cinema.

1 Where's Paul now?

2 Where's Sophia now?

3 *Been* and *gone* are both forms of *go*. Which one means 'go and come back'? Which one means 'hasn't come back yet'?

Lucas has <u>known</u> his best friend Nick for years. They first <u>met</u> when they were at primary school. They <u>got to know</u> each other and they became good friends. Lucas often <u>meets</u> Nick on Saturday afternoons. Lucas sometimes <u>stays</u> at Nick's house when his parents are away.

4 When and how did Lucas and Nick become friends?

5 Do they still see each other? When?

6 When does Lucas sleep at Nick's house?

Scarlett's parents were away and they didn't <u>know</u> about the party. The neighbours phoned Scarlett's parents because of the noise. When they <u>found out</u> about it, they were very angry.

7 Did Scarlett tell her parents about the party?

8 Who told Scarlett's parents that she was having a party?

2 Choose the correct option in *italics*. Use the examples in Exercise 1 to help you.

1 Have you ever *been / gone* abroad? Where?

2 Imagine all your friends have *been / gone* on holiday and you are on your own. What do you do?

3 Have you got a best friend? How long have you *known / met* them? How did you first *meet / know* each other?

4 Do you usually *meet / stay* with your friends at the weekend? What do you do?

5 Do you enjoy *knowing / getting* to know new people? Why (not)?

6 How often do you use the internet to *find out / know* information? Have you used it this week? What for?

3 Work in groups. Ask and answer the questions from Exercise 2.

Listening Part 1

1 In Listening Part 1, you may hear someone describing clothes. Look at the pictures on page 57 and find examples of the things below. Write the picture number.

1 a plain jumper ....1A....

2 a pocket ....

3 a round neck ....

4 a striped jumper ....

5 a skirt ....

6 a V-neck ....

2 Work in pairs. Read the questions carefully and <u>underline</u> the key words. Then decide what each picture shows and the difference between each one.

1 What would the girl like to try on?

A   B   C

6 What's the latest time visitors can buy a ticket today?

A   B   C

2 Where has the boy left his keys?

A   B   C

7 What sorts of TV programmes does the girl like watching?

A   B   C

3 What did Karen buy last weekend?

A   B   C

• The pictures can tell you a lot about what you will hear. Study them carefully before you listen.

• The speakers might mention all the things in the pictures, but only one answer is correct.

Exam advice

4 Which one is Sarah's cousin?

A   B   C

3 Listen. For each question, choose the correct answer. Then listen again and check.
29

4 /P/ Contrastive stress
Read the boy's reply to the girl from question 7. Which words do you think he stresses?

Boy: Oh? I didn't think you liked those sorts or programmes.

5 Now listen to the boy saying his line in three different ways. What makes the meaning of the sentence change?
30

5 Where did Dave get his trainers?

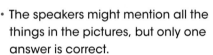   

A   B   C

6 Work in groups. Ask and answer questions about the clothes you usually wear for these occasions. Stress the words you think are important!

• a school trip to the countryside
• family celebrations
• hanging out with friends
• relaxing at home

Speaking Part 3

▶ **Page 159 Speaking bank**

1 **Work in pairs. Read the Speaking Part 3 task below. What do you need to talk about?**

> A school would like to celebrate its 50th anniversary with a special event.
>
> Here are some events the school could organise for students.
>
> Talk together about the different events the school could organise. Say which would be most popular with students.

2 **Work in pairs. Look at these possible events. Which ones do you think would be good ideas for a 50th anniversary celebration?**

> concert   disco   photography exhibition
> fashion show   picnic   talent show

3 **Look at the sentences and decide which you should or should not do in this part of the Speaking exam. Put a tick (✓) or a cross (✗) in each box in the *You* column.**

		You	Noa & Greta
1	Listen carefully to the examiner's instructions.	✓	
2	Discuss your ideas with your partner and the examiner.		
3	Make suggestions and reply to suggestions.		
4	Take turns to speak.		
5	Talk about one picture only.		
6	Agree as quickly as you can.		
7	Speak for at least two minutes.		

4 **Listen to Noa and Greta doing the task. Which things from Exercise 3 do they do? Put a tick (✓) or a cross (✗) in the *Noa & Greta* column.**

5 Underline **two expressions Greta uses to move on to a new picture.**

Greta: Perhaps you're right. Shall we talk about the fashion show?

Noa: OK. I think it's a great idea. The students could all put on their favourite clothes and there could be prizes.

Greta: Um … I'm not very interested in fashion, I'm afraid. We haven't talked about the picnic yet. Do you think it's a good idea?

6 **Work in pairs. Do the Speaking Part 3 task below.**

> A town would like to celebrate its anniversary with a festival.
>
> Here are some activities which the festival could include.
>
> Talk together about the different activities the festival could include, and say which would be most popular with young people.

Writing Part 2 (An article)

▶ **Page 148 Writing bank**
An article

1 Work in pairs. Look at the photo. What can you see? What are the people doing and wearing?

2 Discuss the questions.

1 What celebrations do you have in your country?
2 What's your favourite celebration? Why?
3 What do people wear and do?

3 Read this Writing Part 2 task and <u>underline</u> the important words.

> You see this announcement in an international English-language magazine for teenagers.
>
> > **Let's celebrate!**
> > <u>Tell us about a celebration in your country.</u>
> > *What do people usually wear?*
> > *What do people do?*
> > *Why is it special?*
> >
> > **Write an article answering these questions and we will publish the most interesting articles in our magazine.**
>
> Write your **article**.

4 Work in pairs. Read the first paragraph of two articles. Which is better? Why?

> *The story began on Chinese New Year. People were wearing amazing costumes and they were dancing in the street. We left our flat and we walked to my aunt's house. She was preparing a special meal for us.*

> My favourite celebration in my country is the Venice Carnival in February. The celebrations last for two weeks. There are dances, concerts and performances, but I love the masks and costumes best.

5 Read the complete article about the Venice Carnival. Do you think it is a good answer?

My favourite celebration in my country is the Venice Carnival in February. The celebrations last for two weeks. There are dances, concerts and performances, but I love the masks and costumes best.

My favourite mask is made of leather, it's painted by hand and it has a very long nose. We all wear traditional costumes so Venice looks like an 18th-century city.

We go for walks in our special clothes, we watch actors perform in the street and we go to dances called balls. It's a very special celebration because there is nothing like it anywhere else in the world.

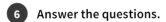

6 Answer the questions.

1 Is it an article and not a story?
2 Is the first paragraph interesting? Does it make you want to keep reading?
3 Does the article include all the information?
4 Is it about 100 words?

> • If you decide to write an article, write an article and <u>not</u> a story.
>
> • Make sure your first paragraph is interesting to make the reader want to keep reading.
>
> **Exam advice**

7 Use your answers from Exercise 2 to write your article in about 100 words.

8 Use the questions from Exercise 6 to think about your work. If you can answer 'yes' to all the questions, then it is probably a good answer.

Vocabulary

1 Choose the correct options in *italics*.

Hi Tamsin,

Sorry I've taken so long to reply. In your last email, you asked what was happening with my friends, so here's my news.

Lucas was disappointed **(1)** *of / on /* (*with*) his last exam results so he's working harder now, but I think he's getting tired **(2)** *about / of / on* studying all the time. He usually goes out in the evenings, so he must be getting very bored **(3)** *with / on / about* life.

Natalie is still very keen **(4)** *of / on / with* football and is quite proud **(5)** *on / with / of* the two goals she scored last Saturday, but she can't play next week and she's sad **(6)** *about / of / with* that. Claire is crazy **(7)** *on / with / about* music and has always wanted to be a singer.

Last week, a local band asked her to sing with them at a concert next Friday. She's really nervous **(8)** *on / about / with* singing in front of all those people, but I don't think she should be frightened **(9)** *with / of / on* doing it. I've told her that some people will be jealous **(10)** *of / on / about* her!

Well, that's all for now.

Lots of love,

Bastian

2 This blog post contains adjectives ending in *-ed* and *-ing*. Underline and correct five more mistakes.

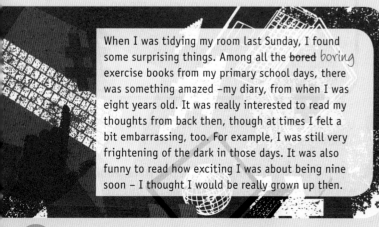

When I was tidying my room last Sunday, I found some surprising things. Among all the ~~bored~~ *boring* exercise books from my primary school days, there was something amazed –my diary, from when I was eight years old. It was really interested to read my thoughts from back then, though at times I felt a bit embarrassing, too. For example, I was still very frightening of the dark in those days. It was also funny to read how exciting I was about being nine soon – I thought I would be really grown up then.

3 Complete the crossword with words from Unit 5.

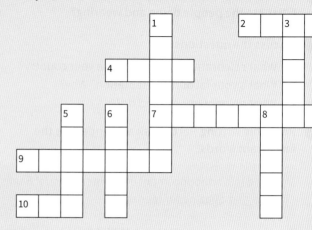

Across
2 the noun form of *afraid*
4 the opposite of *generous*
7 normal and not unusual
9 feeling worried or anxious about something
10 the opposite of 'happy'

Down
1 wanting something that another person has
3 the noun form of *angry*
5 when you're not interested in something
6 the opposite of *ashamed*
8 a word that means 'very bad'

Grammar

4 Choose the correct option in *italics*.

1 **A:** Do you think Dylan and Leah are at the café?
B: They *can /* (*might be*) there, but I'm not sure.

2 **A:** Do you like going to the swimming pool?
B: No, I *can't / couldn't* swim.

3 **A:** I've got a bit of a headache.
B: I think you *shouldn't / should* take an aspirin.

4 **A:** *Could / Might* you run for an hour without stopping?
B: No, I'd be too tired after 30 minutes!

5 **A:** Are the buses to the city centre expensive?
B: No, you *mustn't / don't have to* pay anything if you're under 16.

6 **A:** The weather's not looking very good now.
B: You're right. I think it *can / might* rain later.

7 **A:** What do I need to go to the USA?
B: You *should / have to* take your passport.

Vocabulary

1 Complete the review with words from the box.

> admission   audiences   ~~cartoons~~   interval
> live   performances   reviews

Cirque Eloize

Are you bored of watching **(1)** *cartoons* on TV? Do you fancy doing something new? Why don't you go and see Cirque Eloize's new show?
(2) .... will be amazed by the acrobatics, dance and **(3)** .... music. This touring show has already received very good **(4)** .... in other parts of the country. There are two **(5)** .... each day: one at 2.30 and the other at 7.30. Tickets are still available for many dates with half-price **(6)** .... for under-16s. The show lasts about 85 minutes with no **(7)** ....

2 Choose the correct word (A, B or C).

1 I think I left my keys in the front .... of my jeans.
   (A) pocket   **B** bag   **C** coat
2 My mum often wears bright, ... shirts and long skirts.
   A colour   **B** colourful   **C** coloured
3 I first .... my best friend when I moved to this town.
   A met   **B** knew   **C** found out
4 I'd love to go to New York to get to .... the city.
   A find out   **B** know   **C** meet
5 I've visited Washington DC but I haven't .... to the White House.
   A visited   **B** known   **C** been

Grammar

3 Exam candidates often make mistakes with the present perfect and the past simple. <u>Underline</u> and correct the mistakes.

1 ~~I've~~ | bought some clothes last week.
2 My grandmother has lived here since three years.
3 I haven't seen him for ages because he's gone to Argentina a few years ago.
4 We've gone to the cinema three times this month. Let's do something else.
5 Already I've been to a few shops to look for new shoes.
6 I still can't find my mobile phone. I looked for it everywhere.
7 Milan is the best place I've never been to for clothes.
8 I lost a beautiful pair of gloves which my mother has given me for my birthday.
9 We're planning to go out, but we didn't decide where to go yet.
10 There's a wonderful cinema in my town. It has opened six months ago.

4 Read the article about living in a big city and think of the word which best fits each gap. Use only one word in each gap.

My dad moved to Tokyo when he got a new job about two years **(1)** ....*ago*........ . My mum and I have lived here **(2)** .... about a year. I have to say that I **(3)** .... never lived in such an exciting city and I love it here. I've been at this school **(4)** .... September and I've known my best friend since then. We **(5)** .... to know each other when I sat next to him in class and we soon became good friends. We both love going to the cinema to see new films. We've **(6)** .... been to the cinema twice this weekend.

A

B

D

C

Starting off
Weather

1 Work in groups.

1 What kinds of weather do the photos show?

> cold   foggy   freezing   frost   hot   ice   icy
> lightning   rainy   showers   snowy   storm   sunny
> sunshine   temperature   thunderstorm   windy

2 How do people experiencing this weather feel?

> People often feel sad in cold, foggy weather.

3 What kind of weather do you like most/least? Why?

4 What do you think the underlined expressions mean?

a I hope the sun will <u>come out</u> soon.   *start shining*

b I put on a jumper because it was a bit <u>chilly</u>.

c It's <u>pouring</u> outside, so take your umbrella.

d Open the window. It's <u>boiling</u> in here!

e Even in summer, it gets quite <u>nippy</u> at night.

f It was cloudy earlier, but then it <u>cleared up</u>.

g Because of the <u>soaring</u> temperatures, lots of people have gone to the mountains.

Listening Part 4

1 Look at questions 1–6 in the exam task on page 63.

1 What is the main speaker's name?

2 What is the topic?

3 What do you need to listen for?

2 You will hear an interview with a girl called Olivia talking about her experience of travelling through a snowstorm with her parents. For each question, choose the correct answer.

32

- Quickly read the instructions and the questions to get an idea of what you will hear.

- Listen for reasons why one option is correct – and reasons why the other two are wrong.

Exam advice

THE DAILY NEWS

VOL. 117, NO. 341   DAILY 50 CENTS

1 When it started to snow heavily, Olivia and her family were
- **A** talking about what to do next.
- **B** driving along a main road.
- **C** having a snack in a café.

2 How did Olivia feel as heavy snow began to fall?
- **A** annoyed with her parents for getting lost.
- **B** sure that the snow would stop soon.
- **C** scared about what might happen.

3 Why did the car stop moving?
- **A** It had run out of petrol.
- **B** The snow was too deep.
- **C** They had hit another vehicle.

4 How did they try to keep warm in the car?
- **A** They put on lots of clothes.
- **B** They kept the heater on all night.
- **C** They drank some hot liquids.

5 They were in the car nearly all night because
- **A** it became impossible to open the doors.
- **B** they were told not to leave it.
- **C** nobody knew where they were.

6 The following day, they travelled to a village in
- **A** a rescue vehicle.
- **B** an ambulance.
- **C** their own car.

3 Listen again and check.

32

4 Work in pairs. Discuss the questions and give reasons.
- Would you like to experience a lot of snow?
- Would you like to visit a very cold place?

Grammar

extremely, fairly, quite, rather, really **and** *very*

▶ **Page 130 Grammar reference**
Adverbs of degree

1 Read the sentences from the recording. Then complete the rules with the underlined words.
- Really heavy snow started coming down.
- I was quite certain it wouldn't last long.
- It was rather annoying we'd gone the wrong way.
- It was getting quite difficult to see.

Rules

1 Adverbs of degree such as *very*, *extremely* and .... always make an adjective stronger.

2 The adverbs *fairly* and .... always make it weaker.

3 The adverb .... usually makes it weaker, but with adjectives like *sure*, *true* and *different*, it can mean 'completely'.

2 Discuss the questions, using adverbs of degree.
- Have you ever experienced extreme weather, e.g. *really hot, very stormy weather*?
- What was it like?
- How did you feel and what did you do?

Last year we had an extremely hot summer. The temperatures were very high and I felt really uncomfortable so I went to the shopping mall. It was quite cool there!

too and *enough*

▶ **Page 130 Grammar reference**
too and *enough*

1 Read what some people say about the weather. Complete each rule with the correct option in *italics*.

'In summer it's too hot to work!'

'We had enough time to get indoors before the storm hit our town.'

'It was a hot July day in the city. There were too many cars and there was too much noise.'

'It was winter, so it wasn't warm enough to swim in the sea.'

Rules

1 In the examples above, *too* means *as much as / more than* you need or want. It does not mean the same as *very*.

2 The word *too* goes *after / before* an adjective, often followed by the *-ing / to + infinitive* form of the verb.

3 We use *too much* before *countable / uncountable* nouns and *too many* before *countable / uncountable* nouns.

4 In the examples above, *enough* means *as much as / more than* you need or want.

5 The word *enough* usually goes *after / before* a noun, but *after / before* an adjective, often followed by the *-ing / to + infinitive* form of the verb.

2 Exam candidates often make mistakes with *too* and *enough*. Some of these sentences contain mistakes. <u>Underline</u> the mistakes and correct them.

1 It was hot enough to spend the whole day in the water.
2 In the streets, there are too much cars.
3 My sister is very young to travel alone.
4 In summer it would be too hot to cycle.
5 We did not have plenty of time to see the University of Cambridge.
6 I think you are enough old to spend this summer with your friends.

3 Work in groups.

1 Write down six places you'd like to visit.
2 Talk about which of the places you could visit for a weekend, using *too* and *enough*.
3 Try to decide which is the best place to visit.

I'd love to go to the mountains, but they are too far away and we don't have enough time!

How about the lake? That's nice, and it's not too far.

Reading Part 1

1 Look at the signs and messages below. Where could you see each one?

A

DANGER
Thin ice!
Deep water!

B
CYCLISTS
Leave bicycles in parking spaces provided on ferry
Go to passenger area
Return to bicycles when ferry reaches harbour

C
City Trams
Children aged under 14 travel free (if accompanied by an adult)

D
Sign up for our new teenage phone contract in 5 days and you'll get £30 of extra credit!

E

NO SKATEBOARDING IN PEDESTRIAN-ONLY AREAS

2 Match the texts (A–E) with the purposes (1–5). <u>Underline</u> the words in the texts which tell you the purpose.

1 giving information about prices *C*
2 saying what you must do
3 warning you of something
4 saying what you must not do
5 advertising something

3 For each question, choose the correct answer.

1

ATTENTION
**In case of fire, use this emergency exit.
Alarm bell rings when open.**

A Ring the bell before opening the emergency exit.

B You must find another exit if there is a fire.

C Only go out this way if there is an emergency.

2

To: parents and pupils

Subject: end of term

This Friday all school buses will depart at 3.15 instead of 4.15. For safety reasons, they will leave from the main entrance, rather than the car park.

A Students must get the bus at a different location on Friday.

B Parents should collect their children by car on Friday.

C Buses will leave the school later than usual on Friday.

3

FOR SALE
Fashionable girl's
winter jacket
(Size: medium)
Hardly ever worn
Small tear on left sleeve
but now mended
£20, or make me an offer!
Contact Alex (Class 4C)

A The jacket is in perfect condition.

B The seller may accept a lower price.

C Alex has worn the fashionable jacket many times.

4

FOREST NATURE PARK
- No fires or barbecues
- No camping permitted except at Forest Campsite
- No rubbish – take it all away with you!

A There is a particular location where people can camp in the park.

B Rubbish must be left in the bins provided by the park.

C Pay special attention when cooking food on fires at the park.

5

February's ski trip
Places are still available, but the school must
receive all forms by January 31st. Your parents
must sign the form, or it will
not be accepted.

A Parents may accompany their children on the ski trip.

B Students must apply for the ski trip before February.

C It is now too late to apply for the ski trip.

Grammar
The future

▶ **Page 131 Grammar reference**
Future forms

1 Listen to this conversation between Mia and Owen and fill in the missing verbs. You can use short forms like *'s* (*is*), *'ll* (*will*) and *'m* (*am*).

🎧 33

Mia: Look at the rain, Owen.

Owen: Yes, I know. I'm hoping it **(1)** ....'ll stop......... soon, but I don't think there's much chance of that.

Mia: No, the weather forecast said it's a big storm, so it **(2)** .... for hours. What time do you have to be at the station?

Owen: I **(3)** .... Jason and Mark there at 8.30, in the café near the main entrance. The train **(4)** .... at 8.45.

Mia: It's quite a long walk to the station, isn't it? And it's 8.15 already. Look, I **(5)** .... my mum to take you in the car.

Owen: Thanks!

2 Match the verb forms from 1–5 above with uses a–e.

a for timetables and future dates
b for decisions at the moment of speaking
c for things that aren't certain, e.g. after *I think* or *I hope*
d for future arrangements
e for predictions based on evidence, and plans

3 Put the words in order to make questions. Then ask and answer the questions in pairs.

1 the photos / will / send / you / when / me ?
  1 When will you send me the photos?
2 this evening / are / where / go / going / you / to ?
3 a new bike / get / when / will / you ?
4 the Earth / get hotter / going / is / to ?
5 will / think / cloudy / it / do / tomorrow / you / be ?

4 Work in pairs. What would you say in each of these situations? Tell your partner, using future forms.

1 'Do you want to come to a party with me?'
  (Tell your friend you can't.)

> I'm sorry but I'm going to a concert with friends.

2 'I'm having trouble with my computer.'
  (Offer to help your friend.)
3 'When's the last day of term?'
  (Tell your friend which date.)
4 'The wind is getting stronger.'
  (Say a storm is likely to happen soon.)
5 'Which other language do you plan to study next year?'
  (Tell your partner.)

Vocabulary
Compound words

1 Match the words from box A with the words from box B to make compound words. Then match the compound words with definitions 1–8.

A

~~back~~ camp cross guide over sight sign suit

B

book case night ~~pack~~ post roads seeing site

1 a bag that you carry on your back   *backpack*
2 a book that gives information about a place
3 a bag with a handle for carrying clothes, etc.
4 a place where two roads meet and cross each other
5 a sign by the road that gives information
6 during the night and until the morning
7 a place where people can stay overnight in tents
8 visiting interesting places

2 Use compound words from Exercise 1 to complete Lewis's blog. Then listen to check.

34

Travel Blog

HOME   POST   PHOTO   CONTACT

Next week I'm going to Australia! I'm arriving in the north, so first I'm going to stay **(1)** ......*overnight*...... in Darwin. My **(2)** .... says it's an interesting city, so I think I'll do a bit of **(3)** .... there. Then I'm getting the train to Alice Springs, right in the middle of the country, where I'll spend the night at a **(4)** .... The next day I'm hoping to get a lift down the main road. I'm taking all my things in a **(5)** .... so that I don't have to carry a heavy **(6)** .... around. About 200 kilometres south of Alice, I'll reach a **(7)** .... where there's a **(8)** .... that says 'Uluru 247 km'. Uluru is also known as Ayers Rock – one of the most amazing sights in the world.

UPLOAD ⤒   LIKE ✓

3 **/P/ Word stress in compound words**

34 Listen again to Lewis. Does he stress the first part of answers 2–8, or the second? <u>Underline</u> the correct part of each word.

4 Tell your partner about an exciting journey you would like to go on. Use compound words from Exercise 1 with the correct stress.

> I'd love to go sightseeing in New York ...

Grammar

Prepositions of movement

▶ **Page 132 Grammar reference**
Prepositions of movement

1 Complete this phone message about travelling around a city with the missing prepositions (*in*, *off*, etc.). Then
35 listen to check.

Hi Leon, Toby here. I'm really pleased you're coming to our new house next week. The quickest way here is **(1)** .....*by*..... train to the city centre, which takes an hour and is usually **(2)** .... time. Then you can get **(3)** .... the number 64 bus to Edgely, getting **(4)** .... by the stadium. From there it's a 15-minute walk. Or, if you don't feel like walking, you could jump **(5)** .... a taxi and ask the driver to take you to the end of Valley Road. When you get **(6)** .... of the taxi, you'll see our place right in front of you. See you soon!

2 Use words from the message to complete the rules.

Rules

1 For cars, we use *get* (or *jump*, *climb*, etc.) *into* or .... , and .... when we leave them.

2 For most other road vehicles, plus trains, planes, boats and horses, we use .... or *onto*, and .... when we leave them.

3 We travel .... bus, train, plane or boat, or in other words, ... road, rail, air, land or sea. We also say we are *on* (*board*) a train, plane or ship, or *at sea*.

4 If you arrive neither late nor early, you say you are (or the bus, train, plane, etc. is) .... time.

3 Some of the sentences contain mistakes made by exam candidates. <u>Underline</u> the mistakes and correct them.

1 You can get here in plane.
2 I jumped into my car.
3 The bus drivers are on strike, so everybody has to go by car.
4 Could you come at time, please?
5 I will travel with train.

4 Work in groups. Think of a place you like in your town or city. Describe how to get there using public transport. Use prepositions of movement.

Speaking Part 2

▶ **Page 154 Speaking bank**
Speaking Part 2

1 Work in groups. Describe what you can see in the photo.

2 Listen to Ava. Which of the things you said in Exercise 1
🎧 36 did she mention? Did she describe anything else?

3 Listen again and complete the sentences.
🎧 36

1 It shows a white and blue plane at an airport and there
are .... *Also* .... a lot of people.

2 There are people .... the
plane and they're on the ....
.... to the ground.

3 .... some people .... past the
plane and .... to each other.

4 She's carrying a kind of little case and maybe a
backpack, ...

5 Behind the plane I can see a ....
.... at the airport, in a
yellow jacket.

6 They're on a ....
.... that carries cases from
the plane.

7 The weather looks too nice, ...
.... , quite nice.

4 Match the words and phrases you wrote in Exercise 3 to
the uses (a–d).

a adding a point *Also*   c describing actions
b correcting yourself   d describing things you
                                don't know the name of

Exam advice

• It's fine to correct yourself if you make a
mistake.

• Before the exam, practise talking
about pictures for a minute. Time
yourself!

5 Work in pairs, choose one of the photos below and
describe it to your partner.

• Use prepositions of movement and phrases from
Exercise 3.
• Use adverbs such as *quite*, *really* or *rather*.
• Speak for at least one minute.
• After you finish speaking, ask your partner if you have
described everything.

Writing Part 1

▶ **Page 145 Writing bank**
An email

1 Where can you put these expressions in an email? Write
B for beginning or *E* for end.

Lots of love, *E*
Hi,
Looking forward to hearing from you / seeing you.
Well, that's all for now.
All the best,
This is just a quick message to say
It was great to hear from you.
Give my love to everyone.
Take care,
See you soon.
Don't forget to write soon.
Sorry I've taken so long to write back.
Bye for now.
Dear,

2 Look at the exam task and answer the questions.

1 Who is the email from and what is it about?

2 Which expressions from Exercise 1 does Tony use?

3 Which future forms and adverbs of degree does he use?

4 Which points (a–e) should you put in your reply? What else should you include?

a It doesn't matter that the writer has been slow to reply.

b What you will do before Saturday.

c Why you want to go

d Where you want to eat.

e Where you want to meet.

> Read this email from your English-speaking friend Tony, and the notes you have made.
>
> To:
>
> From: Tony
>
> Hi,
>
> I'm going to the fair with my family on Saturday morning. Would you like to go with us? There will be some really fantastic rides, including all your favourites! — *Say yes*
>
> We'll be there a few hours, and will probably get quite hungry there, so do you want to take some food or buy something? — *Tell Tony.*
>
> By the way, where will you meet us on Saturday? — *Suggest ...*
>
> And do you think it's better to go in the morning or the afternoon? — *Afternoon is easier.*
>
> All the best,
>
> Tony

Write your email to Tony in about **100** words, using **all** the **notes**.

3 Read the reply and answer the questions.

1 Is Jamie's letter about 100 words?

2 Which paragraph covers each of the notes?

3 Which language points (a–e) does Jamie use? Give examples.

a expressions from Exercise 1

b adverbs of degree

c future forms

d *too* and *enough*

e prepositions of movement

> Hi Tony,
>
> Thanks for your email. Yes, I'd love to go on Saturday. It'll be great to go on the water rides there, especially the very steep ones!
>
> Snacks at the fair will be really expensive, so I think I'd better take sandwiches and drinks. Do you think that'll be enough?
>
> I can meet you at the fair – the 56 bus will take me directly there. How about we meet at the main gates? I'll text you as soon as I arrive there.
>
> Can we go in the afternoon? It's easier for me because I need to help my mum in the morning.
>
> See you soon,
>
> Jamie

> **Exam advice**
> - If you are writing to a friend, use informal language.
> - Always put the opening (e.g. *Hi Sam*) the closing (e.g. *Bye for now*) and your own name on separate lines.

4 Plan and write your email in about 100 words. Use expressions from Exercise 1.

5 Work in pairs. Read and check your partner's email.

1 Where you think there are mistakes, use a pencil to write *G* for grammar, *V* for vocabulary, *WO* for word order, or *Sp* for spelling.

2 Discuss your corrections together.

8 Influencers

1. **Zinedine Zidane**'s parents were from Algeria but he grew up in France where he played for the international football team. Now retired from playing football, he's a coach. All four of his sons have played football for Real Madrid's youth teams.

2. American singer, songwriter and actress **Miley Cyrus** is the daughter of the country singer, Billy Ray. Her brother Trace is a singer and guitarist while her grandfather Ron was a politician.

3. **Marie Curie** was the first woman to win a Nobel priz and the only person ever to win a prize in both physic and chemistry. Marie shared her prize in physics with her husband Pierre. Later her daughter and son-in-law were given a Nobel Prize in chemistry.

4. **Indira Gandhi** came from a family of Indian politicians. She was the daughter of India's first prime minister and then she became India's first female prime minister. Although Indira and the social leader Mahatma share the same family name, they aren't relatives. Indira changed her surname when she got married.

Starting off

1. Work in pairs. What do you know about the famous families in the photos?

2. Match the descriptions of famous families (1–4) with the photos (A–D).

3. Work in groups. Discuss the advantages and disadvantages of being famous and being part of a famous family.

Reading Part 6

1 Work in pairs. Read part of a website. What do you think an *influencer* is? Are there any *influencers* in your country?

HOW YOUNG PEOPLE ARE USING SOCIAL MEDIA TO BECOME CELEBRITIES, ADVERTISE THEIR PRODUCTS AND MAKE MONEY

INFLUENCER #1

Amanda Steele (born in 1999) has set up a YouTube channel where she gives advice on beauty and fashion to more than 3 million people. Her own products include make-up and sunglasses.

INFLUENCER #2

Jacob Sartorius (born in 2002) became famous after posting music videos on the social network, Musical.ly. He's already got millions of followers who download his singles.

2 Read the rest of the website quickly. Do not complete the gaps for now. In what ways is Hannah Alper an *influencer*?

INFLUENCER #3

Are all influencers just interested (0) ......*in*...... being famous and making money? Not in the case of Hannah Alper, born in 2003. Hannah (1) .... born in Canada and brought up there. At the age of nine, she took up blogging. She wanted (2) .... share her worries about the world with other people. She hopes that we will all think more about the environment and how our actions might have an effect (3) .... animals.

Hannah doesn't only write about her opinions. She (4) .... also spoken to large audiences on a range of topics. These have been topics (5) .... protecting wildlife to respecting one another. Hannah hopes that her words will encourage others to go out and do something. (6) .... doesn't matter how young someone is, Hannah believes we can all do something to help protect the environment.

- You must complete each space with one word only and your spelling must be correct.
- If you can't fill in a gap, go on to the others and come back to it later.
- When you have filled in all the gaps, check that your completed text makes sense.

Exam advice

3 For each question, write the correct answer. Write one word for each gap. There is an example at the beginning.

4 Exam candidates often make spelling mistakes. Underline the mistakes in the sentences and correct them.

1. She's clever. She's very funny, to.
2. We where both young when I first met her in school.
3. He plays soccer very well, an he's the junior world champion in shooting.
4. At first, I thought she was shy, because she was a very quite girl.
5. I love spending time whit him. I can say that he is my best friend.
6. I like to do my homework with Daniela becouse she is intelligent.

5 Work in groups. Discuss the questions.

- What's your favourite website? Why do you like it?
- How often do you watch video clips online? Do you have a favourite channel?
- Do you follow anyone online? Who? Why?

Vocabulary
Phrasal verbs

1 Look at the underlined phrasal verbs. Decide what each one means by looking at the complete sentence.

1 Zinedine's parents were from Algeria, but he <u>grew up</u> in France.
2 Amanda Steele has <u>set up</u> a YouTube Channel where she gives advice.
3 Hannah Alper was born in Canada and <u>brought up</u> there.
4 At the age of nine, she <u>took up</u> blogging.

2 Replace each <u>underlined</u> expression with the correct form of a phrasal verb from the box, so that the meaning stays the same.

> find out   ~~grow up~~   bring up
> take up   make up   set up
> get on with   run out (of)

1 I was born in a small village, but I <u>became older</u> in Athens with my parents and two brothers. *grew up*
2 If I <u>discovered</u> that my parents were reading my emails, I wouldn't get angry.
3 When my phone <u>doesn't have any more</u> battery, I borrow my friends' phones.
4 I'd love to <u>start</u> my own YouTube Channel. I would let people know about new music.
5 If I had to choose another sport, I would <u>start playing</u> hockey.
6 I <u>have a good relationship</u> with my older sister. We often go out together.
7 If I didn't know an answer in an exam, I would never <u>invent</u> an answer.
8 I was <u>looked after</u> by my grandparents in the countryside when I was a small child.

3 Rewrite three or four of the sentences from Exercise 2, so that they are true for you. Use phrasal verbs.

1 I was born in Naples, but I grew up in Rome, the capital city of Italy.

4 Work in groups. Compare your sentences. Find things that you have got in common.

Grammar
Zero, first and second conditionals

▶ **Page 133 Grammar reference**
Conditional sentences

1 Work in pairs. Kristian wants to go to drama school to be an actor, but his parents want him to stay at school. What advice can you give him?

2 Kristian is talking to Mr Edwards, a teacher at his school. Listen and answer the questions. *(37)*

1 Why has Kristian's dad contacted Mr Edwards?
2 What two pieces of advice does Mr Edwards give?

3 Listen and complete the sentences with the correct form of the verbs. *(38)*

1 If I ....*stay*....... (stay) at school until I'm 18, it ....*will be*...... (be) too late.
2 If I .... (want) to be an actor, I .... (have) to start training at an early age.
3 I .... (have) to give up football if I .... (go) to classes after school.

4 The sentences from Exercise 3 are all examples of conditionals. Conditionals are often divided into different types. Match each type of conditional (sentences 1–3) with the rules (a–c).

• Sentence 2: Type 0 (Zero conditional)   Rule ....
• Sentence 1: Type 1 (First conditional)   Rule ....
• Sentence 3: Type 2 (Second conditional)   Rule ....

> **Rules**
>
> a This is used when the speaker is not thinking about a real possibility, but is imagining a situation that will probably not happen.
>
> b This expresses things which are always or generally true.
>
> c This expresses a real possibility in the future.

5 What form of the verb do we use in each conditional type? Do we use a comma in all conditional sentences?

Type 0 (Zero conditional): If + present simple, present simple

6 Look at this conversation between Kristian and Josh.

1 Does Josh want Kristian to join the drama club?
2 Does Josh talk about a real possibility in sentence (a)?
3 Does Kristian talk about a real possibility in (b)?

Kristian: Can you take a photo of me? When you join the drama club, you need to send a photo.

Josh: What? But **(a)** <u>if you join the club, you'll have to give up football</u> and you're our best player!

Kristian: I know. **(b)** <u>If the drama club met on Wednesdays, I could do both</u>.

Josh: But the club doesn't meet on Wednesdays. What are you going to do?

7 Listen and count how many words are missing from each sentence. Contractions (*I'll*, etc.) count as two words.

🎧39

1 I *'ll need my parents' permission if I want* to go to drama school. (*8 words*)
2 If I .... too old. (..............................)
3 If I .... enough time for everything. (..............................)

8 **/P/** Conditional sentences: contracted words

🎧39 Listen again and complete the sentences in Exercise 7.

9 Complete these sentences with the correct form of the verbs in brackets.

1 If it ....*rains*............ (rain) today, I'll go to the cinema.
2 I often get bored when I .... (watch) sport.
3 If I .... (get) home late, my parents don't mind.
4 I .... (not go out) next Saturday if our teacher gives us a lot of homework.
5 I .... (buy) some crisps if I get hungry.
6 If I .... (not study), I still do well in exams.

10 Rewrite the sentences from Exercise 9 so that they are true for you. Then compare with a partner.

11 Complete these sentences with your own ideas.

1 If I lost my mobile phone,
I'd go to the nearest police station.
2 If I saw a friend cheating in an exam, ...
....
3 If I didn't live here, ...
....
4 If I found a lot of money in a bin, ...
....

12 Write a question for each of the sentences from Exercise 11. Then ask and answer the questions.

> What would you do if you lost your mobile phone?

> I'd go to the nearest police station.

▶ **Page 133 Grammar reference**
Conjunctions: *when, if, unless* + present, future

1 Work in pairs. Kristian, Josh and Hayley are going to an activity camp for a week. Read their messages and decide which person will <u>definitely</u> contact their family.

Have a great trip, Josh!

> Thanks, Mum. I'll send you a message if I run out of money. 😊

Keep in touch, Hayley!

> OK, Dad! I'll let you know when we get there. 😊

Safe trip, Kristian!

> Sure, Mum! 👍 I'll call you tonight, unless we get there really late.

2 Complete the rules about using *if, unless* or *when*.

> **Rules**
>
> We use **(1)** .... for things we are sure will happen. We use both **(2)** .... and **(3)** .... for things we think will possibly happen. However, **(4)** .... generally has the meaning of *except, if*.

3 Choose the best option in *italics*.

1 I'll write again *if* / *when* I finish my exams on Friday.
2 I wouldn't be able to write very well *if* / *when* I broke my right hand.
3 We'll miss the bus *if* / *unless* we run.
4 Paula won't play tennis tomorrow *if* / *unless* it rains.
5 She can't hear you well *when* / *unless* you shout.
6 Dad will give us a lift *when* / *unless* he gets home.

Influencers

Listening Part 3

1 Work in pairs.

- Student A, you want to be famous. Ask for advice.
- Student B, give advice using conditionals. Does your partner agree with the advice?

> I'd love to be a famous singer. What can I do?

> If you upload a video, people will find out about you.

2 You will hear a man called Bob Richards talking about how to get famous on YouTube. Before you listen, read the information below. What is missing in each space (a number, date, time, noun, verb, etc.)?

How to become famous on YouTube ▶▶ ▶

About **(1)** .... hours of videos are uploaded onto YouTube every minute.

Videos about **(2)** .... are usually more popular than all other types.

People want to find out about the video presenter so be **(3)** ....

Add at least ten videos to your **(4)** .... before telling people about it.

Make sure each new video has a **(5)** .... , which is easy to understand.

And be patient! It may take 2 or 3 **(6)** .... to become well known.

- There is always enough time between the six answers for you to write down the missing words.
- Be careful with spelling, especially if the word is spelt out in the recording or if it is a very common word, e.g. *day*.

Exam advice

3 Listen to the talk. For each question, write the correct answer in the gap. Write one or two words or a number or a date or a time. Then listen again and check.

4 Work in pairs. Your school wants to create a video introduction for English-speaking students about you and your country. Discuss what information you could include in this video.

- you and your friends
- your town or city
- famous places in your country

5 Share your ideas with the whole class.

> We can have interviews with people in our city and ask them what they like about it. We can also show photos of the most beautiful places, like …

Vocabulary

Describing people

1 Carter is talking to his friend Will about finding a presenter for his new YouTube channel. Listen and look at the pictures. Who does Carter choose

A

B

C

D

2 Work in pairs. Complete the mind map with words from the box.

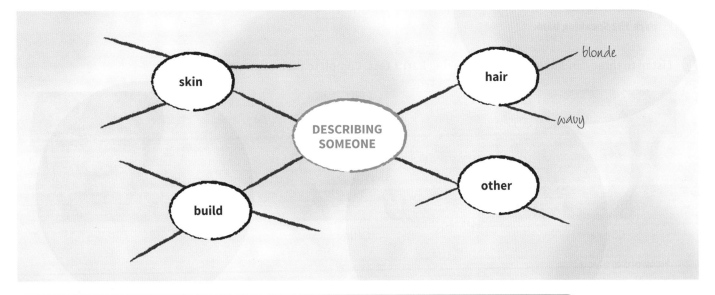

attractive   bald   beard   beautiful   blond(e)   broad shoulders   curly   dark   fair
good-looking   grey   long   medium height   moustache   pale   plain
red   scar   short   slim   straight   wavy

3 Write the opposite of the adjectives.

anxious   ~~easygoing~~   generous   lazy   polite
quiet   shy   stupid

1	strict	*easygoing*	
2	hard-working		**5** mean
3	smart		**6** rude
4	noisy		**7** calm
			8 confident

1 strict *easygoing*
2 hard-working
3 smart
4 noisy
5 mean
6 rude
7 calm
8 confident

4 Will describes one of the people as *honest* and *reliable*. Add *un-*, *im-* or *dis-* to make these adjectives negative.

.....*un*.....friendly .... honest
.... patient .... reliable
.... pleasant

5 Add *-ful* or *-less* to the nouns to make adjectives. Watch your spelling!

1 success ......*successful*.....
(someone who has a lot of success)

2 cheer ....
(someone who is usually happy and positive)

3 beauty ....
(someone or something who looks good)

4 help ....
(someone who likes to help)

5 help ....
(someone who can't help themselves)

6 Exam candidates often make mistakes with adjective order. Read the rules and correct one mistake in each example (a–f).

Rules

1 Adjectives generally go <u>before</u> the noun. We don't normally use more than two adjectives before each noun.

a *In my youth club, there are four girls very nice.*

b *My best friend has hair and eyes brown.*

2 When there are two adjectives together, we generally put the 'opinion' adjective before the 'fact' adjective.

c *At the beginning of the film, a young handsome man is sitting in a café.*

d *She is wearing a white beautiful dress.*

3 When there are two fact adjectives together, we generally put those that describe shape or size before those describing colour.

e *I've made a new friend with black short hair.*

f *He lives in a house with a green big garden.*

7 Work in pairs. Take turns to describe the people below. Don't say who it is. Talk about appearance and character. Guess who your partner is describing.

• a famous person   • a member of your family
• a good friend   • a teacher

> He's almost bald and medium height. He's often cheerful and he's always patient.

> Is it your dad?

Influencers

8

Speaking Part 1

▶ **page 152 Speaking bank**

1 Listen to three candidates doing a Speaking Part 1 test. Complete their answers.

Chiara

How old are you?
14

Where do you live?
Italy

Who do you live with?
My parents and my sister.

Tell us about a teacher you like.

1 My favourite teacher is
....
....

Celine

2 ....

3 ....

4 ....
....

How often do you use a mobile phone?

5 My mum says I use it
....
....

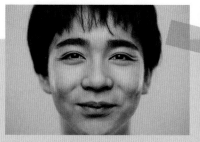

Akihiko

6 ....

7 ....

8 ....

What do you enjoy doing in your free time?

9 I really enjoy
....
....

2 Listen again and answer the questions.

1 Do you think the candidates answer their last questions well? Why? / Why not?
2 What does Celine say when she doesn't understand the examiner's question?
3 Does the examiner repeat the same question to Celine?

- The examiner will ask you general questions about where you live, your daily routine, things you like, etc.
- Always try to give more than a one-word answer.
- Don't try to repeat sentences you have already prepared.

Exam advice

3 Read this part of a Speaking Part 1 test. How could you improve Enrico's answers?

Examiner: What's your name?
Enrico: Enrico.
Examiner: Thank you. How old are you?
Enrico: Fourteen.
Examiner: Where do you live Enrico?
Enrico: Porto, Portugal.
Examiner: Who do you live with?
Enrico Family.

4 Work in groups of three. Take turns to be the examiner. Ask and answer the first three questions from Exercise 1, and one extra question.

Writing Part 2 An article

▶ page 148 Writing bank
An article

1 Work in small groups. Look at the information from the *Cambridge Learner's Dictionary* about punctuation on page 163. Which of the uses are the same in your language?

2 Exam candidates often make mistakes with punctuation. There is no punctuation in sentences 1–6. Correct the mistakes.

1 dear sam i had a great time with my friends last weekend too
2 what about you who is your best friend
3 on saturday i took my cousins dog to the beach
4 after that we ate pizza chicken and ice cream
5 he loves english he thinks that its easy
6 im looking forward to seeing you soon

3 Read this Writing Part 2 task and underline the important words.

> You see this notice in an international English-language magazine.
>
> > **A person who I admire**
> > *Who is it? Is it a member of your family, a friend or perhaps someone famous?*
> > *What does he or she look like?*
> > *What is he or she like?*
> > *Why do you admire him or her?*
> > Write an article answering these questions and we will publish the most interesting articles in our magazine.
>
> Write your **article**.

4 Read Zahra's answer. Do you think her teacher will give her full marks? Why? / Why not?

If i had to choose one person, it would be my cousin Hasan. He was born in Istanbul but he grew up in London. Hes medium height with curly dark hair an brown eyes. Everybody gets on well whit him becaus he's easygoing honest and reliable.

Apart from being such a nice person, Hasan is hardworking and generous to. He's always been keen on drawing. When he was just 14 years old, he set up his own online company wich sells his T-shirt designs. he gives some of the money he earns to help an international childrens charity

5 Answer the questions in pairs and check your ideas for Exercise 4.

1 Does the article include all the information for the task?
2 Does the article use adjectives to describe the person?
3 Does the article give reasons and examples? (e.g. Why is Hasan generous?)
4 Is the punctuation and spelling correct?
5 Is the article about 100 words?

6 Read Zahra's article again. Underline and correct her five spelling mistakes and her five punctuation mistakes.

> • If you have to describe someone or something, don't write long lists of adjectives. Give reasons and examples instead.
>
> • Always check your punctuation and spelling.
>
> **Exam advice**

7 Now write your own answer to the task from Exercise 3 in about 100 words.

8 Use the questions from Exercise 5 to check your work.

Grammar ▶

1 Complete sentences 1–8 using *too* or *enough* and these adjectives.

> big cold dark expensive old
> sleepy thick ~~warm~~

1 Put the heating on, please. It's not _warm enough_ in this room.

2 I'd like to wear those shoes but they aren't .... for me. I'm size 44.

3 It was nearly midnight and it was .... to see anything.

4 You can't skate on the lake. The ice isn't .... to be safe.

5 I must go to bed. I'm .... to stay awake any longer.

6 You're only 16, so you're not .... to drive a car.

7 Put a jumper on. It's .... to go outside in just a T-shirt and jeans.

8 I really liked that laptop but it was .... for me to buy.

2 Choose the correct option in *italics*.

1 A: How's Andrea these days?
B: She *'ll /* (*'s going to*) have a baby.

2 A: Have you got any plans for tonight?
B: Yes, I *meet / 'm meeting* Ryan at 9 o'clock.

3 A: You look tired.
B: Yes, I think I *'m going/ 'll go* to bed early.

4 A: When's the last bus?
B: The timetable says it *leaves / is leaving* at midnight.

5 A: My computer has just crashed!
B: Don't worry. I *'m going to/ 'll* repair it.

6 A: The score's now England 0, Brazil 5!
B: Brazil *will / are going* to win.

Vocabulary ▶

3 Match the beginnings of the sentences with the endings.

1 It's much healthier to go by ...... *d* ......
2 We left the terminal and got onto ....
3 The driver and passenger got into ....
4 In big cities, many people go by ....
5 You should let other people get off ....
6 The police told the thief to get out of ....

a the car and drove to the airport.
b train instead of taking the car.
c the train before you get on.
d bike than to sit in a car or a bus.
e the car and put his hands up.
f the plane, after a six-hour delay.

4 Complete the crossword with words from Unit 7.

Across

1 below a temperature of 0°C
4 the opposite of 'hot'
6 a place where two roads meet
7 a bag you carry when you travel somewhere
8 a word which means the same as 'very much'
9 a bright light you see in a thunderstorm

Down

2 something you read before or when you travel to a new place on holiday
3 visiting interesting places
5 a type of weather when you can't see things very well

Vocabulary

1 Choose the correct word for each gap.

ANGELIQUE KIDJO

Angelique, also **(1)** *known* as The Queen of African music, is one of the greatest female singers **(2)** .... the world. She was born in Cotonou, Benin, West Africa, and she **(3)** .... in Cotonou with eight brothers and sisters. Her uncles, aunts and grandparents come from Ouidah, a small village. She was **(4)** .... in a family of performers. Angelique took **(5)** .... singing when she was six years old. Angelique is good **(6)** .... languages and sings in French, English and two African languages: Fon and Yoruba.

By the 1980s, the political situation in Benin was difficult. Angelique realised, 'Unless I **(7)** .... Benin, I'll have problems.' In 1983 she left for Paris, France, where she studied both Jazz and Law. She couldn't decide between being a lawyer or a musician but thought, 'I will make a bigger difference to the world **(8)** .... I become a musician' and so she developed her music career. She first **(9)** .... her future husband, who is musician Jean Hebrail, at Le CIM, a jazz school in Paris. Now they both live in New York. She has also been a Goodwill Ambassador for UNICEF **(10)** .... 2002, helping to bring education to children all over the world, in particular in Africa.

1	**A**	told	**B**	called	**C**	named	**D**	known
2	**A**	of	**B**	in	**C**	on	**D**	at
3	**A**	grew up	**B**	got on with	**C**	grew	**D**	born
4	**A**	set up	**B**	made up	**C**	brought up	**D**	grown up
5	**A**	on	**B**	off	**C**	out	**D**	up
6	**A**	in	**B**	at	**C**	on	**D**	of
7	**A**	leave	**B**	don't leave	**C**	will leave	**D**	won't leave
8	**A**	when	**B**	unless	**C**	if	**D**	so
9	**A**	knew	**B**	found out	**C**	made up	**D**	met
10	**A**	for	**B**	in	**C**	since	**D**	ago

2 Exam candidates often make mistakes with punctuation and spelling. Underline and correct one mistake in each of the sentences.

1 I only go shopping if I have to becouse most of the shops are expensive.

2 I've just received your email. You ask me wich film stars I like.

3 Since than we have been very good friends.

4 You asked me if i had fun last weekend.

5 After the class on friday, my family and I got on a boat to the island.

6 I think you now him. He is called Patrick.

Grammar

3 Complete the conditional sentences, using your own ideas.

1 If I didn't have to go to school, I'd watch videos all day.

2 If I stay up late, …

3 If I found a wallet on the floor, …

4 I won't go out if …

5 When I leave school, …

6 I'd be annoyed if …

7 Unless the weather is awful, …

8 If I could live in another country, …

4 Read about Debbie's favourite cousin, Axel, and think of the word which best fits each gap. Use only one word in each gap.

If I had to choose a favourite member of my family, I **(1)** *would* choose my cousin Axel. He's rather short **(2)** .... curly blond hair and green eyes. He's **(3)** .... very easygoing person who never gets angry. Now he's studying at university in Germany, but he grew **(4)** .... in Innsbruck in Austria. We haven't seen each other **(5)** .... about two years. He'll come and visit me this summer unless he has **(6)** .... work in his dad's café.

9 Stay fit and healthy

how FIT AND ACTIVE ARE you?

Take this short and simple test to find out …

1 **How do you usually go to school?**
- **A** I go by car.
- **B** I use public transport.
- **C** I walk or cycle all the way there.

2 **What's your perfect way to spend a free afternoon?**
- **A** shopping with friends
- **B** relaxing at home
- **C** rollerblading, playing football, or another sport

3 **How many times a week do you exercise? (You can include things like dancing, or tidying your room.)**
- **A** never
- **B** 3–4 times
- **C** most days

4 **You're bored and want to find something to do. What's your first choice?**
- **A** Go for a bike ride, or go out for a walk.
- **B** Chat online with your friends.
- **C** Message your friends to suggest meeting up somewhere.

5 **If you have to run to catch a bus or train, how do you feel afterwards?**
- **A** I'm exhausted.
- **B** I'm fit, so I feel fine.
- **C** I'm a bit out of breath.

6 **How much time do you usually spend playing computer games or watching TV?**
- **A** more than two hours a day
- **B** 1–2 hours a day
- **C** less than an hour a day

1 Look at the pictures. What are the people doing? How often do you do these kinds of activity?

2 Work in pairs. Do the quiz.

3 Check your score on page 164. Should you make any changes to the way you live?

Listening Part 2

1 Look at the first two lines of questions 1–6 in the exam task below.

1 What's the situation in each question?
2 Who will you hear?
3 What do you have to listen for?

Exam advice

- Make sure you always know which question and which situation you are listening to.
- After you hear each situation and write your answer, forget about that question and move on to the next one.

2 Listen to people talking in six different situations. For each question, choose the correct answer. Then listen again and check.

43

1 You will hear a girl telling her friend about running in a 20-kilometre race. Why did she decide to run in the race?

  A A friend intended to take part.
  B She wanted to win a prize.
  C It would improve her level of fitness.

2 You will hear two friends talking about a film they have just watched. They agree that

  A there was a surprising ending.
  B it was better than the previous film they saw.
  C everyone else in the cinema seemed to like it.

3 You will hear a boy telling his friend about his bicycle. Why does he want to sell it?

  A He rarely uses it.
  B He needs the money.
  C He would like to buy a better bike.

4 You will hear a young man telling his friend about a concert he went to. He thought it was

  A rather boring.
  B too short.
  C very expensive.

5 You will hear a boy telling his friend about his illness. How does he feel now?

  A He has a high temperature.
  B His stomach still hurts.
  C He gets tired very quickly.

6 You will hear two friends talking about their local sports centre. They agree that

  A it offers a good range of activities.
  B it is an easy place to get to.
  C it charges too much for some sports.

Vocabulary

Illnesses and accidents

1 Listen to this sentence and answer the questions.

44

I had a nasty cough, a sore throat and a stomach ache.

1 How do we say the underlined words?
2 What do they mean?

2 The words *cough*, *sore throat* and *stomach ache* are types of illness. Decide if the words from the box are types of illness, accident, or treatment.

> aspirin bandage bruise cut earache fever flu
> fracture high temperature ~~injury~~ medicine
> operation pill plaster plaster cast
> sprain test wound X-ray

injury — accident

3 What are the verb forms of these nouns?

1 injury *injure*
2 cut
3 bruise
4 cough
5 sprain

4 Look at the examples. Complete the rules with *illnesses*, *treatments* or *parts of the body*.

I've cut my thumb.
He's got the flu.
I've had an operation.
Joe took a pill for his headache.
A nurse put a bandage on my arm.

Rules

1 We normally use *me*, *your*, etc. with ....
2 We use *have got* with ....
3 We use *have*, *take* or *put* with ....

5 Find someone in the class who has done the things from the box. Ask them what happened, how they felt and how they got better.

> sprained an ankle had the flu taken an aspirin
> broken a bone had a bandage put on
> had a sore throat taken medicine
> had a stomach ache put a plaster on

Have you ever sprained your ankle?

Yes I have, when I was running.

How did you feel?

It was very painful and I couldn't walk easily.

Grammar
Relative clauses

▶ **Page 134 Grammar reference**
Defining and non-defining relative clauses

1 Read about sports injuries and choose the correct option in *italics*.

Most people **(1)** *which / that* do regular sport are healthier and often feel happier than those **(2)** *who / whose* do little or no exercise. We should be careful, though, to avoid the injuries **(3)** *when / which* sport can sometimes cause. People **(4)** *whose / that* favourite sports include running or jumping, for example, may injure their ankles or knees. Training **(5)** *where / that* involves doing the same exercise again and again can cause serious damage, particularly to athletes in their early teens, **(6)** *when / which* their bodies are still developing. It is important not to do too much too soon. Everyone should warm up before they begin – if possible in the place **(7)** *who / where* they are going to exercise. It is important, too, for people to follow any advice **(8)** *when / that* they receive.

2 Complete the rules with the correct words from Exercise 1.

Rules

Defining relative clauses

We use defining relative clauses to give essential information about someone or something we are talking about.

We use:
- **(1)** ......*that*...... and **(2)** .... for people
- **(3)** .... and **(4)** .... for things
- **(5)** .... for times
- **(6)** .... for places
- **(7)** .... for possessions.

3 Complete the sentences with *where*, *which*, *when*, *who*, *whose* or *that*. Sometimes there may be more than one possible answer.

1 The TV series ...*which / that*... starts tonight is about doctors.
2 People .... swim a lot are usually quite fit.
3 This is the park .... I fell over and injured myself when I was younger.
4 I had a horrible cough .... took about two weeks to go away.
5 Elena has a brother .... name is Ryan.
6 Winter is the time .... people get the flu.

4 Work in pairs. Make as many sentences as you can beginning with these words.

1 Getting presents is something which *I really enjoy!*
2 My room is the place where …
3 Watching sport is something that …
4 Summer holidays are the time when …
5 A good friend is someone who …
6 I know somebody whose …

Rules

Non-defining relative clauses

- We use **non-defining** relative clauses to add **extra information** about someone or something.
- Commas separate this clause from the rest of the sentence.
- We cannot use *that* to begin a non-defining relative clause.

5 Look at the rules. Then answer the questions.

1 What is the relative pronoun in the sentence below?

*Cycling to school, **which is very healthy**, is getting more and more common.*

2 What is the relative clause?
3 Does the sentence make sense <u>without</u> the relative clause?
4 Can we leave out the relative pronoun from the non-defining relative clause?

6 Make one sentence in 1–6, using non-defining relative clauses.

1 My arm is better now. I hurt it last week.

My arm, which ......*I hurt last week, is better now*........

2 My aunt works at the hospital. You met her.

My aunt, who you ....

3 We went to the lake in the next valley. We hired a boat.

We went to the lake in the next valley, where ....

4 Ricky is my best friend. His sister is a nurse.

Ricky, whose ....

5 In 2018 the sports centre opened. I was 12 then.

The sports centre ....

6 Surfing is popular in my country. It's a new Olympic sport

Surfing, which ....

7 Exam candidates often make mistakes with relative clauses. <u>Underline</u> the mistakes in the sentences and correct them.

1 I want to know who sport is your favourite.

2 I can play my favourite sport, that is tennis.

3 They filmed pupils which were playing football.

4 This is the book who my best friend Joey gave me.

5 One sport who I think is good is swimming.

6 I want to learn more about tennis, that is my hobby.

Vocabulary

Sports

1 Match comments 1–3 with photos A–C. Do you like, or watch any of these sports? Why? / Why not?

1 Doing <u>Taekwondo</u> is great and I'm going to get my black belt soon!

2 I really enjoy playing <u>volleyball</u> – it's so fast-moving.

3 I always look forward to going <u>surfing</u> in the summer.

A
B
C

2 Look at comments 1–3 again. Which verb do we use with each sport? Is it *go*, *do* or *play*?.

3 Do we use *go*, *do* or *play* with these sports?

> athletics   baseball   basketball
> climbing   cycling   football   golf
> gymnastics   ice hockey   jogging
> rollerblading   mountain biking
> running   skateboarding   skiing
> surfing   swimming   tennis
> volleyball

4 Choose the correct option in *italics*.

We often use…

1 *go / play* with sports that use balls.

2 *do / go* with outdoor sports.

3 *do / play* with the word *sports* and activities which we do alone.

5 Exam candidates often make mistakes with verbs and nouns. <u>Underline</u> and correct the mistakes.

1 I practise horse riding twice a week.

2 You can make a lot of sports and activities.

3 In winter you can make snowboarding.

4 We have done table tennis.

5 At first, we made aerobics.

6 We played windsurfing.

6 Work in groups. Write down sports that are played in these places. How many do you know?

- on a court
- in a gym
- on a pitch
- in a stadium
- on a track

7 Which of these clothes and pieces of equipment are used in each sport?

> bat   boots   gloves   helmet
> net   racket   trainers

8 Complete the sentences with verbs from the box.

> beat   draw   lose   score   win

1 You ....*beat*.......... a player or team.

2 You .... a goal.

3 You .... , ... or .... a match or game.

9 Work in groups. Which sports do you like or dislike? Which is the most popular sport?

Reading Part 3

1 Work in pairs.

- Which photo is more like you early in the morning? Why?
- How many hours do you usually sleep at night?
- Do you think it's too much, too little or about right? Why?
- What helps you to go to sleep easily, and what keeps you awake?
- How do you feel when you don't sleep well? How does it affect your school work and what you do in your free time?

2 Read the exam instructions and follow these steps.

1 Look at the title of the text and the first line of each question. Decide which questions ask you to understand the whole text, or only part of the text.

2 For each of the questions where you only have to read part of the text, find the paragraph you need.

3 Write the question number next to that paragraph.

4 Read what the text says about that question and decide on your answer.

- Some of these questions focus on opinion and attitude, not fact.

- The last question may ask about the meaning of the whole text.

Exam advice

3 For each question, choose the correct answer.

TEENAGER JULIA RYAN TALKS ABOUT SLEEP

Do you find it difficult to get out of bed in the morning? Have you ever fallen asleep in class? If the answer is yes, then you're not the only one. Across the world, bedtimes are getting later and teenagers are sleeping less. Health experts recommend that 15-year olds should get around nine hours' sleep, but only a third of us even get eight hours.

So what are the reasons for this? Well, stress is an important factor. Like many young people, I find it hard to go to sleep before a big event such as an exam. Our increasing use of technology may also be to blame. New research at Kings College London, involving 125,000 children and teenagers on four continents, shows that using a phone or tablet before going to bed makes it twice as likely you'll sleep badly that night. And the following day, this lack of sleep can make it difficult to concentrate on studying.

But while many schools are attempting to solve this problem by starting the school day later, some schools in New Mexico in the United States are trying something a bit different – they have installed sleeping areas, where students can sleep for 20 minutes in specially designed chairs. I recently tried one of these chairs and my first thought was that it looked like something from a science-fiction film. When I lay down on it, the top part slowly covered my head and upper body so that it became dark inside. Some people might find that scary, but I didn't mind, and the gentle music was quite nice. I started to feel sleepy, and that was all I could remember until the lights came on and I woke up. Then, when I got up, I noticed I was a bit calmer than I'd been before. I'm sure someone who had slept badly before they went to school would feel a lot better.

Some parents might say that their children should be studying during school hours, not sleeping. What I'd say is that sleepy students don't pay attention, but this way they can return to class ready to concentrate on their work. The real solution, though, is to find ways to make sure we all get enough sleep at night, so that nobody has to go to school feeling tired.

1 What is Julia's main purpose in writing this text?

  A To describe how she learnt how to sleep better at night.

  B To discuss the problem of teenagers sleeping too little.

  C To explain how using technology at night can help us sleep better.

  D To show that nowadays we need less sleep than we used to.

2 Julia has trouble getting to sleep

  A just before something important happens.

  B when she has to get up early the next morning.

  C if she leaves her phone switched on all night.

  D the night after she has taken an exam.

3 What was Julia's opinion of the chairs she tried in New Mexico?

  A She decided to start going to bed earlier.

  B She was rather frightened at first.

  C She was convinced they would help people.

  D She thought they were rather uncomfortable.

4 In the final paragraph, what does Julia say about the use of these chairs in schools?

  A Students always sleep better the night after they use them.

  B They can help students learn when they are lying on them.

  C Parents want their children to use them more often.

  D They can improve students' ability to learn in class.

5 What might Julia say to a teenager who feels sleepy at school?

  A Sleeping during the day is not a good idea.

  B Schools should do more to help students sleep well.

  C At night, you should relax more, avoid doing things that can make you feel stressed and try to sleep longer.

  D Feeling tired during school is normal.

4 **Work in pairs. Look at these tips for getting a good night's sleep. Which do you think might be useful? Why?**

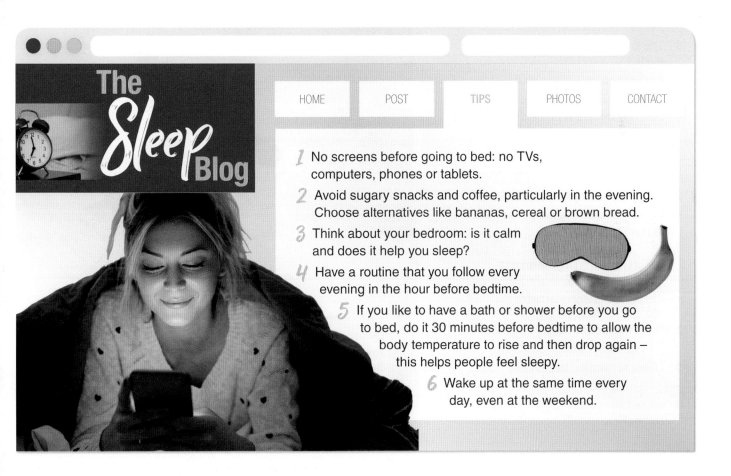

The Sleep Blog

HOME | POST | TIPS | PHOTOS | CONTACT

1 No screens before going to bed: no TVs, computers, phones or tablets.

2 Avoid sugary snacks and coffee, particularly in the evening. Choose alternatives like bananas, cereal or brown bread.

3 Think about your bedroom: is it calm and does it help you sleep?

4 Have a routine that you follow every evening in the hour before bedtime.

5 If you like to have a bath or shower before you go to bed, do it 30 minutes before bedtime to allow the body temperature to rise and then drop again – this helps people feel sleepy.

6 Wake up at the same time every day, even at the weekend.

Grammar
Past perfect

▶ **Page 135 Grammar reference**
Past perfect

1 We use the past perfect when we are already talking about the past and we want to talk about something earlier. Look at the example. Then answer the questions.

I was a bit calmer than I'd been before ...

1 How do we form the past perfect? What do you think is the negative form?

2 Does the past perfect describe the first situation or the second situation?

2 We often use the past perfect to form longer sentences and give more information about the past. Join the sentences using the past perfect.

1 I sprained my ankle. I didn't go to school.
I didn't go to school
......*because I'd sprained my ankle*......

2 I walked all the way home. I felt tired.
I felt tired because ....
....

3 The match started. I arrived at the stadium.
By the time I ....
....

4 I left my trainers at home. I couldn't run in the race.
Because I ....
....

3 Work in pairs. Complete the sentences by saying why something happened. Use the ideas from the box.

> hurt myself   ~~run the fastest~~
> leave their trainers there
> the lesson started

1 I won the race because,
I'd run the fastest...............................

2 I went to hospital because ....
....

3 When I went into the gym, I noticed someone ....
....

4 The bus was late and by the time I got to school ....
....

Writing Part 2: A story

▶ **Page 150 Writing bank**
A story

1 Look at the exam instructions and answer the questions.

> • Your English teacher has asked you to write a story.
> • Your story must begin with this sentence:
>   *Last month, I did something frightening.*

1 Do the instructions give you a first line?
2 Should you write in the first person (*I*) or the third person (*he/she/it*)?
3 Which are the key words?

2 This story has three paragraphs. Read it and decide in which paragraph the things happened.

a describes the main events   2
b sets the scene for the action
c describes the writer's feelings afterwards
d tells us about the final event
e explains what really happened
f introduces the story, saying who did what, where and when

1 Last month, I did something frightening. I went snowboarding in Canada with my friend Lucy, who is a champion snowboarder. I was feeling nervous when we reached the top of the mountain because it had started to snow heavily and I couldn't see much.

2 Lucy went first, but by the time I went, she had disappeared. I went down faster and faster and I thought I saw her go off to the right, so I turned right, too. But soon I came to some cliffs and had to stop. I was terrified. Had she gone over the edge?

3 I waited and shouted, and suddenly, Lucy was there. I'd gone the wrong way but she'd heard me calling and then she'd found me. I felt safe at last.

3 <u>Underline</u> this language in the story.

1 a verb used with a sport
2 a non-defining relative clause
3 six examples of the past perfect

4 Look at the Writing Part 2 task. Answer the questions from Exercise 1.

- Your English teacher has asked you to write a story.
- Your story must begin with this sentence:
  I felt nervous when the game began.

5 Write your story in about 100 words. Use three or four paragraphs and include points a–f from Exercise 2.

> • Use a range of past tenses in your story (the past simple and past perfect for events, and the past continuous for background information).
>
> **Exam advice**

Speaking Part 4

▶ **Page 161 Speaking bank** Speaking Part 4

1 Listen and complete the expressions for agreeing and disagreeing.
45

1 You may be .... right .... , but …
2 I'm not really .... about that.
3 Yes, I .... agree with you.
4 I don't think .... because
5 That's not the .... I see it.
6 I don't agree at ....
7 That's ....
8 I think so ....

2 Match the expressions from Exercise 1 to the uses (a–c).

a agreeing   3
b disagreeing strongly
c disagreeing politely

3 **/P/ Word stress: agreeing and disagreeing**
45 Listen again. <u>Underline</u> the stressed word(s) in each expression from Exercise 1.

You may be <u>right</u>, but . . .

4 Listen again and repeat. Stress the same words.
45

5 Work in pairs. Discuss the questions for at least four minutes. Give reasons for your answers.

Which sports do you think are …

- the most popular in your country?
- the most/least exciting to play?
- the most/least exciting to watch?
- the best for people's fitness and health?
- on TV too often/not often enough?

> • You can talk about your own experiences, but you must not change the topic.
>
> • When your partner is speaking, show you're listening to them.
>
> • Remember there are no right or wrong answers. Say what you think!
>
> **Exam advice**

10 Looks amazing!

A

B

C

D

E

Reading Part 2

1 Work in pairs. Look at the title of the guide, the names of the stalls and the pictures. What do you think you have to do in this Reading Part 2 task?

2 The following people all want to have lunch at the Street Food market. Read the descriptions and <u>underline</u> the important information.

1  Katie's family have tried most of the stalls so want to try something brand new on Tuesday. They would much rather have fish and they want a hot drink with their meal.

2  Jack and his classmates have read that some of the stalls have won prizes and want to try one of those. They would like a vegetarian main meal but they are short of money.

3  Sara and her friends fancy having a light lunch together on Saturday. They would like to sit down to eat at the stall.

4  Samuel's grandmother would like to take him for a meal on Sunday, but she doesn't want to walk too far around the market. Samuel would like a proper meal, but she just wants a dessert.

5  Tania and her mum feel like trying a spicy vegetable dish before the cinema on Sunday. They won't have much time before the film, so they will need to take away their dessert.

Starting off

1 Work in groups. Look at the pictures. What groups of food can you see? Add at least two more examples of food or drink to each group.

2 Discuss the questions.

1 What are your favourite things to eat and drink?

2 Are there any types of food you don't eat? Which ones? Why not?

3 How often do you eat out? Where? Who with?

3 Answer questions 1–5, without reading the text.

1 Katie's family want a hot drink with their meal. *What type of drink could they have?*

2 Jack and his classmates fancy a vegetarian meal. *What sort of food do they not want to eat?*

3 Sara and her friends aren't willing to pay very much. *What words do you expect to read in the description of their most suitable restaurant?*

4 Samuel's grandmother doesn't want to walk too far around the market. *What sort of words do you need to look for in the descriptions?*

5 Jack and his classmates fancy a <u>main</u> meal while Sara and her friends fancy having <u>a light lunch</u>. *What words do you expect to read in the descriptions?*

> • To match the people with an answer, look for a text that says the same things, but in different words.
>
> • For each person or group of people, only one option is correct. Three options are not needed.
>
> **Exam advice**

4 Read the Street Food market guide, and decide which food stall (A–H) would be the most suitable for each group of people (1–5).

5 Work in pairs. Which food stall would (or *wouldn't*) you like to eat at? Remember to say why.

• OUR TOP PICKS AT THE •
STREET FOOD
MARKET

A *Amazing Food by Jason*

If you're looking for a main meal, try the delicious curry from Mauritius here. Don't miss the Creole Chicken, which is spicy fried chicken cooked in tomatoes and served with rice and salad. Not cheap, but visit the stall on Tuesdays for a free glass of hot tea.

B *Scandinavian Kitchen*

Looking for a light lunch? Order the picnic box at this stall which opens this week and you won't be disappointed. We recommend the top-quality turkey with bread and cheese. Or why not try the salmon special, which comes with free coffee and cake? Perfect for those who feel like a change but don't have much time!

C *Just Right Burgers*

All reviews recommend these reasonably priced beef or tuna burgers. The vegetarian burger is grilled vegetables and just the right amount of mushrooms, with or without cheese. Something new for those who fancy a light lunchtime meal. Order a homemade soft drink with your meal.

D *Aladdin's Cave*

Expect to queue for a light middle-eastern meal from this stall. Their lunchbox contains fresh salad, spicy potato chips, garlic sauce and bread. Even meat eaters will consider becoming vegetarians here. Not cheap, but their homemade desserts are amazing!

E *Barbecue Hut*

If you fancy a main meal, sit down here and for less than €10, the prize-winning chefs will barbecue a juicy steak and serve it with fries. Try their range of sauces, from hot pepper to yoghurt. Finish with their famous apple pie and a hot drink! Right next to the market entrance.

F *Blue Dog*

You must try a piadina (an Italian flatbread) from the newly opened Blue Dog. Vegetarians should try the Spinach and Mushroom piadina, which is very reasonably priced. Perfect for those who don't want a heavy meal. Ask for a piadina with chocolate sauce for dessert! - not suitable for a takeaway. Opposite the front gate - you can't miss it! Seating available.

G *Fred Gonzalez*

Fred Gonzalez has been voted chef of the month many times since he set up his Mexican food stall. His customers are happy to wait while his team prepares freshly cooked burritos filled with fish, beef or vegetables and rice, beans, lettuce and hot peppers. Half-price meals for students, but expect queues.

H *Food Planet*

If you think vegan curry is boring, think again. Their potato and pea curry is hot, but it is one of the most delicious dishes in the market. Ask for a slice of their carrot cake in a bag and save it for later. Above-average prices, but worth it. Very short waiting time. Comfortable seating area.

Looks amazing!

Vocabulary

course, dish, food, meal and *plate*

1 Exam candidates often make mistakes with the words
course, dish, food, meal and *plate*. Match the words (1–5)
with their definitions from the *Cambridge Learner's
Dictionary* (a–e).

1 **course** *noun* [C]
2 **dish** *noun* [C]
3 **food** *noun* [C, U]
4 **meal** *noun* [C]
5 **plate** *noun* [C]

a food that is prepared in a particular way as part of a
meal, e.g. *fish and chips* or *lasagne*
b a flat, round object which is used for putting food on
c when you eat, or the food that you eat at that time,
e.g. *breakfast, lunch and dinner*
d a part of a meal, e.g. *starters and desserts*
e something that people and animals eat to keep
them alive

2 Which of the words from Exercise 1 are countable nouns?
Which are uncountable nouns? How do you know?

3 Elsa wrote an email to her friend, Lee, about the food in
her country. Complete Elsa's email using *courses, dish,
food, meals* and *plate*.

Hi Lee,

I'm from Quito, Ecuador. There are many different
types of **(1)** ....food........ in Ecuador – for
example: meat, fish, vegetables, etc. We eat three
(2) .... a day: breakfast, lunch and
dinner. In the morning, my mum often leaves
different cakes or bread on a **(3)** ....
on the table. Lunch and dinner are usually a little
heavier than breakfast. Lunch is three
(4) ....: a starter, which is often soup, a
main course and a dessert. My favourite
(5) .... is *fanesca*, which is a fish soup,
often made with cod.

Write back soon,

Elsa

Grammar

Commands and instructions

▶ **Page 136 Grammar reference**
Commands and instructions

1 Work in pairs. Look at the photos of three dishes from
around the world and answer the questions.

1 Where do you think the dishes are from?
2 What ingredients do you think you need to make these
dishes?

2 Listen to three short recordings about the dishes from
Exercise 1 and check your ideas.
46

3 Listen again. Complete instructions 1–6 with a verb.
46

1 First of all, ...*mix*........ the chicken together with
salt, pepper and chili.
2 .... it on a high heat, or the burrito will be
rather dry.
3 .... one and a half cups of sushi rice.
4 .... cucumber, carrot and tuna for your
first sushi rolls and then .... other things.
5 .... the dosa from an Indian supermarket.
6 .... to serve your dosa with lassi, an Indian
yoghurt drink.

4 What words do we use in the instructions (1–6) to tell
people what to do? What words do we use to tell people
what **not** to do?

5 Choose one of your own favourite dishes and write some
instructions on how to make it. Don't forget to say what
not to do.

6 Work in groups. Take turns to read your instructions
from Exercise 5 without saying the name of the dish.
Guess what each other's favourite dish is.

Listening Part 1

1 Look at the first question from Listening Part 1 and the three pictures. What do we know about Natalie?

1 What will Natalie buy for the picnic?

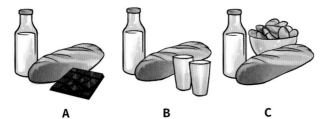

A   B   C

- We know that Natalie will get a **(1)** .loaf.of.bread. and a **(2)** .... (Pictures A, B and C).
- We don't know if Natalie will take a **(3)** .... (Picture A) or some **(4)** .... (Picture B) or some **(5)** .... (Picture C).

2 Listen to the first part of the recording. What do you think the answer is?
47

3 Listen to the last part of the recording. Choose the correct answer, A, B or C.
48

4 Look at questions 2–7 from Listening Part 1. <u>Underline</u> the key words. Then look at the pictures and think about the information you need to listen for.

2 What did the girl take to the party?

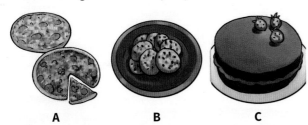

A   B   C

3 What food will the boy try?

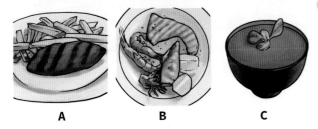

A   B   C

4 Where did the girl go yesterday?

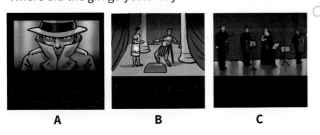

A   B   C

5 What do the students need to bring for their sports lesson?

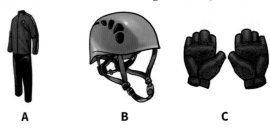

A   B   C

6 What activity did the boy do for the first time on holiday?

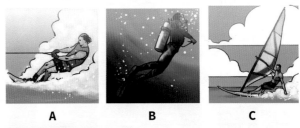

A   B   C

7 Where has the girl been?

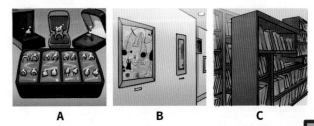

A   B   C

- Listen carefully to the beginning, middle and end of each recording. The information you need may come anywhere.
- When one question has finished choose an answer, and think about the next one.

Exam advice

5 Listen and for each question, choose the correct answer. Then listen again and check.
49

6 **/P/ Connected speech: linking sounds**
Listen to this sentence. What do the linking lines mean?
50

I'm going to get her some earrings or a necklace from that new jewellery shop on the corner.

If a word ends with a consonant sound and the next word begins with a vowel sound, it often sounds like these words are connected.

7 Read the sentences and draw linking lines between the connected words. Then listen and practise saying the sentences.
51

1 I baked a cake instead.
2 It's a plate of mixed fried fish.

8 Work in groups. Do you enjoy shopping? What are your favourite kinds of shop?

Vocabulary
Shops and services

1 Look at the photos of shopping streets from around the world. What can you see in each one?

2 Match the types of shop from the box with the things you can do (1–6).

> book shop bakery butcher's chemist dentist
> dry cleaner's garage supermarket
> hairdresser's library travel agent's

1 make an appointment
2 buy or pay for something
3 borrow something
4 book a holiday
5 have something repaired
6 complain and ask for your money back

3 Listen to three short conversations. Match the speakers to places from Exercise 2.
52

1 ....

2 ....

3 ....

4 Listen again. Discuss what you think Layla, Lewis and Charlie should do next.
52

Grammar
Have something done

▶ **Page 136 Grammar reference**
Have something done

1 Look at the sentences from the recording. Choose the correct options in *italics* in the rules.

Layla: I normally have my hair cut at Gabrielle's.
Lewis: We're having the scooter repaired.
Vicki: I had this dress cleaned last week.

Rules

When we talk about an action **(1)** *we do for ourselves / somebody does for us*, we can use *have something done*.

Layla does not cut her own hair, she has *her hair* **cut**.

Get something done (e.g. *She* **gets** *her hair* **cut**) is also possible, but usually in **(2)** *formal / informal* situations.

2 Look at the pictures. Complete the sentences with *Polly* or *Ginny*.

My cousin Polly

My neighbour Ginny

1 .... rarely has her hair cut.
2 .... gets her hair cut every three weeks.
3 .... tries to clean her own nails.
4 .... often has her nails done.
5 .... always cleans her bedroom.
6 .... had her bedroom cleaned last year.
7 .... got her bike fixed two years ago.
8 .... washed her scooter this morning.

3 Complete the table.

	I do it myself	someone does it for me
present simple	I cook my own meals	**(1)** I .... *have my meals cooked* ....
present continuous	I'm cleaning my room	**(2)** I'm ....
past simple	I cut my hair	**(3)** I ....

4 Complete the conversations with *have* or *get*. Write *both* if they are both possible.

Receptionist: Good morning! Linda's Hair Salon. How can I help you?
Ginny: I'd like to book an appointment to **(1)** .... my hair done.

Mother: Polly, can't you do something with your hair? It looks awful!
Polly: Don't worry, mum! I'll **(2)** .... it cut when I'm ready.

5 Write a sentence about each situation using the words given. Check you have used the correct form of the verb *have* by looking at the time expression (*at the moment, a week ago*, etc.).

1 I / hair / cut / three times a year
  I have my hair cut three times a year.
2 I can't do my homework because I / laptop / mend / at the moment.
3 My bike is broken again and I / it / repair / a week ago.
4 Jack isn't at school today. He / teeth / check today by the dentist.
5 Keith and Pete are going to a party. They / suits / clean last week.
6 In the summer, my brother often / his head / shave.
7 A nurse came to our school last week. We / our eyes and ears / test.
8 My cousins are staying with us right now because they / their house / decorate.

6 Work in groups. Ask and answer questions about the things people do for you.

How often do you When did you last	have	your hair cut? your photo taken? your teeth checked? your computer mended? your bedroom painted? your eyes tested?

How often do you have your hair cut?

I have it cut every six weeks.

Speaking Part 2

▶ Page 154 Speaking bank

1 Listen to Luna describing one of the three photos. Which photo is she describing?

53

2 Which things does Luna talk about?

1 the place in the photo

2 the weather

3 what the people are doing in the photo

4 what the people are wearing

5 everyday objects

3 Listen again. Luna uses two phrases to describe objects she doesn't know the word for. Complete the sentences.

53

One of them is carrying something. I can't remember the word for this object.

(1) .... the rain. We open it when it rains.

On her back, she's got a ... a ... **(2)** .... a bag.

4 Work in pairs. Take turns to describe some of the objects in the pictures using phrases from the table. Can your partner guess which object you are describing?

What is it?	What is it made of?	What is it used for?
It's a kind of ...	It's made of ... (metal/ plastic/wood/ glass, etc.)	It's used for ...
It's something like a ...		

- Imagine you're talking to somebody who can't see the photo.

- If you don't know the word for an object, use another phrase to describe it.

Exam advice

5 Work in different pairs. Take turns to describe one of the photos for a minute. Listen to your partner and tick (✓) the things from Exercise 2 your partner describes.

Writing Part 2: an article

▶ **Page 148 Writing bank**
An article

1 Read the Writing Part 2 task and <u>underline</u> the key words.

Articles wanted!

<u>Going Shopping</u>
Where do young people go shopping nowadays?
Do they prefer going to indoor shopping centres or to town centres?
Or perhaps they'd rather do all their shopping online?
Tell us what you think!

Answer these questions and we will publish the best articles in our next magazine.

Write your **article**.

2 Work in pairs. Discuss the questions from the Writing Part 2 task. Make a note of your answers.

3 Now discuss the questions in this Writing Part 2 task. Make a note of your answers. Then decide which exam task you would have more to write about.

You see this notice in an international English-language magazine.

We're looking for new writers for our magazine!

A good meal
What makes a good meal?
Is it the place, the people, the food – or all of these things?
How important is it to eat out and try different kinds of food from different countries?
Tell us what you think!

We will publish the most interesting articles in our next magazine.

Write your **article**.

• In the exam, you can choose between an article and a story. Choose the one which you are more interested in and which you can write more about.

• If you choose the article, make sure you include all the points in the question.

• Check your work for mistakes. Make sure you have written about 100 words.

Exam advice

4 Choose <u>one</u> of the Writing Part 2 tasks and write your answer in about 100 words. Use your notes from Exercise 2 or 3 to help you.

5 Check your work. If you can answer 'yes' to all the questions, then it is probably a good answer.

1 Have you written an interesting article?

2 Have you included all the information?

3 Are your ideas connected with words like *because*, *and* etc.?

4 Have you checked the article for mistakes, in particular with spelling and punctuation?

5 Have you written about 100 words?

Grammar

1 Match the sentence beginnings with the endings. Then add relative pronouns from the box to form complete sentences.

> when (x2)   where   which   who   whose

1	Sunday is the day	a	cut his hand.
2	All the races	b	tennis is played.
3	Winter is the time	c	I relax at home.
4	James is the boy	d	took place were exciting.
5	A court is a place	e	husband is very ill.
6	That's the woman	f	people catch the flu.

1 *Sunday is the day when I relax at home.*

2 ....

3 ....

4 ....

5 ....

6 ....

2 Put the words in the correct order, starting with the word that has a capital letter. Add commas to form non-defining relative clauses.

1 a swimming champion / is / Zara / only 14 / is / who
   Zara, who is only 14, is a swimming champion

2 we play tennis / the weather / good / In summer / when / is
   ....

3 won / the best player of all / was / whose / Stevie / team
   ....

4 we live / a lot of pollution / is / where / In the city centre / there
   ....

5 better now / who / My brother / an accident / is feeling / had
   ....

6 a team sport / on a court / which / is / Volleyball / is played
   ....

3 Complete the story using the past simple or the past perfect form of the verbs in brackets.

My first match

At ten o'clock last Saturday morning, I **(1)** *was* (be) ready to play my first real match at the tennis club. I **(2)** .... (practise) all the previous week and I really **(3)** .... (feel) good, especially as I **(4)** .... (bring) my lucky trainers.

When I **(5)** .... (put) them on, I walked onto the court. I noticed that the grass **(6)** .... (be) very wet, as it **(7)** .... (rain) a lot the night before, but that **(8)** .... (not seem) important.

Jack, the other player, **(9)** .... (be) a little late because he **(10)** .... (leave) his racket at home, but as soon as he arrived we **(11)** .... (start) the match. I quickly **(12)** .... (realise) that in the past I **(13)** .... (play) against stronger players than him, and I **(14)** .... (be) sure that I could win.

Suddenly, I **(15)** .... (slip) on the wet grass and **(16)** .... (fall). I **(17)** .... (know) immediately that I **(18)** .... (injure) my ankle badly, so that was the end of the game. I **(19)** .... (go) to hospital, and fortunately I **(20)** .... (not broke) it. But after that I never **(21)** .... (wear) my 'lucky' trainers again!

Vocabulary

4 Choose the correct option in *italics*.

1 Skiers have to wear good *gloves* / *boots* / *trainers* to keep their hands warm.

2 Last week I was coughing and I had a really *hurt* / *sore* / *injured* throat.

3 In last night's football match, Brazil *won* / *beat* / *drew* the United States 6–0.

4 I was practising hitting the ball with a baseball *racket* / *bat* / *net*.

5 Sophia is good at *jogging* / *gymnastics* / *athletics*, especially the long jump and 100 metres.

6 If I have a headache, I usually take a *medicine* / *pill* / *test* with a glass of water.

7 After I fell off my bike, I had a big purple *bruise* / *flu* / *disease* on my leg.

Vocabulary

1 Complete sentences 1–5 with a suitable verb.

1 If you have toothache, you should ...make/book... an appointment to see the dentist.

2 If you are not happy with something in a shop, you should always .... and ask for your money back.

3 If you want to go on a trip, it's better to .... it through a travel agent than online.

4 You don't need to buy books, you can .... them from the library.

5 You can save time and money if you learn how to .... broken things yourself.

2 Read the email below from Shane and choose the correct word for each gap.

> Dear Ryan,
>
> Let me tell you something about myself. I **(1)** ....was........... born in Hong Kong but now I live in Singapore. One of the most amazing things about Singapore is the variety of **(2)** .... and other places to eat out. You can eat in expensive restaurants or **(3)** .... street food stalls where the cooks prepare your food in front of you. My favourite **(4)** .... is 'Chicken Rice'. This is boiled chicken **(5)** .... is served on top of rice with cucumber. And if you prefer to eat at home, there are plenty of **(6)** .... where you can buy your own meat, fish, fruit and vegetables.
>
> Shane

1	**A** am	**B** be	**C** was	**D** have
2	**A** plates	**B** food	**C** courses	**D** restaurants
3	**A** cheap	**B** cheaper	**C** more expensive	**D** richer
4	**A** drink	**B** plate	**C** course	**D** dish
5	**A** which	**B** who	**C** whose	**D** what
6	**A** dry cleaners	**B** markets	**C** bakers	**D** travel agents

Grammar

3 Complete these sentences using the correct form of *have something done*. Use an object, like in the example (*his car*).

1 My uncle didn't have time to wash his car before my cousin's wedding, so he *had his car washed* at the garage.

2 My sister tried to cut her own hair but it looked terrible so she went to the hairdresser to ....

3 We wanted to have a photo of the whole class so we .... by a professional photographer.

4 We live on the ninth floor and we can't clean the windows ourselves because it's dangerous. Once a month, we .... by a professional.

5 When I had problems with my bike, I tried to repair it with a friend but we couldn't. In the end I .... at a bike shop.

4 Read about a wedding and think of a word which best fits each gap. Use only one word in each gap.

> My cousin Max **(1)** ....met.......... his girlfriend when they were at university and a few years later, they decided to get married. I went to their wedding two weeks **(2)** .... Before the wedding, I went to the hairdresser with my mum and we **(3)** .... our hair cut and we went to the dry cleaner to **(4)** .... our dresses cleaned. It was a fantastic day and we all **(5)** .... a really good time there. As Max and his new wife **(6)** .... leaving on their honeymoon, I shouted 'Don't forget to send me a postcard!' They haven't written to me yet!

11 The natural world

Starting off
Animals

1 Work in groups. Match the <u>underlined</u> animals with the photos (A–H). Then decide if statements 1–8 are true or false. Check your answers on page 164.

1 <u>Tigers</u> can swim very well.   F
2 <u>Flamingos</u> sleep standing on one leg.
3 <u>Kangaroos</u> can't walk backwards.
4 <u>Ostriches</u> bury their heads in sand.
5 <u>Bears</u> can run faster than horses.
6 <u>Elephants</u> are afraid of mice.
7 <u>Penguins</u> can fly short distances.
8 <u>Camels</u> carry water in humps on their backs.

2 Where do the animals in the photos usually live?

> cool forests   coasts   deserts   grassland
> jungles   lakes   mountains

Listening Part 4

1 Work in pairs.

- Which wild animals have you seen? Where? What were they doing?
- Which animals are important in your country? Why are they important?
- Which animals are becoming less common in your country? Why?

> - For each question or statement, underline the key word(s). Then do the same for options A, B and C.
> - Listen for words with similar or opposite meanings to the ones you underlined. This will help you choose your answers.

Exam advice

2 You will hear a young woman called Ellie talking about her trip to southern Spain to see the Iberian lynx. For each question, choose the correct answer.

1 <u>Why</u> did Ellie and her friend decide to <u>go</u> to that location?

  A <u>Both</u> of them had <u>been</u> there <u>before</u>.

  B A <u>lynx</u> was <u>seen</u> there <u>recently</u>.

  C There were <u>no other animals</u> in the area.

2 As they walked to the stream, they felt

  A glad because they could see where they were going.

  B very tired because of the steep hills they had to climb.

  C uncomfortable because the weather was so hot.

3 Where did the girls hide when they arrived at the stream?

  A among the trees.

  B behind the rocks.

  C in a small building.

4 When they saw the first animal, they were

  A surprised that it was a little cat.

  B delighted that it was a young lynx.

  C disappointed that it was a rabbit.

5 What did the young lynx do after it came out of the bushes?

  A It waited for its mother.

  B It caught a rabbit.

  C It saw Ellie and her friend.

6 Ellie and Marta started walking back to the village

  A as soon as the sun went down.

  B when it was completely dark.

  C very early the next morning.

3 Work in pairs. Which wild animal would you most like to see close up? Why?

Vocabulary
Noun suffixes

1 Look at the <u>underlined</u> nouns and answer the questions.

… which <u>location</u> did you choose, and why?
… I can imagine your <u>excitement</u>!
… we kept going in the right <u>direction</u>.

1 What is the verb form of each noun?

2 Which suffix does each noun have?

3 Which noun drops the letter 'e' from the verb form? Why?

2 Complete the table with the noun form of the verbs from the box. Be careful with any spelling changes.

> ~~admire~~ announce attract celebrate collect
> complete confirm connect create develop
> disappoint discuss educate enjoy entertain
> examine explore improve inform invent
> invite move pollute prevent protect relax
> replace reserve translate

-ment	-ation	-ion
	admiration	

The natural world   99

3 Complete the news article with the noun form of the verbs from the box.

> disappoint explore improve
> inform ~~invent~~ move

Scientists use robot chick to study penguins

Scientists in Antarctica have used a new **(1)** .....*invention*...... to help them study penguins close up: a tiny robot on wheels that looks like a baby penguin. The robot, similar to those used in the **(2)** .... of the moon and Mars, provided lots of exciting new **(3)** .... about the birds. Scientists, working some distance away, controlled every **(4)** .... the robot made and it was immediately accepted by penguin families as one of them. The adults even sang to it, though to their great **(5)** .... the 'baby' didn't reply. The scientists are now working on a new model with one important **(6)** .... – it will be able to play penguin songs.

4 Listen and check your answers to Exercise 3.

🎧 55

5 **/P/ Word stress in longer nouns**

🎧 55

Listen again and <u>underline</u> the stressed syllable in nouns 1–6 in Exercise 3. Then answer the questions.

• Which syllable is stressed in each word? *invention*
• Which syllables are stressed in the other noun forms from Exercise 2?

6 Practise saying the words with the correct stress.

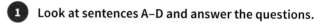

Grammar

The passive

▶ **Page 137 Grammar reference**
The passive: present simple and past simple

1 Look at sentences A–D and answer the questions.

A Tigers very rarely <u>attack</u> people.
B People are very rarely <u>attacked</u> by tigers.
C The guides <u>allowed</u> the tourists to take photos.
D The tourists <u>were allowed</u> to take photos.

1 Which sentences are active? Which are passive?
2 Which two sentences describe an event in the past?
3 Which two sentences use a form of *be* and the past participle of the verb?
4 What is the subject and what is the object in A? How is B different?
5 What is the subject and what is the object in C? How is D different?
6 What information is in sentence C, but not in D?

2 Complete the rules with *active*, *passive* and *by*.

Rules

1 We often find the ....*passive*........ in formal texts (e.g. news reports, textbooks, etc.).

2 In .... sentences, we always use the past participle form of the verb.

3 We often use the .... when we are speaking, or writing informal letters, etc.

4 We use the .... when we focus on who or what did an action.

5 We use the .... when we focus on the action rather than who or what did it.

6 We can add .... + noun if it is important to say who or what did it. In the passive, we often leave this out.

3 Complete the sentences with the present or past passive form of the words in brackets.

1 The mountain road ....is not used...... (not use) in winter.
2 When ......was the island discovered..... (the island / discover)?
3 I wanted to go to the zoo, but it
.... (close).
4 The young zebra ....
(chase) by a hungry lion, but it escaped.
5 What time ....(crocodiles /
feed) today?
6 The sharks .... (not notice)
until they were very close to the boat.

4 Write passive sentences. Begin with the <u>underlined</u> words and only use *by* where necessary.

1 They catch <u>a lot of fish</u> here.
  A lot of fish are caught here.
2 People saw <u>two giraffes</u> near the trees.
3 One small cloud hid <u>the moon</u>.
4 They don't allow <u>cars</u> in the national park.
5 They grow <u>rice</u> in the east of the country.
6 Somebody wrote <u>a poem</u> about this waterfall.
7 Fire partly destroyed <u>the forest</u>.

5 <u>Underline</u> nine more passive forms in the article. What is the infinitive form of each main verb?

In the past, bears and wolves <u>were considered</u> a danger to both people and farm animals, so in many countries their numbers were reduced, often to zero. Nowadays, however, a lot more is understood about how they form part of nature, and some years ago, international agreements were made to bring back these magnificent creatures. A lot of money was spent, large areas where they could move freely across borders were created, and they are now protected by law.

In Europe, bears and wolves are once again found in many countries, from Spain to Scandinavia, where they are allowed to live in places with few people. They are sometimes seen in mountain areas or forests, but usually they prefer to keep away from humans. So if we keep well away from them, we are not in any danger.

6 **/P/ Word stress in passive forms**
56 Listen. Which part of the underlined passive form is stressed? What happens to the other part?

   . . . bears and wolves <u>were considered</u> a danger both to people and farm animals.

7 Look at your answers to Exercise 4. How do you think
57 the passive verb forms are pronounced? Listen and check.

Reading Part 5

1 **Work in pairs.**

- What are the people doing in the photos?
- How will their work help animals?
- Which of these jobs would you like to do? Why?

2 **Quickly read the text and answer these questions.**

1 What kind of text is it?
2 Where did the people go?
3 What kind of things did they do there?
4 Who paid for the expedition?
5 How did they get more money?

3 **Try to fill in gaps 1–6 without looking at options A–D. Use these questions to help you.**

1 Which noun forms a phrase that means 'with the purpose of'?
2 Which noun forms a phrase that means 'join other people in an activity'?
3 Which noun means 'different things of the same type'?
4 Which verb that means 'give' goes with the preposition *for*?
5 Which verb often goes before *care of*?
6 Which noun means 'the knowledge you get from doing a job'?

- For each gap, decide what kind of word the four options are. This can help you with the grammar of the sentence.
- When you've chosen your six answers, check that the completed text makes sense.

Exam advice

4 **For each question, choose the correct answer.**

	A		B		C		D	
1	A	aim	B	plan	C	order	D	reason
2	A	part	B	time	C	place	D	turns
3	A	row	B	range	C	chain	D	crowd
4	A	provide	B	serve	C	benefit	D	support
5	A	made	B	had	C	got	D	took
6	A	background			B	curriculum		
	C	experience			D	qualification		

A SCHOOL EXPEDITION ABROAD

A group of Highfield Secondary pupils have worked extremely hard on a school expedition to East Africa. In **(1)** .... to pay for the expedition, the students decided to grow vegetables in the school garden, and then sold them to local shops, family and friends. They also took **(2)** .... in a local radio show to advertise all the events they had organised to raise money.

These hard-working students have recently returned from East Africa, where they spent a month in a nature park working on a **(3)** .... of environmental projects. The pupils planted trees to **(4)** .... food for wild animals, **(5)** .... care of sick and injured wildlife in an Animal Rescue Centre, and helped to dig water holes for elephants. The expedition was an educational **(6)** .... that they will never forget.

5 Work in groups. Think of ways you could raise money for a school expedition abroad or for an environmental project in your country. Then decide which is the best way. Use these ideas or your own.

- Organise a class sale. Students brings things they or their family don't want.
- Take part in a long-distance race. Adults pay you for each kilometre you run.
- Give up something you really like, such as eating crisps or playing video games. Adults pay you for each day you stop doing these things.
- Offer to walk people's dogs or babysit young children.

Grammar

Comparative and superlative adverbs

▶ **Page 137 Grammar reference**
Comparative and superlative adverbs

1 Look at examples a–d. Then answer questions 1–5.

a This is a conservation area, so the number of lions is increasing more quickly.

b We should speak more quietly …

c In a check on local water pollution, the lake did even worse than the river.

d Nowadays, the animals we see most frequently are rabbits and foxes.

1 Underline three examples of comparative adverbs and one example of a superlative adverb.

2 How do we usually form comparative adverbs?

3 Which adverb in a–d doesn't follow this rule?

4 When we compare two actions, which word normally follows the adverb?

5 How do we usually form superlative adverbs?

2 Complete the table.

adverb	comparative	superlative
quietly	more quietly	
		(the) most carefully
slowly		
		(the) most easily
	faster	
badly		(the) hardest
	better	
	earlier	

3 Work in pairs. Ask and answer questions using comparative adverbs.

1 you ride your bike / quick?
2 you work / hard?
3 you talk / loud?
4 you speak / clear?
5 you sing / good?
6 you finish your homework / early?

> Do you ride your bike more quickly than you used to?

> Yes, I used to ride very slowly.

4 Work in small groups. Ask and answer questions about other students in the class using superlative adverbs.

1 who runs / fast?
2 who sings / beautiful?
3 who gets to school / early?
4 who plays football / good?
5 who speaks / quick?
6 who passes their school exams / easy?

> Who runs the fastest?

> Emilio runs the fastest. He's faster than anyone else.

Speaking Part 4

▶ **Page 161 Speaking bank**

1 Work in pairs.

  1 How are the people in the pictures wasting water?

  2 How could they reduce this waste, do you think?

2 Listen to Ethan and Lily. What three suggestions do they make for saving water?

58

3 Listen again and complete the phrases Ethan and Lily use to give examples.

  1 At home, ...*for instance*................ , you can have …

  2 … when you're brushing your teeth, ... , you should …

  3 … when you're doing other things, ... washing your hair.

  4 … especially in places .... school.

  5 … a tap which loses just one drop a second, ... , wastes 20 litres a day!

58

4 Work in groups. In what other ways can you save water? Use phrases from Exercise 3 to discuss your ideas.

> • Give reasons and examples to support what you say and feel.
>
> • Help your partner to talk by asking them for their opinions.
>
> **Exam advice**

5 Work in different pairs. Discuss the questions for at least four minutes. Give examples and stress important words.

- What do you think are the best ways to save electricity at home?
- Which do you think is better for the environment – travelling by car or by bus? Why?
- Which do you think is the most interesting kind of animal in your country? Why?
- Do you like watching TV programmes about animals? Why? / Why not?
- Do you think we are doing enough to protect wild animals? Why? / Why not?

Writing Part 1: An email

▶ **Page 145 Writing bank**
An email

 1 **Look at the exam task and answer the questions.**

1 How do you know that Chloe has received a message from you?
2 What have you already told Chloe you are going to do?
3 Which four things must you put in your reply?

Read this email from your English-speaking friend Chloe, and the notes you have made.

To:

From: Chloe

Hi,

It was great to hear from you and I'm really glad you're coming to visit. Shall we go to the countryside while you're here? — *Good idea!*

My grandparents live in a cottage in the area, so we can take a day trip or go all day Saturday and Sunday. Which would you rather do? — *Tell Chloe.*

We could take a bus and then walk, or cycle there. It's not far and I've got a spare bike. — *Say which and why.*

There's lots of wildlife there, too. What would you most like to see? — *Suggest …*

All the best,

Chloe

Write your email to Chloe using all the **notes**.

---

2 **Work in groups. Read Leo's reply and answer the questions.**

1 Which paragraph deals with each of the four notes on Chloe's message?
2 Leo has written a good email but has made one mistake in each paragraph. Can you correct each one? Mark the mistakes *G* for grammar, *V* for vocabulary, *WO* for word order, or *Sp* for spelling.
3 What does Leo write to avoid using these words and phrases from Chloe's message?

• go to the countryside   *get out of the city*
• walk
• Saturday and Sunday
• wildlife
• rather

Dear Chloe,

Yes, it'd be great to get out of the city. This sounds like a great idea – besides, the city has too much noise and <u>polluteion</u>.

I'd love to stay overnight in the country, so I think I'd prefer to spend the <u>weekend whole</u> there. I really like cottages!

Let's <u>drive</u> there by bike. We can get around much more quickly than on foot, and go to more places.

The animals I'd most like to see are butterflies, but I don't know if they <u>find</u> there. I like watching birds too, especially really big ones.

Looking forward to seeing you,

Leo

• Try to use your own words instead of copying words from the email you received.

• Check you have included all the points in the email you received.

• Write clearly and make sure you haven't made any mistakes.

Exam advice

---

3 **Look again at the exam task. Then plan and write your own email in about 100 words. Try to include comparative/superlative adverb forms.**

4 **Work in pairs. Check your partner's email. Where you think there are mistakes, write *G, V, WO* or *Sp* in pencil. Then discuss your corrections.**

12 Express yourself!

Starting off
Collocations: using your phone

1 Work in pairs. What do you and your friends use your phones for? Talk about the things from the box, and add your own ideas.

> call friends   check the time   go online
> listen to music   play games   share videos
> take selfies   text friends

2 Work in groups. Read about how young people use their phones. Is it true for you and the people you know? Do you think it's different for older generations?

33% Young people spend of their time using a smartphone.

18% of 18–24 year-olds send over 200 phone messages every day.

Most communication is done through text messages.

Around **51%** of young people use their phones when they're with their friends.

Reading Part 4

1 Look at the title of the article on page 107 and read the first sentence in bold.

- What is the 'challenge'?
- Would you agree to take up the challenge?
- Would you find it easy?

2 Read the complete article but do not complete the gaps for now. Did Becky find the challenge easy?

3 Read the second paragraph of the article again. Is sentence A or B the correct answer for gap 1? How do you know?

4 Five sentences have been removed from the text below. For each question, choose the correct answer. There are three extra sentences which you do not need to use.

Can you live without technology for a week?

Teenager Becky Barnes takes up the challenge

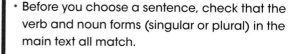

Day 1
Most mornings, I check my phone for messages, read quickly through Facebook and have a look at Instagram. Not this morning! And surprisingly, I was ready for school much earlier than usual.

On the way to school. I began to count the number of people on their phones – my dad, some young kids, my friends. **(1)** _____ This was going to be a long week.

Day 2
I set my alarm for later than usual, but I was still out of the house before my brother. When I got to school, my friends told me about some news that had been posted the night before. **(2)** _____ This conversation was unexpected. We don't usually talk to each other first thing in the morning because we normally spend most of the previous evening sending each other messages.

Day 3
I woke up feeling positive until I remembered that I had sports practice that afternoon and I didn't have a lift. Normally, I can arrange this quickly by posting a message. **(3)** _____ It was stressful but I learnt that I needed to plan if I wanted to live without my phone.

Day 4
I felt more prepared today. My friends and I had planned to meet at Jason's house after school to work on a project and I managed to get a lift there. We started well by talking about the project. **(4)** _____ Everyone was checking their phone.

Day 5
On Friday evening, I was at home. I'd just seen my favourite series and I wanted to talk about it. **(5)** _____ I wanted my phone back but I knew I would hate myself if I gave up.

A I wanted to use my phone, I wanted to be like him.	**E** I spent an hour organising transport.
B I felt jealous of them, I was missing mine.	**F** However, fifteen minutes later, we were all sitting in silence.
C I could imagine the messages my friends would post about the show.	**G** I really enjoyed hearing all about it.
D I enjoyed having a real conversation about them.	**H** Everyone had left their phones at home.

5 Work in pairs. Prepare for a discussion by writing down three reasons for and three reasons against the following opinion.

> We should all turn off our phones for at least three days every week.

6 Work in groups. Discuss the opinion from Exercise 5. Remember to give reasons for and reasons against. Then decide together whether you agree or disagree.

> We need our phones to keep in touch with our friends.

> Young people don't know how to talk to each other.

Vocabulary

ask, ask for, speak, talk, say and tell

1 Choose the correct words in *italics* in the rules.

Rules

ask or ask for

We use **(1)** *ask / ask for* if we want someone to do something.

I asked my friends to bring some food to the party.

We can use **(2)** *ask / ask for* when we want someone to give us something.

I asked the teacher for the answers to the homework.

speak or talk

We **(3)** *speak / talk* a language. We do <u>not</u> **(4)** *speak / talk* a language.

She speaks French. ~~She talks French.~~

say or tell

We can use *say* or *tell* with direct or indirect speech, but **(5)** *say / tell* is always followed by the person. **(6)** *Say / Tell* is never followed by the person.

She said ~~me~~ she was unhappy.
He told me he lived in Rome.

We also use **(7)** *say / tell* to report instructions

Our football coach told us to sleep well before the match.

Note:

- We use **(8)** *say / tell* with greetings: *hello, goodbye, goodnight,* etc.
- We use **(9)** *say / tell* with the following nouns: *the truth, a lie, a joke, a story* etc.

---

2 Exam candidates often make mistakes with these verbs. Choose the correct option in *italics*.

1 Olga knows how to *speak / talk* English well.
2 He *said / told* me to go to 6th Avenue.
3 I'll *ask / ask for* more information about the new pool.
4 At first we were bored but then we started to *say / tell* jokes.
5 When we are together, we *say / talk* about lots of different things.
6 A waiter came and *told / asked* us what we wanted.

3 Complete the mind map with *ask, ask for, say, speak, talk* and *tell*. Add at least one more phrase to each verb.

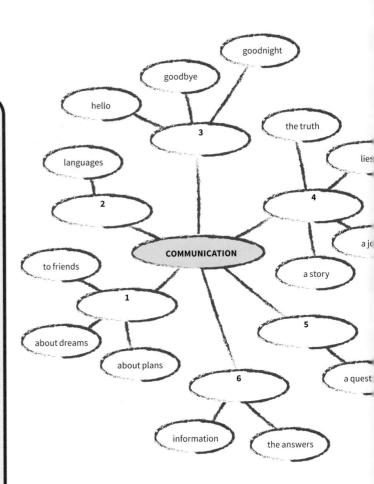

4 Complete the questions with a noun from Exercise 3.

1 When you're doing your homework, how often do you ask for .... ?
2 Do you say .... when you come into the classroom?
3 Has someone told you a .... recently?
4 Can you speak two .... ?
5 Who do you go to when you want to talk about your .... ?
6 Is it easy or difficult for you to tell a .... ?

5 Work in pairs. Ask and answer your questions.

6 Answer the questions using the verb + noun combinations from the mind map. Then compare your answers with a partner. Do you agree?

What makes ...

- a great friend?
- a great parent?
- a great teacher?
- a good sports trainer?

> I think someone who always tells the truth makes a good friend.

Grammar

Reported speech

▶ **Page 138 Grammar reference**
Reported speech

1 Work in groups. Marsham School is taking part in a charity project which helps children all over the world. List things the students could do to raise money (e.g. *a sponsored walk*).

> **raise money**
> *verb* to collect money from other people: *They're raising money for charity.*
> **sponsor**
> *verb* to give money to someone to support an activity or an event: *a sponsored walk* (= a walk for charity)

2 Listen to Adam, John and Nina talking about how they can raise money. What events do they suggest?
59

3 Rewrite Adam, John and Nina's words in reported speech.

1 Adam: Last year we organised a disco to collect money. Adam said that they .... the year before.
2 Adam: We can organise a similar event again. Adam said they ....
3 John: We've thought about organising a football match. John said they ....
4 John: In my sister's school, the students are going to play against the teachers. John said in his sister's school, the students ....
5 John: It doesn't have to be just teachers. John also said ....
6 Nina: We're all using our phones right now. Nina said they .... then.
7 Nina: We'll turn off the electricity and hold some special technology-free events instead. Nina said they .... the electricity and hold some special technology-free events instead.

4 Listen to Sonia telling Lisa about the meeting. Check your answers from Exercise 3.
60

5 Use your answers from Exercise 3 to complete this table.

direct speech	reported speech
present simple	(1) .... *past simple* ....
present continuous	(2) ....
present perfect	(3) ....
past simple	(4) ....
will + infinitive	(5) ....
is/are going to	(6) ....
can	(7) ....

6 Use the underlined words from Exercise 3 to complete the table.

direct speech	reported speech
today	(1) .... *that day* ....
last year	(2) ....
my	(3) ....
we	(4) ....
right now	(5) ....

7 Work in pairs. What can you say in situations 1–4? Complete the sentences.

1 Mark says: 'I can't play tennis. I've hurt my arm.' Later you see him playing basketball.
'You said .... *you couldn't play tennis because you'd hurt your arm* .... ,'
2 Ruth says: 'Someone left their phone in the kitchen after the party.' Later your cousin tells you that she has lost her phone.
'Ruth said .... ,'
3 Your brother is studying abroad. He phones you and says: 'I'm having a great time here.' Later his teacher asks you if you've spoken to your brother.
'My brother said .... ,'
4 Harry says: 'I want to sell my bike so I can buy a new one.' Later your sister tells you she wants to buy a bike.
' Harry said .... ,'

8 Choose a situation from Exercise 7 and write a story in reported speech.

Last week I wanted to play tennis with Mark, but he told me he couldn't play because . . .

Reported commands

▶ **Page 138 Grammar reference**
Reported commands

9 In the meeting about the project, Helen told the other students to do four things. Complete the reported commands.

1 'Be quiet!'
Helen told them to .... *be quiet* ....
2 'Close the door, Paul!'
Helen told Paul ....
3 'Think about the suggestions!'
Helen told them ....
4 'Don't forget about the meeting!'
Helen told them not ....

10 Rewrite each instruction 1–4 as a reported command.

'Keep in touch.'
1 Lisa's family told her ....

'Don't be late!'
2 She told her brother ....

'Don't bring more pizza!'
3 Dave told his friend ....

'Don't forget to download Season 3 for me!'
4 Charlie's mum told him ....
for her.

Listening Part 3

1 You will hear a woman called Catherine Bryant talking about a competition on the radio. Read the notes. Is the answer a singular or a plural noun? What do you learn about the competition?

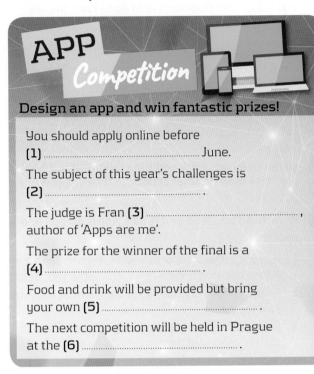

APP *Competition*

Design an app and win fantastic prizes!

You should apply online before
(1) .... June.

The subject of this year's challenges is
(2) ....

The judge is Fran **(3)** .... ,
author of 'Apps are me'.

The prize for the winner of the final is a
(4) ....

Food and drink will be provided but bring
your own **(5)** ....

The next competition will be held in Prague
at the **(6)** ....

2 Read the notes again carefully. What kind of information is missing in each gap?

3 Look at gap 4. Which answer is more likely: *laptop* or *phones*? Why?

- Write clearly, so that you can read your answers later.
- Make sure your answers are grammatically correct.

Exam advice

4 Listen, and for each question, write the correct answer in the gap. Write one or two words or a number or a date or a time.

5 Listen again and check.

6 Work in groups.

1 How many apps have you got on your phone?

2 What's your favourite app? Why?

3 What app would you like that you don't have at the moment? (If it doesn't exist yet, what would you like it to do?)

Grammar

Reported questions

▶ **Page 139 Grammar reference**
Reported questions

1 🎧 62 **Listen. Write the questions that people ask Catherine about the app competition.**

1 *Can I choose the the members of my team?*
2 ....
3 ....
4 ....
5 ....

2 🎧 62 **Listen again. Complete the questions with the students' names:** *Connor, Charlotte, Emily, Samir* **or** *Peter.*

1 ....*Emily*.......... asked if she could choose the members of her team.
2 .... asked if they needed to pay anything to take part.
3 .... asked how they registered for the competition.
4 .... asked what they did if they had technical problems.
5 .... asked what the prizes were.

3 **Look at the reported questions from Exercise 2. Choose the correct option in** *italics* **for a–e, to complete the rules about reported questions.**

Rules

In reported questions …

a the normal question order stays *the same / changes*.

b the tense stays *the same / changes*.

c we *always / never* use an auxiliary verb (e.g. *do, does* or *did*).

d we use *if* when there *is / isn't* a question word (*what, when*, etc.).

e we *use / don't use* a question mark at the end.

4 🎧 63 **Emily's team wins the competition. Listen to her friends asking about the winning app. What does the app do? Do you think it's a good idea? Why? / Why not?**

5 **Write her friends' questions in reported speech.**

1 Cindy asked Emily ....
2 Harry asked her ....
3 Phil asked her ....
4 Diana asked her ....
5 Lily asked Emily ....

1 What does the app do?

5 Will the app do my exams for me?

2 Does it do anything else?

4 Where did you get the idea from?

3 Can I use it to share stuff with my friends?

Vocabulary

Negative prefixes

1 **Emily said that an app which did our exams would be** <u>unfair</u>. **Make these adjectives negative by writing** *im-, in-* **or** *un-.*

1 .... friendly, comfortable, believable
2 .... correct, expensive, complete
3 .... possible, polite, patient

2 **Add** *im-, in-* **or** *un-* **to make negative adjectives.**

1 Would you like to have an app that does exams for you? Or would it be *un*fair?
2 Many young people use the internet for more than four hours a day. Is this .... healthy?
3 How often do you get .... patient when you're using new technology?
4 Do you think that using your phone when you're with your friends is .... sociable?
5 Do you need to spend a lot of money on a phone? Or is an .... expensive one just as good?
6 Will we ever be able to communicate without speaking or writing, just thinking? Or will it be .... possible?

3 **Work in pairs. Ask and answer the questions.**

Speaking Part 1

▶ **page 152 Speaking bank**

1 🎧 64 Listen to three students answering questions for the Speaking Part 1 exam. Complete the table with a tick (✓) or a cross (✗).

		Anton	Eleni	Victoria
1	Does he/she give a suitable answer?	✗		
2	Does he/she answer in full sentences?			
3	Does he/she use a range of grammar and vocabulary?			

2 Who do you think gives the best answer and why?

3 How could you improve Anton and Eleni's answers?

Examiner: Do you walk to school every day?
Anton: Bus.

Examiner: Eleni, tell us about your best friend.
Eleni: My best friend is Maria. She's tall. Her hair is long and straight. She is very nice. I like her.

4 🎧 65 Listen to Eleni and Victoria doing the complete Speaking Part 1 exam. Complete the questions.

1 What's .... ?
2 How .... ?
3 Where .... ?
4 Who .... ?
5 .... use the internet?
6 .... your best friend.

> • Listen carefully to the examiner's questions. You can ask the examiner to repeat the question.
> • Answer the questions in full sentences, using a range of grammar and vocabulary.
> • Look at the examiner when you're answering the questions.

Exam advice

5 Work in groups of three. Take turns to ask a question from Exercise 4 and another question below.

• Who uses the internet the most in your family? What for?
• Do you use the internet mainly for fun or mainly for school? Why?
• Do you often buy things online? Describe the last thing you bought.
• Do you usually do your homework by hand or on a computer? Which do you prefer?

Grammar

Indirect questions

▶ **Page 140 Grammar reference**
Indirect questions

1 Work in groups.

1 How many different kinds of social media do you use?
2 What do you use each one for?
3 What are some of the dangers of using social media?

2 🎧 66 Listen to a TV journalist talking to Bradley. What are Bradley's answers to the questions from Exercise 1?

3 🎧 66 Listen again and complete the indirect questions.

direct questions	indirect questions
Could I ask you some questions?	**(1)** I was wondering if I ......*could ask you*...... some questions.
What is your name, please?	**(2)** Could you tell me what .... please?
How many different kinds of social media do you use?	**(3)** I'd like to know how many different kinds of social media ....
What do you use each one for?	**(4)** Could I ask you .... each one for?
What are some of the dangers?	**(5)** Do you have any idea what some of the .... ?

4 Answer the questions.

1 Can we use question words in indirect questions?
2 Do we change the tense in indirect questions?
3 Do we change the word order in indirect questions?
4 Are indirect questions more polite than direct questions?
5 What phrases can we use to start an indirect question?
6 Do we always use a question mark at the end of an indirect question?

5 **/P/ Intonation in direct and indirect questions.**
🎧 67 Listen to the direct questions in Exercise 3. Does the speaker's voice go up or down at the end?

6 🎧 68 Listen to the indirect questions again. Does the speaker's voice go up or down?

7 Work in pairs. You are doing some research into how young people do things. Choose <u>one</u> of the topics below and write indirect questions for people in the class.

> following celebrities online   keeping in touch
> keeping up-to-date with the news
> making plans   playing games

8 Work in groups. Ask and answer your questions.

Writing Part 2 A story

▷ **Page 150 Writing bank**
A story

1 Work in groups. Look at the pictures and sentences. What do you think happened next?

1 The message began, 'Congratulations! You've won first prize!'

2 I was in class when my phone rang.

2 Read the Writing Part 2 tasks and answer questions 1–3.

1
- Your English teacher has asked you to write a story.
- Your story must begin with this sentence:
  The message began, 'Congratulations! You've won first prize!'

2
- Your English teacher has asked you to write a story.
- Your story must begin with this sentence:
  I was in class when my phone rang.

1 What do you have to write for each question?
2 Who do you have to write it for?

3 Now read this story, and answer the questions.

I was in class when my phone rang. I couldn't believe it. I had forgotten to switch it off. I didn't know what to do, because it was still ringing. Should I answer it? The teacher stopped talking and looked directly at me. She asked all the students what the noise was, and we said that it was a phone. Suddenly, she looked embarrassed. She told us that she had to leave the classroom for a minute. She picked up her bag and left the room. As soon as the teacher closed the door, the ringing noise stopped.

1 Which task does it answer?
2 Why did the phone stop ringing when the teacher closed the door?

4 Work in pairs. Decide if these sentences are true or false.

1 The story is about 100 words.
2 It is well organised.
3 The story has a clear ending.
4 The ideas are connected using *and*, *because*, etc.
5 There are different tenses.
6 There are some reported questions and some reported speech.

5 Write a story in about 100 words using one of the tasks from Exercise 1. Make sure the sentences from Exercise 4 are true for your answer, too.

- Make sure you write a proper ending for the story. Try to surprise your readers.
- Check there are no mistakes in your story and it is the correct length.
- In the exam, you will need to choose between **a story** and **an article**. You <u>won't</u> be able to choose between two different stories.

Exam advice

Grammar

1 Choose the correct option in *italics*.

My family and I **(1)** *are lived* / (*live*) in an old house on the coast. When it **(2)** *built* / *was built* in the 19th century, it was over 500 metres from the sea, but now the water **(3)** *seems* / *is seemed* to be getting closer. The sea level **(4)** *is risen* / *is rising* every year, and the sand **(5)** *washes* / *is washed* away by the waves.

Sometimes, when there's a storm, the water **(6)** *is reached* / *reaches* the house. Last February, for instance, the ground floor **(7)** *completely flooded* / *was completely flooded* by sea water, and a small building near our house **(8)** *disappeared* / *was disappeared* overnight. Unless something **(9)** *does* / *is done* immediately, we **(10)** *are known* / *know* that our home will be next. Some other houses along the coast **(11)** *saved* / *were saved* when a strong wall **(12)** *put up* / *was put up* in front of them, and we want the same here.

2 Complete sentences 1–8 with the comparative or superlative adverb form of the words in the box.

> bad careful ~~early~~ frequent
> good hard heavy quick

1 You should get up .... *earlier* .... in the morning.
2 The ice melted .... as the temperature increased.
3 Of all the people at the meeting, Lauren spoke .... She made a great speech.
4 Buses stop here .... now – every ten minutes.
5 We must try .... to find solutions to environmental problems.
6 They're all bad musicians in that band, and the guitarist plays .... of all.
7 It began to rain .... when the storm approached.
8 If we all use energy ...., we can reduce the amount of pollution we cause.

Vocabulary

3 Complete the sentences with the noun form of the verb in brackets.

1 My ..... *education* ..... (educate) began at the local primary school nearly ten years ago.
2 I was so pleased when I got an .... (invite) to my friend's sister's wedding!
3 The new school gym is a big .... (improve) on the old building.
4 The mathematics .... (examine) will be held in the last week of term.
5 There was great .... (excite) when our local team's match began.
6 In my town, the New Year .... (celebrate) often go on all night.
7 In class we had a .... (discuss) about ways of using less plastic.
8 There was some really good live .... (entertain) at last night's party.

4 Complete the crossword with words from Unit 11.

Across

3 a large animal that lives in forests or mountains
5 a very high place
7 the noun of 'explore'
8 a hot place with lots of trees and animals
9 a bird which cannot fly and lives in a cold place

Down

1 an animal that lives in Australia and jumps well
2 the noun of 'discuss'
4 the noun of 'move'
6 a hot, dry place

Vocabulary

1 Complete the sentences with the correct form of the verbs from the box. You will need to use some verbs more than once.

> ask   ask for   say   speak   talk   tell

1 Most of my friends can ...._speak_........ two or three languages really well.
2 Ben .... 'thank you' to everyone for his presents.
3 My friend .... me if I wanted to go to the cinema that night.
4 There's a boy in my class who likes .... jokes all the time.
5 In your email you .... me about my plans for the summer holidays.
6 I'm going to .... some help with this exercise. It's really hard.
7 I became very nervous and decided to .... my parents the truth.
8 When I get to school on Monday, I love .... to my friends about the weekend.
9 Can you .... a little more slowly, please? I don't understand.
10 In class today, we .... in groups about how to prepare for exams.

2 Add *im-*, *in-* or *un-* to the words from the box to complete the sentences.

> expensive   fair   healthy   patient   polite   possible

1 I can't live without my mobile phone. It's ...._impossible_........ .
2 My mum got a tablet online for €40. It was quite ....
3 It's .... to charge children the same price as adults.
4 My neighbour spends all day playing video games. That must be ....
5 Wait for the app to download completely. Stop being so ....
6 Don't eat with your mouth open. It's ....

Grammar

3 Underline and correct the mistake in each sentence.

1 In my maths class, the teacher asked me what ~~was my name~~. _my name was_
2 A friend asked me what was my dog called.
3 Marta asked me why didn't I go to the exam.
4 My sister asked me why was I crying.
5 Nicky asked me what was I going to do.
6 Danny asked me what new sport should he take up.
7 I imagine you are wondering when am I going to visit.

4 Bryony is talking about how she spends her free time. Rewrite her sentences in reported speech.

1 'I like hanging out with my friends and watching films with them.'
She said _she liked hanging out_ with her friends and watching films with them.
2 'We're looking forward to seeing the new film.'
She said .... to seeing the new film.
3 'I've just bought a new tablet to watch my favourite series online.'
She said .... a new tablet to watch her favourite series online.
4 'I'm going to invite my friends round to my house tonight because …'
She said .... her friends round to her house that night.
5 '… we finished all our exams yesterday.'
She said .... their exams the day before.
6 'I'm sure we'll have a lot of fun.'
She said .... a lot of fun.

5 Read the text and think of the word which best fits each gap. Use only one word in each gap.

I was in class when my phone rang. I **(1)** ...._said_........ sorry to the teacher and switched it off. My partner asked me **(2)** .... I knew who had called and I said that I didn't know. She **(3)** .... me that someone had called her **(4)** .... day before during her physics class and the teacher had taken away her phone. She thought it **(5)** .... very unfair. At that moment, our teacher told us **(6)** .... be quiet and she gave us extra homework. Now that's unfair!

Grammar reference

PREPOSITIONS OF TIME

We use *at*:

- for times of the day: *at* 7 o'clock, *at* breakfast time
- in expressions like: *at* the weekend, *at* night, *at* New Year

We use *on* for:

- days: *on* Tuesday
- dates: *on* May 17th

We use *in* for:

- years: *in* 2017
- seasons: *in* summer
- months: *in* August
- parts of the day: *in* the morning

PRACTICE

1 Complete the conversation with *at*, *in* or *on*.

A: Are you busy (1) .... Saturday?

B: Yes, I'm with my grandmother (2) .... the morning. I have to be there (3) .... 11 o'clock. It's her birthday party. Her birthday is (4) .... August 28th – that's Monday, but everyone's busy then.

A: Do you want to meet (5) .... the evening (6) .... Saturday?

B: OK!

FREQUENCY ADVERBS

| always (100%) |
| usually |
| often |
| sometimes |
| occasionally |
| hardly ever |
| never (0%) |

- We usually put frequency adverbs before the main verb.
  I **usually/sometimes/never** go to college in the evening.
  I don't **often** go to college at the weekend.

- We don't use *never*, *hardly ever* and *always* at the beginning or end of sentences.

- We put frequency adverbs after the verb *be*.
  I am **often** ill in the winter.
  She is **usually** at college at 8 o'clock.

There are other expressions that we can use to talk about frequency. These expressions are used at the beginning or end of sentences, not in the middle.

- *every day, every week, every month, ever year …*
- *once a day, twice a week, three times a month …*
- *on Fridays, at weekends …*
- *most days, most nights, most weeks …*

On Fridays, I go to college by bike.

I go running **twice a week**.

PRACTICE

1 Put the words in order to make sentences.

1 a / go / gym / I / the / to / twice / week.

....

2 an / hour / I / more / hardly ever / spend / than / there.

....

3 an / for / half / hour. / I / run / sometimes

....

4 I / I'm / listen / music / running. / to / usually / while

....

5 always / exhausted. / get / home, / I / I'm / When

....

6 every / Friday. / friends / go / I / my / out / with

....

PRESENT SIMPLE AND PRESENT CONTINUOUS

Present simple

Positive/Negative forms

I/You/We/They	take	photos.
	don't take	
He/She/It	takes	
	doesn't take	

Question forms

Do	I/you/we/they	take	photos?
Does	he/she/it		

Short answers

Yes,	I/you/we/they	do.
	he/she/it	does.
No,	I/you/we/they	don't.
	he/she/it	doesn't.

We can use the present simple to talk about something that:

* happens regularly (and routines):
  *I **play** tennis every Tuesday.*

* is generally true and permanent at the present time:
  *My brother **lives** in France.*

* is a fact or always true:
  *The sun **rises** in the east.*

Present continuous

Positive/Negative forms

I	am/'m	working at the moment.
	am/'m not	
You/We/They	are/'re	
	are not / aren't / 're not	
He/She/It	is/'s	
	is not / isn't / 's not	

Question forms and short answers

Am	I	working at the moment.
Are	you/we/they	
Is	he/she/it	
Yes,	I	am.
	you/we/they	is.
	he/she/it	are.
No,	I	am / 'm not.
	you/we/they	isn't.
	he/she/it	aren't.

We can use the present continuous to talk about

* something happening now:
  *They**'re living** with friends while their house **is being decorated**.*
* a temporary situation which is true now:
  *He**'s doing** his homework in his bedroom.*
* something happening in the present but not necessarily at the moment:
  *My sister**'s studying** art.*

PRACTICE

1 Choose the correct option in *italics*. Sometimes there may be more than one possible answer.

Many people (1) *take up / are taking up* cycling these days. Cycling is great because it (2) *helps / is helping* our general fitness. When we cycle, we (3) *use up / are using up* more energy than when we (4) *walk / are walking*. (5) I *go / am going* cycling regularly, but only on small roads where there aren't many cars. At the moment, (6) *I train / I'm training* for a race so (7) *I spend / I'm spending* a lot of time on my bike.

STATE VERBS

State verbs refer to a state or a condition, rather than an action. They are not normally used with continuous verbs.

✓ I **prefer** apples to oranges.

✗ I'm preferring apples to oranges.

- This is a list of common state verbs.

> agree appear believe depend hear hope
> know like look love need own possess
> prefer see seem smell suppose taste
> think understand want weigh wish

- There are verbs which can be both state verbs and action verbs, but have a different meaning.
  She **looks** tired. (look = appear)
  She**'s looking** for her phone. (look = search)
  He **has** an apartment. (have = own)
  He**'s having** breakfast. (have = eat)

PRACTICE

❶ Complete the sentences with the present simple or present continuous form of the verbs in the box.

> cost have help own prefer
> smell think want weigh

1 **A:** How much .... you .... , Ben?

   B: I don't know. About 60 kilos, maybe? I .... not to know actually.

2 Paul is a computer expert. He .... people with their IT problems.

3 The flowers in our garden .... beautiful.

4 My dad .... a lot of problems with his car at the moment.

5 A cinema ticket .... €15! I .... that's a lot of money!

6 Lucas .... a new bike, but he .... to sell it.

COUNTABLE AND UNCOUNTABLE NOUNS

Countable nouns

Countable nouns refer to nouns which can be counted. They have singular and plural forms: **tree – trees**; **knife – knives**; **child – children**; **man – men**.

- Singular countable nouns can be used with a/an:
  a **book**, an **elephant**.
- Plural countable nouns can be used with numbers, some and any:
  Our family has some **animals** – a dog and three **cats**.

Uncountable nouns

Uncountable nouns refer to nouns which <u>cannot</u> be counted. They have no plural form: **advice** advices, **furniture** furnitures, **information** informations, **homework** homeworks, etc.

Both countable and uncountable

Some nouns can be countable and uncountable.

I love **lambs**, but I don't eat **lamb**.

lamb (countable) = animal

lamb (uncountable) = meat from a lamb.

- To make uncountable nouns countable, use countable nouns like piece, slice, spoonful, box, etc.
  a **piece of advice**
  three **slices of bread**
  two **spoonfuls of sugar**
  a **bowl of rice**

PRACTICE

❶ <u>Underline</u> the countable nouns and (circle) the uncountable nouns in this short text.

> As well as giving us energy, sugar in our diet makes our food taste better. Sometimes we add sugar to our breakfast cereals. Sugar is also used in biscuits, ice cream, chocolate and many other things we eat. It is also in fruit and vegetables and even in a glass of milk!

A FEW, A LITTLE BIT OF, MANY, MUCH, A LOT OF AND LOTS OF

These words and phrases are quantifiers. They tell us how much or how little of something there is.

- For small quantities, use a few with plural countable nouns:
  A few people in my class speak Russian.

- Use a little bit of or a little with uncountable nouns:
  I'd like **a bit of / a little** advice about going to university, please.

- For large quantities, use many with plural countable nouns:
  There aren't **many** trains at night.
  How **many** times have you been to London?

Use *much* with uncountable nouns in questions and negative sentences.
*How **much** money do you need?*
*We don't have **much** time.*

Use *a lot of* or *lots of* with plural countable nouns or uncountable nouns.
__A lot of__ / __Lots of__ students ride bikes to college.
You can save __a lot of__ / __lots of__ money if you cycle or walk.

PRACTICE

Underline and correct the mistakes in these sentences.

1 We haven't got many time.

2 I drink a little waters when I wake up.

3 There are lot of things we need to talk about.

4 Can you help? I need some informations about train times.

5 How much friends do you have online?

6 We have a lot of furnitures in our house.

PREPOSITIONS OF PLACE

We use prepositions of place to say where something is.

- We use *at* with points: ***at*** *the bus stop,* ***at*** *the station,* ***at*** *home,* ***at*** *school*

- We use *in* with spaces or to say something is inside another thing: ***in*** *the kitchen,* ***in*** *the sea,* ***in*** *the car,* ***in*** *France*

- We use *on* with surfaces: ***on*** *the wall,* ***on*** *the floor,* ***on*** *the ceiling,* ***on*** *the table*

PRACTICE

❶ Complete the sentences with *at*, *in* or *on*.

1 My computer is .... the desk .... my bedroom.

2 I live .... the end of the road.

3 Your shoes are .... a box .... the shelf.

4 There's someone .... the door.

PAST SIMPLE

be

Positive/Negative forms

I/He/She/It	was	here yesterday.
	wasn't	
You/We/They	were	
	weren't	

Question forms and short answers

Was	I/he/she/it	here yesterday?
Were	you/we/they	
Yes,	I/he/she/it	was.
	you/we/they	were.
No,	I/he/she/it	wasn't.
	you/we/they	weren't.

Other verbs

play (regular)
go (irregular)

Positive/Negative forms

I/You/We/They/He/She/It	played didn't play	tennis yesterday.
	went didn't go	to school yesterday.

Question forms and short answers

Did	I/you/we/they/he/she/it	play	tennis yesterday?
		go	to school yesterday?
Yes,	I/you/we/they/he/she/it		did.
No,	I/you/we/they/he/she/it		didn't.

Spelling of regular past simple verbs

For regular verbs, we add *-ed* to the base form of the verb, or *-d* if the verb already ends in *e*.

for verbs:	present simple	past simple
• ending in a consonant + *-y*, add *-ied*	study carry	stud**ied** carr**ied**
• ending in a vowel + a consonant (with stress on last syllable), double the final consonant and add *-ed*	plan prefer drop	plan**ned** prefe**rred** dro**pped**
• ending in a vowel + *-l*, double the *-l* and add *-ed*	travel control	trave**lled** contro**lled**
• ending in a vowel + consonant (with no stress on the last syllable)	happen visit	happen**ed** visit**ed**

We use the past simple to talk about
- past actions/events/states which have finished:
  *Jenny **was** tired after she **went** ice skating.*
- repeated past actions:
  *I **cycled** to school every day when I was a student.*
- a sequence of past actions:
  *We **left** home, **walked** to the station and **caught** the train.*

PAST CONTINUOUS

Positive/Negative forms

I/He/She/It	was	studying all evening.
	wasn't	
You/We/They	were	
	weren't	

Question forms and short answers

Was	I/he/she/it	studying all evening?
Were	you/we/they	
Yes,	I/he/she/it	was.
	you/we/they	were.
No,	I/he/she/it	wasn't.
	you/we/they	weren't.

We use the past continuous to talk about
- a particular moment in the past:
  *Emily **was walking** the dog at 5 pm.*
- temporary actions which give extra (less important) information:
  *It **was raining**, so I decided not to go out.*
- two or more actions happening at the same time:
  *While I **was doing** my homework, he **was playing** the guitar.*
- an action happening when another action happened:
  *He **was cleaning** his bike when he hurt his hand.*

when, while and as

We can use these words with the past continuous to introduce an action happening at the same time as another.
***When** Joe was walking home, it started to rain.*
*The phone rang **while** I was having breakfast.*
*They arrived **as** we were leaving.*

PRACTICE

1 Choose the correct option in *italics*.

1 While I *watched / was watching* TV, my sister was doing her homework.

2 My friends *often phoned / were often phoning* me when my parents were out.

3 While I was talking to my friend, I *realised / was realising* that something was wrong.

4 It was a lovely day. The sun *shone / was shining* and the birds *sang / were singing*.

5 Lionel Messi *won / was winning* a gold medal for Argentina in the Beijing Olympics.

2 Complete the sentences with the past simple or past continuous form of the verbs in brackets.

1 While I .... (tidy) my room, I .... (find) some old photographs.

2 As I .... (leave) the cinema, I .... (realise) that I'd left my phone behind.

3 While Simon .... (watch) television, his brother .... (cook) dinner.

4 When we .... (hear) the fire alarm, we all .... (stop) what we .... (do) and .... (walk) out of the building.

5 My computer .... (crash) while I .... (update) my web page.

USED TO

Positive/Negative forms

I/You/He/She/It/We/They	used to	enjoy watching football.
	didn't use to	

Question forms and short answers

Did	I/you/he/she/it/we/they	use to	play football?
Yes,	I/you/he/she/it/we/they	did.	
No,		didn't.	

We use *used to* to talk about the past. There is no present form of *used to*.

Note:
In negative and question forms, the spelling is *use* not *used*.

We use *used to* + an infinitive form to talk about:

• things that happened regularly in the past but don't now.
*I **used to** drink milk for breakfast, but now I always drink orange juice.*

• actions that didn't happen in the past, but happen now.
*I **didn't use to** drink orange juice, but now I love it.*

• past states or conditions that are different from the past.
*I **used to** have long, dark hair. (= I don't any more)*

PRACTICE

1 Rewrite the sentences so that they mean the same as the original sentence. Use the correct form of *used to*.

1 I like hot weather now, but I didn't in the past.

....

2 My brother played football until he broke his leg.

....

3 My hair was blond, now it's brown.

....

4 Did you go on holiday with friends when you were a child?

....

5 When I was younger, I didn't get up late.

....

SO (DO) I AND NOR/NEITHER (DO) I

We can use *so (do) I* and *nor/neither (do) I* to show that you think the same as another person.

• We use so in positive sentences when we have the same feelings or experiences.
A: *I love chocolate.* B: *So do I.*
A: *I ate a lot of chocolate yesterday.* B: *So did I.*

• We use the same auxiliary verbs or modal verbs in the reply.
A: *I **am** hungry.* B: *So am I.*
A: *I **will** have lunch at one o'clock.* B: *So will I.*

• We use *nor* or *neither* in negative sentences. We use the same auxiliary verbs or modal verbs in the reply.
A: *I **don't** like chocolate.* B: *Nor/Neither do I.*
A: *I **haven't** had coffee for ages.* B: *Nor/Neither have I.*

Note: We use *don't* to respond to positive statements. We use *do* to respond to negative statements.

A: *I love chocolate.* B: *I don't!*
A: *I don't like chocolate.* B: *I do!*

PRACTICE

1 Write replies to these sentences using *so* or *nor/neither*.

1 I spent a long time doing my homework yesterday.

....

2 I didn't understand the question.

....

3 I like ice cream.

....

4 I don't like hot weather.

....

5 I have two brothers.

....

VERBS FOLLOWED BY *TO* OR *-ING*

- Some verbs are always followed by an infinitive (*to* + verb):
  *When I was 15, I **decided to become** a professional musician.*

- Others are always followed by the *-ing* form of the verb:
  *Mike **kept falling** asleep during the lesson.*

- There are some verbs which can be followed by either an infinitive or the *-ing* form. Unfortunately, there are no rules to help you work out whether verbs are followed by the infinitive or the *-ing* form, or either, so you will need to learn them.

Verbs followed by the infinitive

> afford agree arrange attempt choose decide expect help hope intend learn manage offer plan promise refuse seem want would like

Verbs followed by *-ing*

> admit avoid can't stand* consider dislike* don't mind* enjoy* fancy* feel like finish give up imagine mind miss postpone practise put off prevent suggest

Note: The verbs marked * all express likes or dislikes.

Verbs followed by the infinitive or *-ing* with no difference in meaning

> begin continue intend start

Verbs followed by the infinitive or *-ing* with little difference in meaning

> hate like love prefer

There is a small difference in meaning between the two forms.

- *-ing* form: the action or experience is more important.
  *He likes **baking** cakes.*
- infinitive form: result of the action is more important, or to describe a habit/something we prefer.
  *He likes **to bake** cakes for special occasions.*
- The *-ing* form is more common after *hate* and *love*:
  *I hate **playing** ball sports. I love **doing** gymnastics.*

Verbs followed by the infinitive or *-ing* where there is a clear difference in meaning

	infinitive	-ing
forget	I **forgot to say** thank you. (= I didn't say thank you.)	I **forgot saying** that. (= I have no memory of this.)
go on	He **went on to talk** about his childhood. (= This was the next thing he talked about.)	He **went on talking**. (= He continued talking.)
remember	I **remembered to lock** the door. (= I did something I had to do.)	I **remember locking** the door. (= I have a memory of this.)
stop	Let's **stop to buy** flowers. (= in order to do something)	Let's **stop buying** flowers. (= not continue)
try	I **tried to learn** Japanese, but it was too difficult, so I stopped. (= try something, and not succeed)	I **tried eating** spinach, but I didn't like it. (= try something and find out what it's like)

- In negative sentences, we put *not* after the first verb.
  *He's **decided <u>not</u> to go** to university next year.*
  *She **considered <u>not</u> going** away for the weekend. (= but now she is going.)*
- In sentences which include an object, we put the object after the first verb.
  *I **helped <u>my friend</u> to do** his homework.*
  *We should **stop <u>people</u> using** their phones or eating while they're driving.*

PRACTICE

1 Complete the conversation with the correct form of the verbs in brackets.

A: It's really hot here, isn't it? Do you fancy
(1) .... (go) for a swim?

B: Yes, I'd love (2) .... (have) a swim.

A: Can I suggest (3) .... (go) this afternoon?

B: I'd planned (4) .... (go) to the cinema this afternoon, but I don't mind (5) .... (do) that tomorrow instead.

A: I can't imagine (6) .... (live) in a hot country all the time.

B: I'm sure you'd manage (7) .... (have) a nice time.

A: Maybe I'd get used to it. I certainly enjoy
(8) .... (spend) my summer holidays here.

Tick (✓) the pairs of sentences which have the same meanings.

1 **A** The teacher continued to talk even though the bell had rung for the end of class.
   B The teacher continued talking even though the bell had rung for the end of class. ☐

2 **A** I began to learn German two years ago.
   B I began learning German two years ago. ☐

3 **A** Ben stopped to phone his parents.
   B Ben stopped phoning his parents. ☐

4 **A** I prefer to watch football than to play it.
   B I prefer watching football to playing it. ☐

5 **A** I like to watch the sunrise.
   B I like watching the sunrise. ☐

6 **A** They went on to tell us about their holiday.
   B They went on telling us about their holiday. ☐

PHRASAL VERBS

A phrasal verb is a verb with two or three parts. The meaning of the verb is sometimes different from the meaning of its separate parts. Phrasal verbs can combine verbs with prepositions or adverbs. For example: *to take off*, *to put on*, *to catch up with*, *to look forward to*.

There are two main types of phrasal verbs

• verbs which need an object:
  *She **took off** her hat.*
  *He **put on** his shoes.*
  *We're **looking forward to** our holiday.*

• verbs which do not need an object:
  *They **set off** early.*
  *We **got up** late.*

• Sometimes, it is possible to put the object in between the verb and the preposition/adverb. Sometimes, it is not.
  ✓ *He **took** his hat **off**.*
  ✓ *He **took** it **off**.*
  ✗ *He **took off** it.*

  ✓ *We're **looking forward** to the weekend.*
  ✗ *We're **looking** the weekend **forward to**.*

PRACTICE

1 Underline the phrasal verbs in questions 1–6. Then match them with answers a–f.

1 What should you do if your TV breaks down?
2 Which of your parents do you take after?
3 Do you like to dress up when you go to a party?
4 Who do you really look up to?
5 Do you ever have to look after anyone?
6 What do you think about people who show off?

a No, I prefer to wear my normal clothes.
b I don't like them.
c Ask someone to repair it.
d I'm like my mother.
e My father. He's my hero.
f I sometimes babysit my little brother.

2 Rewrite the underlined words with a phrasal verb from the box. Make any other necessary changes.

| get on with give up look forward to sign up for take up |

1 I have a good relationship with everyone in my family.

....

2 I've put my name down for an English course.

....

3 I can't wait to see my friend again.

....

4 My father has stopped eating sugar.

....

5 My brother has just started playing basketball.

....

4 COMPARATIVE AND SUPERLATIVE ADJECTIVES

We use comparative adjectives (e.g. *bigger than*) to compare two people or things and to say if one has more of a quality (e.g. size, height, etc.) than the other.

- Comparative adjectives are usually followed by *than*.

- We use superlative adjectives (e.g. *the fastest, the most important*) to say that in a particular group, something has the most of a quality.

Regular adjectives

	comparative	superlative
• For most adjectives, add -er or -est.	*small* ➔ *smaller* *Italy is* **smaller** *than Spain.*	➔ *the* **smallest** Vatican City is **the smallest** country in the world.
• For short adjectives ending in -e, add -r or -st.	*large* ➔ *larger* *Canada is* **larger** *than China.*	➔ *the* larg**est** Russia is **the largest** country in the world.
• For short adjectives with a vowel + a consonant, double the consonant and add -er or -est.	*hot* ➔ *hotter* *Algeria is hotter than Mexico.*	➔ *the* hot**test** Libya is the hottest country in the world.
• For two-syllable adjectives ending in -y, change the y to i and add -er or -est.	*heavy* ➔ *heavier* *Elephants are* **heavier** *than crocodiles.*	➔ *the* heav**iest** Blue whales are **the heaviest** animals in the world.
• For some two-syllable adjectives, we can either add -er, -est or use *more, the most*. These are adjectives ending in -ow, -le, -er and *polite, quiet, common* and *stupid*.	*Mia is* **more polite** *than me. (= Mia is* **politer** *than me.)*	*Mia is* **the most polite** *girl in the class.* *(= Mia is* **the politest** *girl in the class.)*
• For longer adjectives, or two-syllable adjectives ending in -ful, put *more/less the most/least* in front of the adjective.	*difficult* ➔ *more/ less difficult* *Some people think it's* **more difficult** *to make friends when you are older.*	➔ *the most/ least difficult* *Is it true that Japanese is* **the most difficult** *language for English speakers to learn?*

Irregular adjectives

There are three irregular adjectives: *good, bad, far*.

bad ➔ *worse* ➔ *the worst*

good ➔ *better* ➔ *the best*

far ➔ *farther/further** ➔ *the farthest/furthest**

*There is no difference in meaning, but *further/the furthest* is more common.

PRACTICE

1 Complete the comparative and superlative adjectives.

1	thin	thinner than	
2	nice	than	the nicest
3		lazier than	the laziest
4	comfortable	than	the most comfortable
5	good	better than	
6	bad	than	the worst
7		farther/further than	the farthest/ furthest

2 Complete the sentences with the comparative or superlative form of the adjectives in brackets.

1 It rained every day in December 2015 in Portland, USA. It was .... December for 75 years. (wet)

2 A blue whale is .... than an elephant. (heavy)

3 I felt ill all weekend, but I'm much .... now. (good)

4 This writer's new book is .... than her others. (bad)

5 We've moved house. Now, we live .... from my school than we used to. (far)

6 Some people think that the Sydney Opera House is .... modern building in the world. (beautiful)

a bit, a little, slightly, much, far, a lot

We can use these words with comparative adjectives.

We use *a bit*, *a little*, *slightly*, *not much* or *not a lot* to describe a small difference:
My brother is **a little** younger than me.
I'm **a bit** older than him.

We use *much*, *a lot*, or *far* to describe a large difference:
I'm **much** fitter than my brother, but he's **a lot** faster than me.
He's **much** more polite than his cousin.

(not) as ... as

We use *as* + adjective/adverb + *as* to say that two things are the same.
Hannah is **as tall as** Jess.
Today is **as warm as** yesterday.

We use *not as* + adjective/adverb + *as* to say that one thing is less than another.
My brother is**n't as fit as** me. = I am fitter than my brother.
I'm **not as fast as** my brother. = My brother is faster than me.

PRACTICE

Rewrite the sentences so that they mean the same thing as the original sentence. Use the words in brackets.

1 Roman is taller than Josh.
Josh .... (not as)

2 My old phone was cheap. My new phone is very expensive.
My new phone .... (much)

3 Burgers aren't as healthy as fruit.
Fruit is .... (a lot)

4 Spain is a big country in Europe. It's 505,370 km². France is a little bigger, at 643,801 km².
Spain is .... (a bit)

5 The old shopping centre was good, but the new one is much nicer.
The new shopping centre is .... (far)

GRADABLE AND NON-GRADABLE ADJECTIVES

- Most adjectives are gradable. This means we can make them stronger or weaker by using words like *very*.
  We cannot use words like *completely* or *absolutely* with these adjectives.
  ✗ I'm completely cold.
  ✓ I'm **very cold**.
  ✓ Our English is exam was **fairly difficult**.
  ✓ Harry's new car is **quite big**, isn't it?
  ✓ Ben was **pretty tired** after a long day's work.

- Non-gradable or extreme adjectives are adjectives which we **cannot** make stronger or weaker by using words like *very*. We can use these words with non-gradable adjectives: *completely*, *absolutely*, *totally*, *really*.
  ✗ I'm very freezing.
  ✓ I'm **absolutely freezing**.
  ✓ Our English is exam was **absolutely impossible**.
  ✓ Harry's new car **really enormous**, isn't it?
  ✓ Ben was **totally exhausted** after a long day's work.

PRACTICE

❶ Match gradable adjectives 1–7 with non-gradable adjectives a–g.

1	bad	a	amazed
2	big	b	delighted
3	cold	c	excellent
4	good	d	exhausted
5	pleased	e	freezing
6	surprised	f	terrible
7	tired	g	huge

❷ Choose the correct options in *italics*.

1 My friend was absolutely *pleased / delighted* when she heard she'd passed her exam. Her parents were quite *surprised / amazed*, too. They thought she might fail.

2 The school heating system broke down, so we felt very *cold / freezing* all day.

3 I was totally *tired / exhausted* after running 10 kilometres.

4 I had a very *bad / terrible* night's sleep. That's why I'm pretty *tired / exhausted* now.

5 I really enjoyed the film last night. I thought it was absolutely *good / excellent*.

6 The audience for the concert was absolutely *big / huge*. I think there were thousands of people there.

MODAL VERBS: *CAN, COULD, MIGHT* AND *MAY* (ABILITY AND POSSIBILITY)

Talking about ability and inability

- We use *can/can't* and *could/couldn't* to talk about ability or inability. They are followed by the infinitive without *to*.
  Anna **can speak** French, but she **can't speak** Chinese.
  Max **could walk** when he was a year old, but he **couldn't talk** until he was two.

Can Anna speak French?	Yes, she **can**.
Can she speak Chinese?	No, she **can't**.
Could Max walk when he was one?	Yes, he **could**.
Could he talk when he was one?	No, he **couldn't**.

Talking about possibility

- We use *might, may* and *could* to talk about possibilities in the present or the future.
  We use *can* to talk about possibilities in the present but not the future. These modal verbs are followed by the infinitive without *to*.
  It **might be** very hot tomorrow.
  We **may go** swimming this afternoon.
  There **could be** a storm later this evening.
  It **can snow** here in April, but it doesn't often happen.

- To talk about negative possibilities we can use *may not* or *might not*, but not *can not* or *could not*.
  Laura is not feeling well, so she **may not go** to school today.
  You have to accept that you **might not win** the lottery this week.

- The form of these verbs never changes. For example, we cannot say ~~He cans~~ / ~~They mighted~~.

- We can use *May I … ?* or *Could I … ?* to ask for permission.
  May I sit here?
- We rarely use the short form *mightn't*. We don't use ~~mayn't~~.

PRACTICE

1 Complete the sentences with *can, can't, could, couldn't, may* or *might*. Sometimes more than one answer is possible.

1. I've looked for my phone, but I .... find it.
2. My brother .... swim when he was four.
3. I'm not sure what to do tomorrow. I .... go to Jo's party.
4. She isn't looking well. I think she .... have flu.
5. I .... play the piano but I don't play very often.
6. Kieran .... ride a bike until he was nearly 12.

2 Match the sentence beginnings (1–5) with the endings (a–e). Then choose the best modal verb in *italics*.

1. I don't know where Luis is. He *may / can*
2. I have some free time, so I *can / might*
3. There's someone at the door. It *may / can*
4. We need to tidy up. Our friends *can / could*
5. Working too hard *can / could*

a. be one of my friends.
b. make you stressed.
c. see her.
d. still be at school.
e. arrive at any minute.

MODAL VERBS: *SHOULD, SHOULDN'T, MUST, MUSTN'T, HAVE TO, DON'T HAVE TO* (OBLIGATION AND PROHIBITION)

should/shouldn't

- We use *should/shouldn't* to give or ask for advice.
  Should/shouldn't are followed by the infinitive without *to*.
  You **should join** a gym if you want to keep fit.
  You **shouldn't eat** too much chocolate.
  What **should I do**?

- An alternative to *should* is *ought to* + infinitive.
  This is more formal.

must, have to

- We use *must* and *have to* to express obligation.
  You **must take** your passport with you when you travel abroad.
  We **have to show** our passports when we cross the border.

- We often use *must* to talk about rules or laws which we agree with or believe in.
  We **must wear** a seat belt in the car, even for short journeys.

- We often use *have to* to talk about rules or laws which were made by someone else or which we may not agree with.
  My teacher says that I **have to finish** the homework tonight or I'll be in trouble.

don't have to

- Use *don't have to* or *needn't* (but not *mustn't*) when it's not necessary to do something.
  We **didn't have to show** our passports when we went to Scotland.
  We **don't need to** wear a uniform at our school.

can/can't

- We can also use *can/can't* to express permission or lack of permission.
  You **can leave** any time you like.
  You **can't bring** animals in here.
  Can I use your phone, please?

mustn't

Use *mustn't* to express prohibition, to say that something is not allowed.
You **mustn't use** *your phone in the cinema.*

We can also use *can't* instead of *mustn't.*
You **can't talk** *during the exam.*

There is no past tense form of *mustn't*. Use *not allowed to.*
We **weren't allowed to go** *into the concert without a ticket.*

PRACTICE

Complete the sentences with *can/can't, must* or *mustn't*.
Sometimes there may be more than one possible answer.

1 We .... bring a dog in here.

2 We .... pay in cash. We .... pay by credit card.

3 We .... use wifi here.

4 We .... sit at this table. It's reserved.

5 We .... use our phones here.

2 Choose the correct verbs in *italics*.

When my grandfather was young, children
(1) *must not / didn't have to* stay at school until
the age of 18 or even 16. They (2) *could / couldn't*
leave when they were 14. My grandfather had no
choice. He (3) *had to / didn't have to* go out and
earn money for his family. At the end of every week
he (4) *could / had to* give his wages to his mother.
She gave him a small amount of money which he
(5) *had to / could* spend as he liked. When he was 18,
he wanted to join the army, but he failed the medical
examination so he (6) *had to / couldn't* do military
service. This meant he couldn't fight for his country.
Instead of being a soldier, he drove an ambulance.

ADJECTIVES WITH *-ED* AND *-ING* ENDINGS

Many English adjectives which end in *-ing* or *-ed* are formed from verbs.

verb	adjectives
relax	*relaxed/relaxing*
surprise	*surprised/surprising*

* Adjectives which end in *-ed* tell us how a person feels.
  I'm going to bed because I'm **tired**.

* Adjectives which end in *-ing* describe the effect of something.
  I'm going to bed. I've had a **tiring** *day at work.*

PRACTICE

1 Choose the correct adjectives in *italics*.

1 A: Did you see that *interested / interesting* programme about the moon on TV last night?
  B: No, I'm not really *interested / interesting* in space.

2 A: You look very *relaxed / relaxing*. Did you have a good holiday?
  B: No, it wasn't *relaxed / relaxing* at all! I was ill.

3 A: What do you find most *annoyed / annoying* about your older brother?
  B: Everything he does makes me *annoyed / annoying*.

4 A: What's happened? You look really *excited / exciting*.
  B: Yes, I've just heard that I've won first prize in a competition. It's so *excited / exciting*!

6

PRESENT PERFECT

We use the present perfect to connect the present with the past.

Positive/Negative forms		
I/You/We/They	**have/'ve** **have not/haven't**	**finished** work.
He/She/It	**has/'s** **has not/hasn't**	

Question forms and short answers		
Have	I/you/we/they	**finished** work?
Has	he/she/it	
Yes,	I/you/we/they	**have.**
	he/she/it	**has.**
No,	I/you/we/they	**haven't.**
	he/she/it	**hasn't.**

- The present perfect is formed with the correct form of *have* in the present and the past participle of the main verb. The past participle of regular verbs and some irregular verbs is the same as the past simple. The past participle is underlined in the examples below.

past simple	present perfect
I **finished** work.	I **have finished** work.
He **bought** a sandwich.	He **has bought** a sandwich.

- Some irregular verbs have past participles which are not the same as the past simple form.

past simple	present perfect
She **ate** her lunch.	She **has eaten** her lunch.
She **wrote** a letter.	She **has written** a letter.

We use the present perfect to talk about:
- something which started in the past and is connected with the present.
  *Ed **has broken** his leg, so he can't play football this weekend.*
- something which started in the past and is still true:
  *Ben and Karen **have lived** in London for seven years.*
- past experiences which refer to an unstated time in the past, often with *ever* and *never*:
  *Anna **has been** to Brazil, but she **has never been** to Canada.*
- recent past actions
  ***Have** you **done** your homework?*

just, already and yet

- *just* = very recently, a short time ago:
  *I've **just** emailed Marcus and told him the good news.*

- *already* = before now, often sooner than expected:
  *He's **already** done his homework, so he can go out with his friends.*

- *Just* and *already* are placed between *have/has* and the past participle.

- *yet* = *until now* is used in negative sentences and questions to talk about things we plan to do in the future, but which are not done. *Yet* is placed at the end of a sentence:
  *I haven't finished my project **yet**.*
  *Have you finished your project **yet**?*

PRACTICE

1 Complete the sentences with *already, just* or *yet*.

1 I've .... finished my homework. I finished it a minute ago.

2 **A:** Let's tell our friends the news.
   B: I've .... told them. I told them last week.

3 I'm not hungry because I've .... had lunch. I ate earlier.

4 Have you met Benoit .... ?

5 I haven't got dressed .... because I've just woken up.

since and for

We can use *since* and *for* with the present perfect to talk about a time that started in the past and continues to the present.

- *since* is followed by the beginning of a period of time:
  *We've lived here **since** December 2017.*
  for is followed by a period of time:
  *She's lived there **for** six and a half years.*

PRACTICE

2 Complete the sentences with *for* or *since*.

1 My father has worked for the same company .... 20 years.

2 Megan has played football .... she was six years old.

3 I haven't eaten anything .... 7 o'clock this morning.

4 Sofia can't still be tired. She's slept .... 11 hours!

5 I've made lots of new friends .... I've been at this school.

The present perfect or the past simple?

We use the present perfect to talk about a past experience without saying when it happened.
I've been to the top of the Eiffel Tower.

To say when something happened, use the past simple.
I went to the top of the Eiffel Tower last summer.

We use the present perfect to talk about the continuing effect of a past event or action on the present.
There has been an accident on the motorway. Now there are long queues of traffic into the city centre.

We use the present perfect to talk about the time period up to the present.
I've been to town this morning. (= It is still the morning.)
My brother has written a short story. (= He may write more stories.)

If the time period is now over, we use the past simple.
I went into town this morning. (= It is now afternoon or evening.)
Prince wrote over 150 songs. (= He died in 2016, so can't write any more.)

PRACTICE

1 Underline and correct the mistakes in the conversation. Some lines are correct.

A: Have you heard? My oldest sister's getting married.
B: Who to?
A: A guy called Elliot.
B: Really! How long did she know him?
A: Only six months. Apparently they've met at work.
B: Have you met Elliot already?
A: No, not yet, but my sister's told me a lot about him.
B: When have you seen her?
A: I've seen her last week. She drove me to school one day.

4 Complete the conversations with the past simple or present perfect form of the verbs in brackets. Make any other changes necessary.

1 A: You look terrible. Are you OK?
   B: I'm alright. I .... (go) to bed late last night and I .... (just wake up).

2 A: Where's Chloe?
   B: I don't know. Her train .... (arrive) half an hour ago, but I .... (not see her yet).

3 A: Shall we go and see the new Star Wars film tonight?
   B: No, I .... it. (already see)
   A: Really?
   B: Yes, I .... it last week. (see)

4 A: What's the most expensive thing that you .... (ever buy)?
   B: My racing bike. It .... 500 euros. (cost)
   A: I .... as much money as that on anything! (never spend)

5 A: .... gymnastics? (you ever do)
   B: Yes, but I .... karate (never do).

6 A: Where .... on holiday last year? (go)
   B: We .... to Florida. (go)
   A: Really? I've got relatives there, but I .... them. (never visited)

7

ADVERBS OF DEGREE

extremely, fairly, quite, rather, really and *very*

- We can use *extremely, really* and *very* to make adjectives and adverbs stronger.
  We've had an **extremely busy** day.
  I'm going to stay inside today. It's going to be **really hot**.
  It was so warm, they were walking **very slowly**.

- We can use *fairly* and *rather* to make adjectives and adverbs weaker (they mean 'not very').
  I think you'll pass the exam **fairly easily**.
  I'm **rather disappointed** that I failed the exam, but I'm not surprised.

- *Quite* has two opposite meanings: completely (with gradable adjectives) and not very (with non-gradable adjectives).
  I've been working hard, so I'm **quite tired**. (*quite* = a bit tired)
  I'm **quite exhausted** after running a marathon yesterday. (*quite* = completely)

PRACTICE

1 **Put the words in order to make correct sentences.**

1 because / coat / cold / forgotten / had / I / I / my / really / was

  ....

2 exam / fairly / her / is / Mia / pass / she / sure / will

  ....

3 is / moving / slowly / The / traffic / very

  ....

4 Be / busy / careful / cross / extremely / roads / when / you

  ....

5 a / difficult / question / rather / That / was

  ....

too and *enough*

We use *too* to say something is more than is needed, wanted o allowed.

- *too* + adjective/adverb
  Anna's **too young** to drive.
  Hurry up! You're walking **too slowly**.

- *too* + adjective/adverb + *for someone* + infinitive
  This exercise is **too difficult for me to do**.
  They were talking **too quickly for me to understand**.

- *too* + *much* + uncountable noun
  You've made **too much food**.

- *too* + *many* + plural countable noun
  We've got **too many books**. I'm going to give some away.

- *too* + *much/many* + noun + *for someone* + infinitive
  There are **too many books for me to read**.

We use *enough* to say that there is (or isn't) as much as is needed.

- adjective/adverb + *(not) enough* (+ infinitive)
  Anna's **old enough to drive**.
  We're not running **fast enough to win** the race.

- adjective / adverb + *enough* + *for someone* + infinitive
  That car isn't **big enough for us all to get** in.

- *enough* + noun
  There are **enough chairs** for everyone to sit down.

PRACTICE

2 **Complete the sentences with *enough* or *too* and a word from the box.**

| big | good | hours | ill | money | rich | sugar |

1 Jane's staying at home today. She's .... to go to school.

2 I couldn't believe I'd won the lottery. It was .... to be true.

3 Ben's grown so quickly – his shoes aren't .... for him now.

4 I'm really busy. There aren't .... in the day

5 I wish I had .... for that car. But I know I'll never be .... to buy one.

6 Eating .... can be very bad for you.

FUTURE FORMS

will

Positive/Negative forms

I/You/He/She/It/We/They	will/'ll	be late home.
	will not/won't	

Question forms and short answers

Will	I/you/he/she/it/we/they	be late home?
Yes,	I/you/he/she/it/we/they	**will.**
No,	I/you/he/she/it/we/they	**won't.**

We use *will* to talk about:

things we expect to happen or predict will happen:
*More people **will** buy electric cars in the future.*

things which are not certain:
*It probably **won't** be cold tomorrow.*

future facts:
*My app says that the sun **will** rise at 5 o'clock tomorrow.*

quick decisions about what to do next:
*There's someone at the door. **I'll** get it.*

an offer or a promise:
*Don't worry. I **won't** be late.*

be going to

Positive/Negative forms

I	am/'m	
	am not/'m not	
You/We/They	are/'re	**going to** study tonight.
	are not/aren't	
He/She	is/'s	
	is not/isn't	

Question forms and short answers

Am	I	
Are	you/we/they	**going to** study hard?
Is	he/she	
Yes,	I	**am.**
	you/we/they	**are.**
	he/she	**is.**
No,	I	**am/'m not**
	you/we/they	**aren't.**
	he/she	**isn't.**

We use *going to* to talk about:

- things we predict based on what we can see, or something that we think is certain to happen:
I'm going to sneeze.

- future plans and things we intend to do:
I'm going to watch the match on TV.

Present continuous forms for the future

We use the present continuous to talk about:
- arrangements or plans which have already been made.
I'm starting a new course tomorrow.

Present simple forms for the future

We use the present simple to talk about:
- events in the future that are certain because they are facts.
*The film **starts** at 3.30 pm. Don't be late!*
- fixed or planned events.
*The lesson **ends** at 7.30 this evening.*

PRACTICE

1 **Choose the most appropriate option in *italics*.**

1 *We see / We're going to see* the new *Spiderman* film tomorrow. I bought the tickets online.

2 I don't think *I'll be / I am* late home. The lesson usually finishes at 3 o'clock.

3 I've got an important exam tomorrow, so *I go / I'm going to go* to bed early this evening.

4 Our train *leaves / is leaving* at 10.45 am.

5 **A:** We've run out of bread.
B: OK, *I'll go / I'm going to go* and get some more.

PREPOSITIONS OF MOVEMENT

by

- We use *by* to talk about ways of travelling.
  *We went to Holland **by** ship.*
  *We go **by** car to the supermarket.*
  *I prefer to travel **by** train than **by** air.*
  *More goods travel by road than **by** rail.*

Note: We say *on foot* (not ~~by foot~~)
*We usually go to school **on foot**.*

in/into, out of

- We use these prepositions to say how we move into or out of something like a car, taxi, etc.
  *The parents and their two children got **into** the taxi.*
  *Ben got **out of** the car.*

on/onto/off

- We use these prepositions to say how start or stop using something like a bike, bus, plane or train.
  *I got **off** my bike and locked it.*
  *I got **on(to)** the bus near my home and got **off** at the park.*

PRACTICE

1 **Complete the sentences.**

1. The floods destroyed the roads so we travelled everywhere .... foot.

2. In some places it is cheaper to travel .... air than .... rail.

3. We got .... the plane just before it took off.

4. The taxi broke down, so we all got .... it and walked into town.

5. The quickest way to get to France from England is to go .... train.

6. We got .... the car when it started raining, so we didn't get wet.

8

CONDITIONAL SENTENCES

We use conditional sentences to talk about possible situations and their results. Conditional sentences usually have a conditional (*if*) clause and a main clause (*usually a result*).

possible situation or action (conditional clause)	main clause/result
If I see Matt,	*I'll tell him to call you*

There are three types of conditional sentences which can refer to the present or the future.

We use the **zero conditional** about things which are true.

conditional clause: *if* + present verb	main clause/result clause: present simple verb
If the sun is too hot,	*it burns you.*

We use the **first conditional** to talk about likely situations.

conditional clause: *if* + present simple	main clause/result: *will** + infinitive
If we go by bus,	*we'll get there on time.*

*We can also use modal verbs with future meaning (*will, shall, can, etc.*) in first conditional sentences:
If we collect enough money, we can buy our teacher a present.

We use the **second conditional** to talk about unlikely situations. We can use it to talk about the present or future.

conditional clause: *if* + past simple	main clause/result: *would** + infinitive
If I had a lot of money,	*I'd buy a new smartphone.*

*We can also use other modal verbs (*should, might, could*).
If I knew how to snowboard, I could enter the competition.

We can use *were* instead of *was* in the conditional clause.
*If I **were/was** you, I'd look for a new hobby.*

Note: Conditional (*if*) clauses can come before or after the main clause. When the conditional clause comes before the main clause, it is followed by a comma.

PRACTICE

1 Match the sentence beginnings (1–8) with the correct endings (a–h) to make conditional sentences.

1 If I have time,
2 If I had more time
3 If you mix blue and yellow
4 You wouldn't be hungry
5 She would be really angry
6 If he phones her,
7 If my computer breaks again,
8 If I had enough money

a you get green.
b she refuses to speak.
c if she knew the truth.
d I'll phone you.
e I'll throw it in the bin.
f I'd buy a new computer.
g I'd cycle to college.
h if you ate more.

2 Make second conditional sentences.

1 I'd like to do the high jump but I'm not very tall.
   If .....I were/was taller, I'd do the high jump.....

2 She can't study in Canada because she doesn't speak English.
   If ....

3 I haven't got enough free time to learn to play a musical instrument.
   If ....

4 I'd like to buy a laptop, but I haven't got enough money.
   If ....

CONJUNCTIONS: *WHEN, IF, UNLESS* + PRESENT, FUTURE

when

- Use *when* to talk about things that happen at a particular time in the future:
  ***When** I get home this evening, I'll have a shower.*

if

- Use *if* for things that may or may not happen, or to say what happens if something else happens:
  ***If** I finish work early, I'll go swimming.*

unless

- *unless* means the same as 'if not'.
  ***Unless** I get home early, I won't go swimming.*
  (= If I do not get home early, I won't go swimming.)

PRACTICE

3 Complete these sentences with *if*, *when* or *unless*.

1 .... you take me to the station, I'll have to walk there.

2 We'll fail the exam .... we revise.

3 .... we hurry, we'll get there in time.

4 Let's watch the late film .... you are not too tired to watch anything.

5 In the UK, you can't drive .... you are over 16.

6 .... I'm sad, I usually talk to my friends.

7 .... you're not feeling better tomorrow, you should go to the doctor.

8 I'll watch some TV .... I get home tonight.

9

DEFINING AND NON-DEFINING RELATIVE CLAUSES WITH *WHICH, THAT, WHO, WHOSE, WHEN, WHERE*

Relative clauses are used to link different pieces of information in one sentence.

*The film Titanic, **which made Leonardo di Caprio famous**, was made in 1997.*

We use relative clauses to avoid short, simple sentences like these ones.

The film Titanic was made in 1997. It made Leonardo diCaprio famous.

Defining relative clauses

*   These clauses give us essential information which tells us exactly which person or thing we are referring to.
    *The actor **who plays Luke Skywalker** is Mark Hamill.*

*   Without the information in the relative clause, we would not know which actor we are talking about.
    ✗ *The actor is Mark Hamill.*

Non-defining relative clauses

*   These clauses give us extra non-essential information. The sentence still makes sense without this relative clause.
    *The first Star Wars film, **which was directed by George Lucas**, came out in 1977.*
    ✓ *The first Star Wars film came out in 1977.*

Relative pronouns

Use these relative pronouns to introduce relative clauses:

*   *who* refers to people
*   *which* refers to things
*   *that* can refer to people or things
*   *whose* refers to possession or relationships:
    *The student **whose** brother was on TV is in my class.*
*   *where* refers to places:
    *The village **where** I live is on the outskirts of city.*
*   *when* refers to times:
    *The time **when** I was my happiest was my years at school.*
*   *why* refers to reasons or explanations:
    *The reason **why** I got up so early is that I couldn't sleep.*

defining clauses	non-defining clauses
• Do not have commas.	• Have commas. They are like pauses in spoken English.
• Use these relative pronouns *who, which, whose, where, when, why, that.*	• Use these relative pronouns: *who, which, whose, where, when, why.*
• *that* can be used instead of *who* or *which.*	• Don't use *that.*
• *who, which* or *that* can be left out if they are the object of the clause.	• Relative pronouns cannot be left out.

PRACTICE

❶ Complete the sentences with a relative pronoun. Sometimes there may be more than one possible answer.

☐ **1** Ben's the person .... bike was stolen last week.

☐ **2** That's the dog .... tried to bite me.

☐ **3** She doesn't like people .... are unfriendly.

☐ **4** That's the house .... they want to live in.

☐ **5** Where are the keys .... were on the kitchen table?

☐ **6** We're moving to a quiet place .... we can't hear the traffic.

☐ **7** The company .... David works for makes computers.

☐ **8** I read a lot of books .... I was ill.

❷ Tick (✓) the sentences in exercise 1 where it is possible to leave out the relative pronoun.

Rewrite these sentences as one sentence using relative clauses.

1 The music was by Mozart. Gisela was playing the music last night.
The music which ....

2 The violin was not hers. Gisela was playing the violin in the concert.
The violin that ....

3 James is Gisela's music teacher. Gisela borrowed James' violin.
James, ...

4 We've just listened to Gisela's latest recording. Gisela's recording is number 1 in the classical charts.
We've just listened ....

5 Gisela's mother is very proud of her. Gisela's mother was in the audience tonight.
Gisela's' mother, ...
....

6 Tomorrow, Gisela is going back to Vienna. Gisela goes to music school in Vienna.
Tomorrow, Gisela is ....
....

PAST PERFECT

Positive/Negative forms

I/You/He/She/It/We/They	had/'d	finished school by 5 o'clock.
	had not/hadn't	

Question forms and short answers

Had	I/you/he/she/it/we/they	**finished** school by 5 o'clock?
Yes,	I/you/he/she/it/we/they	**had.**
No,	I/you/he/she/it/we/they	**hadn't.**

We use the past perfect to:

- make clear the order of past events. The past perfect describes something that happened before an action/event in the past.
  *My parents **had left** when I arrived home. (= My parents were not there when I arrived home.)*

- say what was completed before a specific past time.
  *By 9 o'clock, I**'d phoned** three people and **had sent** five emails.*

- explain past events or situations or give background information.
  *He**'d drunk** nothing all day, so he was really thirsty.*
  *I**'d got** up at 5 o'clock, so by midday I was very tired.*

- talk about situations that have changed.
  *I**'d planned** to finish writing my essay this morning, but I've got a terrible headache.*

PRACTICE

❶ **Complete the sentences with the past simple or past perfect form of the verbs in brackets.**

1 It .... (rain) all night and, although it .... (stop), the ground .... (be) still very wet.

2 We .... (plan) to have a picnic, but then it started raining, so we .... (have to) think of something else to do.

3 It .... (be) sunny every day for two weeks, but then it .... (start) to snow.

4 We .... (can not) go for a walk in the forest because the snow and ice .... (make) the paths too dangerous.

5 Yesterday, we .... (go) to the cinema because there was a new film that none of us .... (see).

COMMANDS AND INSTRUCTIONS

We use the imperative form for giving commands.
***Stand** up!*

The imperative form of verbs is the same as the infinitive without *to*. Imperative forms have no subject.

✓ ***Wake** up!*
✗ ~~You wake up!~~

✓ ***Do not use** your mobile phone.*
✗ ~~You do not use your mobile phone.~~

We can also use the imperative form for giving:

- instructions, for example in recipes:
  ***Boil** for 10 minutes.*
- advice:
  ***Put** on a warm coat.*
- encouragement:
  ***Keep** trying.*
- warnings:
  ***Be** careful.*

PRACTICE

❶ Complete the meaning of the signs using the imperative form of verbs in the box.

be	drink	eat	turn	use

1 ....or
   .... here.

2 .... left.

3 .... cameras here.

4 .... quiet.

HAVE SOMETHING DONE

- Use *have something done* to talk about things we ask other people to do for us, things that we do not want to, or cannot do ourselves.
  *I'm **having my teeth checked** tomorrow.*

- We can also use *get something done*. It has the same meaning but is more informal:
  *I'm **getting my hair cut** tomorrow.*

- Notice the order of words: *have* + object + past participle. A different word order changes the meaning.
  *She **has her hair cut**. (= Someone does it for her.)*
  She has cut her hair. = (She did it herself recently.)

- Use *have something done* in any tense.
  *I **(don't) have my hair cut** every week.*
  *We're **(not) having our flat decorated**.*
  *We **had (didn't have) our computer repaired** yesterday.*
  *We'll **have our car washed** tomorrow.*

PRACTICE

❶ Put the words in order to make correct sentences.

1 you / your / had / cut / have / hair?
   Have ....

2 bedroom / have / painted / I / might / my / blue
   I ....

3 fixed / had / Michael / yet / bike / his / has / ?
   Has ....

4 get / teeth / I / every / my / months / polished / six
   I ....

5 checked / your / have / computer / viruses / should / you / for
   You ....

❷ Make sentences with *have* something *done* using the words given and the tense in brackets.

1 he – hair cut – beard shave off (present perfect simple)
   ....

2 she – car – wash – yesterday (past simple)
   ....

3 he – shoes – clean (present perfect simple)
   ....

4 they – house – paint (present continuous)
   ....

5 he – tooth – take out – this morning (past simple)
   ....

6 she – eyes – test – tomorrow (*will*)
   ....

THE PASSIVE: PRESENT SIMPLE AND PAST SIMPLE

We form the passive by using the correct form of *be* followed by the past participle.

active	passive
We **feed** our cat twice a day.	Our cat **is fed** twice a day.
They **built** our school in 2012.	Our school **was built** in 2012.

We use passive verbs rather than active verbs when:
we are more interested in who or what is affected by the action of the verb than who or what does the action.
*My car **was made** in France.* (The focus is on *my car* rather than the workers or the company that made it.)
*We **were given** a lot of homework to do in the holidays.* (Here, *we* are the focus, not the homework or the teachers who gave the homework.)
we don't know who did the action:
*My bike **was stolen** yesterday.* (I don't know who stole it.)
when who or what did something is obvious:
*The driver of the car **was arrested**.* (We know that the police arrest people so we don't need to mention them.)

To say who or what did the action we can add a *by* phrase.
*This opera **was composed by** Mozart.* (Mozart is the person who did the action.)

PRACTICE

1 **Complete the sentences with the passive form of the verbs in brackets. Use the present simple or the past simple.**

1 Last year's final, which .... (play) in the new stadium, ... (watch) by over 2 million people.

2 In the past most children walked to school, but now many .... (take) by their parents. Most of them .... (drive) by car.

3 I've just finished reading a science fiction novel that .... (write) in 1980. Many of the things that .... (predict) by the author have come true.

2 **Change the active sentences into passive ones. Mention who did the action, if necessary.**

1 A vet sees our cat twice a year.

....

2 The police closed the roads because of the storm.

....

3 A famous author wrote the book.

....

4 They play cricket in Australia.

....

5 My father taught me how to sing.

....

COMPARATIVE AND SUPERLATIVE ADVERBS

	comparative	superlative
For adverbs with two or more syllables (e.g. *carefully*)	add *more* **more carefully**	add *most* **the most carefully**
For adverbs with one syllable (e.g. *fast, late*)	add *-er* **faster later**	add *-est* **the fastest the latest**
Irregular adverbs: *well, badly*	**better worse**	**the best the worst**

- With comparative adverbs, we often use *than*.

- Although *early* has two syllables, the comparative and superlative forms are *earlier* and *the earliest*.

- Use comparative adverbs to say how things are done or happen at different times.
*Today it's raining **more heavily** than it did yesterday.*

- Use superlative adverbs to say how things are done by someone or something else.
*Everyone in my class works hard, but Jon works **the hardest**.*

PRACTICE

1 **Complete the sentences with the comparative or superlative form of the adverbs in brackets.**

1 I can't read it. Please write .... (clearly).

2 Our team played .... (well) in our group.

3 Cars can travel much .... (fast) than bicycles.

4 My brother works .... (hard) than I do.

5 If you revised .... (serious), you would do .... (well) in your exam.

6 I run .... (quickly) of all my friends.

2 **Underline the mistakes in the sentences and correct them.**

1 Jan dances most beautifully than Lucy.

....

2 We all write well, but Jon writes the better of all.

....

3 Peter waited the more patiently to see the doctor.

....

4 You need to work more hardly, especially at exam time.

....

5 You must go to bed more earlier than you did last night.

....

6 My sister runs more faster than me.

....

12

REPORTED SPEECH

Direct speech is what we call the words people actually say when they speak.
In the example below, the direct speech is <u>underlined</u>.
He said, '<u>I haven't seen you for a long time.</u>'

Indirect or reported speech is how we report (tell) what another person says.
He said he hadn't seen me for a long time.

- Verb tenses often change when we report what people said.

direct speech	reported speech
present simple 'I **go** to a school in the city centre.'	➜ past simple She said she **went** to a school in the city centre.
present continuous 'I**'m waiting** for a bus.'	➜ past continuous He said he **was waiting** for a bus.
present perfect 'I **have** already **had** lunch.'	➜ past perfect He said he **had** already **had** lunch.
past simple 'I **enjoyed** my dinner.'	➜ past perfect She said she **had enjoyed** her dinner.
will future 'I**'ll** call you later.'	➜ would She said she **would** call me later.
can 'I **can** speak four languages.'	➜ could She said she **could** speak four languages

We also need to make other changes when we report what people said.

- Subject and object pronouns:
  '**I** have already told **you**.' ➜ **She** said **she** had told **me**.
  '**We** live in Paris.' ➜ **They** said **they** lived in Paris.

- Possessive adjectives:
  '**I**'ve mended **my** bike.' ➜ **He** said **he**'d mended **his** bike.
  '**We** love **our** flat.' ➜ **They** said **they** loved **their** flat.

- Time references:
  'We're going on holiday **tomorrow**.' ➜ They said they were going on holiday **the next day**.

- Place references:
  'I want to stay **here**.' ➜ He said he wanted to stay **there**.

Reported commands

- We can use *tell* to report commands. We need to include the object (the person who needs to listen to the command) + infinitive after *tell*.

direct commands	reported commands
'Stop talking!' 'Don't be late!'	The teacher **told them to stop** talking The father **told his daughter not to be** late.

PRACTICE

1 Write the reported speech as direct speech.

1 She said she was living in Moscow.
   'I'm living in Moscow.'

2 I said I was sorry, but I couldn't lend her more money.
   ....

3 He says he still feels ill.
   ....

4 She says she's older than me.
   ....

5 They said they'd come and see me later.
   ....

6 Max said he'd left the day before.
   ....

7 She told him to stop worrying.
   ....

2 Write the statements and commands as reported speech.

1 'I'm leaving school at the end of next year.'
   He said
   ....

2 'I've got a surprise for you.'
   She said
   ....

3 'Shut the door!'
   She told him
   ....

4 'We've all passed our English exam.'
   They said
   ....

5 'It's my birthday tomorrow.'
   He said
   ....

6 'You're the only person I know who likes classical music.'
   She said
   ....

7 'Don't drink any more coffee!'
   He told Max
   ....

8 'We went to Morocco for our holiday last year.'
   They said
   ....

REPORTED QUESTIONS

The word order in reported questions is the same as for positive phrases.

positive phrase	direct question	reported question
I **was smiling**.	'Why are you smiling?'	He asked me why I **was smiling**.

We use *ask* when we report questions. We need to make changes to tenses, pronouns, times and places. We don't use question marks.

direct question	reported question
'**Why** are you smiling?'	He **asked** me **why** I was smiling.
'**What** are you doing tomorrow?'	She **asked** us **what** we were doing the next day.
'**When** do you finish football practice?'	He asked me **when** I finished football practice.
'**Why** did you come here?'	She asked me **why** I had gone there.

With *yes/no* questions (questions that need either a *yes* or *no* answer), we need to use *if* or *whether* after *ask*.

'**Are** you feeling OK?' '**Do** you need a break?'	She **asked if/whether** I was feeling OK. He **asked if/whether** I needed a break.

PRACTICE

1 Rewrite the indirect sentences as direct questions.

1 They asked me why I went to Morocco on holiday.

........'Why did you go to Morocco on holiday?'

2 Helen asked me if I was enjoying my new course.

....

3 Alex asked if anyone had found his keys.

....

4 Sasha wanted to know what we'd done the day before.

....

5 I asked Veronika if she could come to my party that evening.

....

6 We asked a policeman if he could tell us where the station was.

....

7 Jan wanted to know who my favourite actor was.

....

8 I asked my brother if he had tried to phone me.

2 Write the questions as reported questions.

1 'Why are you wearing your best clothes?'

My mum asked ....

2 'Where are you going?'

My dad asked ....

3 'What are you going to do there?'

My brother asked ....

....

4 'Are you going with anyone?'

My sister asked ....

5 'Do I know who you're going with?'

My dad asked ....

6 'What time will you be back?'

My mum asked ....

7 'How will you get home?'

My brother asked ....

....

8 'What will you do if you miss the last bus?'

My sister asked ....

INDIRECT QUESTIONS

Indirect questions are a polite way of asking for information. We use expressions like *Could you tell me ...?* or *I was wondering ...* to introduce the question.

direct question	reported question
Are you busy later?	**Could you tell me if** you're busy later?
Do you know the time?	**I was wondering if** you know the time.
Where do you work?	**I'd like to know where** you work.

- The word order in indirect questions is the same as for statements.
  *'How long **have you lived** here?'*
  *'I would like to know how long **you have lived** here.'*

- We do not use the auxiliary verbs *do*, *does* and *did* in indirect questions. However, we sometimes need to change the tense of the verb.
  *'When **does** the train **leave**?'*
  ✓ *Could you tell me **when the train leaves**?*
  ✗ ~~Could you tell me when does the train leave?~~

  *'When **did** you **get** home?'*
  ✓ *Could you tell me **when** you **got** home?*
  ✗ ~~Could you tell me when did you get home?~~

- If there is no question word (*what*, *when*, etc.), use *if* or *whether*.
  'Is the train late?'
  *'Could you tell me **if** the train is late?'*

PRACTICE

① **Write the questions as indirect questions.**

1 'Where do you live?'
   Could you tell me
   ....

2 'Are you doing anything at the weekend?'
   I was wondering ....

3 'What did they do last weekend?'
   Can you tell me ....

4 'What did you think of the film?'
   I'd like to know ....

5 Is my seat number on this ticket?
   Could you tell me ....

A phrasal verb is a verb with two or three parts. The meaning of the verb is sometimes different from the meaning of its separate parts. Phrasal verbs can combine verbs with prepositions or adverbs.

This section focuses on phrasal verbs related to four topics: **relationships**, **travel**, **communication** and **daily routines**.

RELATIONSHIPS

1 Match the phrasal verbs with the definitions below.

> look after someone   go out with someone
> bring up someone   split up with someone
> get together   get on with someone

.... = look after children until they are adults

.... = have a friendly relationship with someone

.... = meet

.... = have a romantic relationship with someone

.... = take care of someone

.... = end a relationship

2 Choose the correct option in *italics*.

1 I *get on / get together* with my friends every weekend to play football.

2 I *split up / get on* with everyone in my family. Everyone's very friendly.

3 My grandparents *brought up / went out* four children in a very small house.

4 I need to *look after / bring up* my little sister when my parents go out.

5 The band *got together / split up* because they didn't enjoy playing together any more.

3 Write a sentence using each of the phrasal verbs.

TRAVEL

1 Match the phrasal verbs with the definitions below.

> turn up   break down   check in
> set off   take off   get back

.... = when something (e.g. a car or computer) stops working

.... = arrive at an airport as a passenger, or a hotel as a guest

.... = return

.... = leave on a journey

.... = when a plane leaves the ground

.... = arrive, come

2 Complete the sentences with the past simple form of the phrasal verbs from the box.

1 We .... for the airport at 7 o'clock in the morning.

2 After we had been driving for ten minutes, our car .... , so my dad called a garage. Five minutes later, a mechanic .... and fixed the problem.

3 When we got to the airport, we parked the car and .... at the departures desk.

4 Half an hour later, our plane .... and our holiday began!

5 When we .... home a week later, we felt very relaxed.

3 Write a sentence using each of the phrasal verbs.

Phrasal verb builder

COMMUNICATION

1 Match the phrasal verbs with the definitions below.

> hang up   fill in something   call someone back
> switch something off   ring up someone

.... = return a phone call

.... = complete a form

.... = end a phone conversation

.... = make a phone call

.... = turn off something (e.g. computer)

2 Choose the correct option in *italics*.

My computer stopped working yesterday, so I
(1) *switched off / switched it off* and **(2)** *called back /
rang up* a help line. But the line was busy so I **(3)** *filled
in / hung up.* I waited ten minutes and then **(4)** *rang up
/ called back.* The person who answered the phone
asked me to **(5)** *ring up / fill in* an online form, and
gave me another number to call. In ten minutes, my
computer was working again!

3 Write a sentence using each of the phrasal verbs.

DAILY ROUTINES

1 Match the phrasal verbs with the definitions below.

> tidy up   wake someone up   get up
> put something on   pick someone up

.... = get out of bed

.... = collect someone in a car

.... = put clothes on your body

.... = make a place look clean

.... = stop (someone) sleeping

2 Complete the sentences with the present simple form of
the phrasal verbs from the box. Add any other words you
need.

I try and help at home, because my parents are really
busy. I always **(1)** .... my room, and help
with my five-year-old brother, too. He has just started
school. Every morning, I **(2)** .... at 7 o'clock.
At 7.15, he **(3)** .... and **(4)** ....
his school clothes. Then he watches TV while he is
having breakfast. At 8.00, his friend's mum
(5) .... in her car and takes him to school.

3 Write a sentence using each of the phrasal verbs.

Irregular Verbs

verb	past simple	past participle
be	was/were	been
beat	beat	beaten
become	became	become
begin	began	begun
bend	bent	bent
bite	bit	bitten
bleed	bled	bled
blow	blew	blown
break	broke	broken
bring	brought	brought
build	built	built
burn	burnt/burned	burnt/burned
buy	bought	bought
catch	caught	caught
choose	chose	chosen
come	came	come
cost	cost	cost
cut	cut	cut
deal	dealt	dealt
dig	dug	dug
do	did	done
draw	drew	drawn
dream	dreamt/dreamed	dreamt/dreamed
drink	drank	drunk
drive	drove	driven
eat	ate	eaten
fall	fell	fallen
feed	fed	fed
feel	felt	felt
fight	fought	fought
find	found	found
fly	flew	flown
forbid	forbade	forbidden
forget	forgot	forgotten
forgive	forgave	forgiven
freeze	froze	frozen
get	got	got
give	gave	given
go	went	gone
grow	grew	grown
hang	hung	hung
have	had	had
hear	heard	heard
hide	hid	hidden
hit	hit	hit
hold	held	held
hurt	hurt	hurt
keep	kept	kept
kneel	knelt	knelt
know	knew	known
lay	laid	laid
lead	led	led
learn	learnt/learned	learnt/learned
leave	left	left
lend	lent	lent
let	let	let
lie	lay	lain
light	lit	lit
lose	lost	lost
make	made	made
mean	meant	meant
meet	met	met
pay	paid	paid
put	put	put
read	read	read
ride	rode	ridden
ring	rang	rung
rise	rose	risen
run	ran	run
say	said	said
see	saw	seen
sell	sold	sold
send	sent	sent
set	set	set
sew	sewed	sewn
shake	shook	shaken
shine	shone	shone
shoot	shot	shot
show	showed	shown
shut	shut	shut
sing	sang	sung
sink	sank	sunk
sit	sat	sat
sleep	slept	slept
smell	smelt/smelled	smelt/smelled
speak	spoke	spoken
spell	spelt/spelled	spelt/spelled
spend	spent	spent
spill	spilt/spilled	spilt/spilled
spoil	spoilt/spoiled	spoilt/spoiled
stand	stood	stood
steal	stole	stolen
stick	stuck	stuck
strike	struck	struck
sweep	swept	swept
swim	swam	swum
swing	swung	swung
take	took	taken
teach	taught	taught
tear	tore	torn
tell	told	told
think	thought	thought
throw	threw	thrown
understand	understood	understood
wake	woke	woken
wear	wore	worn
win	won	won
write	wrote	written

Writing bank

MAKING YOUR WRITING MORE INTERESTING

To make a sentence more interesting, we can add more details.

1 Look at how the second sentence adds information. Match the new information (1–8) with the descriptions (a–h).

- *I went to Spain.*
  ¹Last year, I went to Spain, ²which is my favourite country.

- *I like warm weather.*
  I like warm weather, ³but I don't like cold weather.

- *I've got an exam tomorrow.*
  I've got an ⁴important exam tomorrow, ⁵so I had to walk to school.

- *George was happy.*
  George was ⁶really happy ⁷because it was his birthday.

- *I read the letter.*
- I read the letter ⁸slowly and carefully.

a adding a contrasting idea ......3......

b giving a reason ....

c saying when something happened ....

d giving the result of an action ....

e using a relative clause to give extra information ....

f using an adjective to describe something ....

g using an adverb to make an adjective stronger ....

h using adverbs to describe how something happens ....

2 Complete the table with the words from the box.

> and   beautiful   because   but   completely   delicious
> easily   later that day   loudly   modern   quickly   so
> the next day   this morning   wonderful   yesterday

adjectives	adverbs	linking words	time expressions

3 Make the sentences more interesting. Use the words from the box. Can you think of any other words to use?

> but   early the next morning
> large   really   suddenly

1 It .... started to rain.

2 I called Max, ... he didn't answer his phone.

3 We set out for London ....

4 I ordered a cup of coffee and a .... slice of cake.

5 The film was .... boring!

4 Join the two parts of the sentences with *and, but, so* or *because*.

we didn't play tennis – the weather was bad

We didn't play tennis because the weather was bad.

1 I was very tired – I went straight to bed

....

....

2 we all went to the party – everyone had a great time

....

....

3 Paul wanted to come with us – he couldn't

....

....

4 we all laughed – it was so funny

....

....

WRITING PART 1: AN EMAIL

Read the exam task. What information should you include in the email?

Read this email from your English-speaking friend Sam,
and the notes you have made.

To:

From: Sam

Hi,

Guess what? Do you remember the sports competition I entered last month? They announced the results yesterday, and I've won two tickets to go and watch an international sports event!

Amazing!

Would you like to come to the event with me? We can choose to go in July or August.

Yes — tell Sam when you can make it.

We have to book which sport we want to see in advance. There are football and basketball matches. Which sport do you prefer to watch?

Tell Sam.

They sell lots of souvenirs at the stadium. What do you think we should buy?

Suggest ...

Bye for now,

Sam

Write your **email** to James, using **all** the **notes**.

MODEL ANSWER

Use an informal phrase to start the email.

Hi, Sam,

Thanks for your email. That's amazing news about the competition! Well done!

Yes, I love sport, so it would be incredible to go to a big sports event with you. I can go with you in July, but I can't go in August because I'm on holiday then.

I'm a big football fan, so I'd love to see an international football match. It would be brilliant to see some of my favourite heroes in action.

Why don't we buy football shirts as souvenirs? We can wear them at the match!

See you soon,

Tom

Remember you are replying to Sam's email.

This answers the question about when you can or can't make it, and gives a reason.

This answers the question 'Which sport do you prefer to watch?'

This is a suggestion.

Use an informal phrase at the end.

KEY LANGUAGE AND IDEAS FOR EMAILS

Opening an email:
Hi   Hi, Tom   Hi, there   Hello

Closing an email:
Love,   See you soon,   Take care,   Bye

Responding to an email:
Thanks for your email.   It's good to hear from you.

Responding to good news:
That's amazing news!   I'm so happy for you!   Wow!   How exciting!   Well done!

Responding to bad news:
I'm sorry to hear about …

Making a suggestion:
Why don't you/we …?   You/We could …   If I were you, I'd …   Make sure you …

Making an offer or promise:
I could … if you like.   Would you like me to …?   I can … if you want.

Making a request:
Could you …?   Can you …?   Would you mind … -ing?

Giving good or bad news:
You'll be pleased to hear that …   I'm afraid …   Guess what …?   I'm sorry, but …

Linking words and phrases:
and but so because also as well

Informal language:
• contractions: *I'm   you're   he's*
• informal words and phrases: *awesome   great   keep in touch   take care   I guess …*
• exclamation marks to show emotion: *That's great news!   Wow!*

---

❷ Match the beginnings and endings of these sentences.
Then decide if each sentence is a suggestion (S), an offer (O), a promise (P) or a request (R).

1 Could you   **a** I'd definitely accept the job. ....

2 If I were you,   **b** some useful addresses if you want. ....

3 I can send you   **c** be there to help on the day. ....

4 Don't worry, I'll   **d** let me know what time you're arriving? ....

❸ Correct the <u>underlined</u> mistakes in the sentences giving good or bad news.
Use the Key language and ideas box to check your answers.

1 <u>I afraid</u> I won't be able to come to your party.

2 <u>Guess that</u> I'm doing next week?

3 <u>I'm sorry, and</u> Dan won't be here when you visit.

4 <u>You'll be pleased hear</u> that I've now finished all my exams!

❹ Choose the correct linking words in *italics*.

1 I finish work at six o'clock, *because / so* I can meet you at 6.30.

2 My sister Martha is *also / as well* coming home for the holidays.

3 I'm not very good at singing, *because / but* I still enjoy it.

4 I'm a bit disappointed *because / so* my exam results weren't brilliant.

5 I'll find the document *also / and* send it to you in an email.

5 Read the exam task. What information must you include in your email?

To:	
From:	Logan

Hi,

The weather forecast looks good next weekend, so my family's having a barbecue to celebrate the end of the school year. Would you like to come?

I'd like to invite everyone in our English class. What kind of food do you think our classmates would like to eat at a barbecue?

I'd also like everyone to play some outdoor games after we eat. What game do you think would be best for our classmates?

See you soon,

Logan

great idea!

Yes — say which day.

Tell Sam.

Suggest ...

6 Before you write your reply to Logan, complete the table with ideas.

Paragraph 1 (respond to the invitation)	
Paragraph 2 (suggest some food)	
Paragraph 3 (explain your idea for a game)	
Useful phrases I can use	

7 Write your email, using your notes from Exercise 6. Write about 100 words.

8 Check your email and make changes if necessary.

- [ ] Have you answered all the questions and included all the necessary information?
- [ ] Have you used a suitable phrase to open and close your email?
- [ ] Have you tried to make your writing more interesting by adding details?
- [ ] Have you used informal language?
- [ ] Have you used linking words and phrases?
- [ ] Have you counted your words?

WRITING PART 2: AN ARTICLE

KEY LANGUAGE AND IDEAS FOR ARTICLES

Use adjectives for describing people and things:
attractive brave calm cheerful convenient ...

Use linking words and phrases:
and but so because although also as well ...

Use an introductory sentence for each paragraph:
Paris is a city of variety.
A good job should be creative.   Photography is a great hobby.

Give your opinion:
I think ... It seems to me that ... I would say that ...

2 Choose the best introductory sentence in *italics* for each opening paragraph.

1 *There are many benefits to keeping fit. / I don't really do enough exercise.* Doing regular exercise is good for your heart, and it helps you to lose weight. It can also improve your mood, especially if you feeling tired or unhappy.

2 *Some older people are not used to the internet. / The internet has changed people's lives in many ways.* People can now go online to do their shopping and book restaurants and holidays. Students also have access to lots of information that was difficult to find before the internet.

3 *Teaching is a very difficult job. / I would like to become a teacher.* Students are not always interested in learning, and teachers have to work hard to encourage their students to study. Also, there are sometimes problems with bad behaviour from students.

1 Read the exam task. What should your article be about? What information should it include?

> **Articles wanted!**
>
> ### My favourite city
>
> *What's your favourite city?*
>
> *What's so special about this city?*
>
> *What city would you love to travel to in the future?*
>
> *Tell us what you think!*
>
> **Write an article answering these questions and we will publish the most interesting ones on our website.**

MODEL ANSWER

My favourite city is Paris because it is so lively and interesting. It is also full of surprises.

Paris is a city of variety. It has many beautiful old buildings, but it also feels modern. You can visit expensive designer shops or small, traditional markets. There are hundreds of restaurants which serve French food, or different food from around the world. You can meet all kinds of people, too. There is something for everyone.

I would love to travel to New York in the future because I've seen the city in so many films, and I would love to visit it in real life.

The first paragraph answers the first question and gives a reason

Adjectives make the article more interesting to read.

The second paragraph gives more details and answers the second question in the task.

The third paragraph is about a city the writer would like to go to in the future.

3 Complete the table with the adjectives from the box. Can you add any more adjectives?

> amusing   delicious   freezing   frightening   peaceful
> quiet   old-fashioned   stormy   tasty   tight

clothes	films	food	countryside	weather

4 Read the exam task. What should your article be about? What should it include?

5 Before you write your article, complete the table with ideas.

> ### Articles wanted!
>
> #### My perfect job
>
> *What makes the perfect job?*
>
> *Is it being creative, travelling, meeting people, or something else?*
>
> *How important is it to earn a lot of money?*
>
> *Tell us what you think!*
>
> Write an article answering these questions and we will publish the most interesting articles on our website.

Paragraph 1 (answer the first question)	
Paragraph 2 (give more details)	
Paragraph 3 (give your opinion about money)	
Useful phrases I can use	

6 Write your article, using your notes from exercise 5. Write about 100 words

7 Check your article and make changes if necessary.

- ☐ Have you answered all the questions and included all the necessary information?
- ☐ Have you used adjectives to make your article interesting to read?
- ☐ Have you expressed a personal opinion?
- ☐ Have you used linking words and phrases?
- ☐ Have you counted your words?

WRITING PART 2: A STORY

1 **Read the exam task. Which is the best way to continue the story (1, 2 or 3)? Why?**

- Your English teacher has asked you to write a story.
- Your story must begin with this sentence:

  I opened the letter from my cousins in Brazil.

1 I have three cousins who live in Brazil, and I get on very well with them.
They are all very keen on football.

2 They said they were coming to visit me, and they were arriving on the 15th – today!

3 I think Brazil is a really interesting country, and I would love to go there one day.
There are lots of amazing wild animals there.

MODEL ANSWER

I opened the letter from my cousins in Brazil. They said they were coming to visit me, and they were arriving on the 15th – today!

I was really excited. First, I cleaned everything in the flat. Then I went to the supermarket to buy food. After that, I made a cake to make them feel welcome. By evening, I was completely exhausted. I picked up the letter again to check the time of their flight, and that's when I noticed the date. They were arriving on July 15th, but today was June 15th!

We had a wonderful time together in July, and all laughed about the mistake I had made!

The first paragraph gives background to the story.

The second paragraph gives the main events of the story.

Time expressions make the order of events clear.

Adjectives and adverbs make the story more interesting.

The last paragraph ends the story.

KEY LANGUAGE AND IDEAS FOR STORIES

Use past simple verbs for the main events:
I went to a restaurant.   I found a letter.

Use past continuous verbs for longer actions in the past:
I was waiting for the bus.   The sun was shining.

Use past perfect verbs for background events:
Unfortunately, I had forgotten my purse.

Time expressions:
First   then   later   the next day   finally …

Adjectives to describe people:
friendly   kind   tall

Adjectives to describe places:
busy   quiet   modern

Adjectives to describe feelings:
excited   angry   … delighted

Adverbs to describe how someone does something:
quickly   slowly   carefully

Adverbs to comment on what happened:
luckily   fortunately   unfortunately

Complete the sentences with the correct form of the verbs in brackets. Use the past simple, past continuous or past perfect.

1 I packed my bags and then .... (call) a taxi to take me to the airport.

2 Sara .... (wait) for me when I got to the restaurant.

3 I could finally relax because I .... (pass) all my exams!

4 I found an old key while I .... (walk) along the beach.

5 James was late because he .... (forget) to set his alarm.

6 I opened the door and then quickly .... (close) it again.

Choose the correct time expressions in *italics*.

I was really scared when my car broke down near the forest. (1) *Then / First*, I tried starting the car, but that didn't work. (2) *Finally / Then*, I tried to call a friend, but I had no signal on my phone. (3) *Next / After*, I decided to wait for another car so I could ask for help.
(4) *An hour later / Before an hour*, I was still sitting there! Suddenly, I heard the sound of another car.
(5) *Finally / After*, someone came to help me and I got home safely.

Complete the sentences with adjectives from the box.

> curly   disappointed   entertaining   messy
> smart   spicy

1 The room was .... and not very clean.

2 She was wearing a very nice, ... jacket and skirt.

3 He cooked some delicious, ... food for us.

4 The show was fun and very ....

5 She introduced me to a tall young man with .... hair.

6 I was very .... when she didn't call me.

5 Read the exam task. Before you write your story, complete the table with ideas.

- Your English teacher has asked you to write a story.
- Your story must start with this sentence: Last week, I went to the zoo.

Paragraph 1 (the background to the story)

Paragraph 2 (the main events)

Paragraph 3 (the ending)

Language I can use

6 Write your story, using your notes from Exercise 5. Write about 100 words.

7 Check your story and make changes if necessary.
- ☐ Does your story have a clear beginning, middle and ending?
- ☐ Have you used verbs in the past simple, past continuous and past perfect?
- ☐ Have you used time expressions to order the events?
- ☐ Have you used adjectives and adverbs to make your story interesting?
- ☐ Have you written about 100 words

Speaking bank

SPEAKING PART 1

1 Listen to Maria answering the questions. Does she use full sentences in her answers?

1 What's your name?

2 What's your surname?

3 Where do you come from?

4 Do you work, or are you a student?

2 Listen to Maria answering more questions. Notice how she adds extra information.

1 What did you do yesterday evening?

2 Do you think that English will be useful to you in the future?

3 Tell us about a place you would like to visit in the future.

4 Can you describe your house or flat?

5 What do you enjoy doing in your free time?

KEY LANGUAGE AND IDEAS FOR PERSONAL QUESTIONS

Use frequency adverbs to talk about habits and routines:
I usually have breakfast …
I often watch TV …

Use the past simple and time expressions to talk about the past:
Yesterday I watched …
Last weekend I visited …

Use *be going to* and time expressions to talk about future plans:
Next summer, I'm going to travel to …

Talk about future hopes:
I'd like to visit …
I want to get a job …
I hope I'll work …

Add extra information: *Actually and Also*

Add contrasting information: *but …*

Add reasons and results: *because so That's why …*

Add examples: *For example , …*
For instance, …

---

3 Complete Maria's answers with the words in the box. Listen again and check.

> and   Also   because
> but   For example   often   so

1 I .... watch films with my friends.

2 I hope I'll travel to different countries with my job, ... I'm sure I will need English.

3 I'd love to go to New York one day .... it looks like such an exciting city.

4 The kitchen is very small, ... the living room is quite big.

5 .... , it's got a balcony.

6 I'm quite into sport, ... I do quite a lot of sport in my free time.

7 .... , I sometimes go running in the evenings.

4 Complete the table with the time expressions from the box.

> always   last night   last weekend
> next weekend   sometimes   tomorrow
> tonight   usually   when I was younger

present simple	past simple	*be going to*

Match the questions (1–5) with the answers (a–e). Then choose one extra piece of information (f–j) to add to each answer. Listen and check.

1 Tell us about your English teacher.
2 Would you like to live in a different country?
3 Can you tell us about your home town?
4 How do you usually travel to school or work?
5 What did you do last weekend?

a My home town is Barcelona. …..
b His name's Mr Adam. …..
c On Saturday I played football. ….
d I wouldn't like to for long. ….
e I usually catch the bus. ….

f It's on the coast.
g We usually have a match every Saturday.
h I'd miss my family and friends at home.
i He's really funny.
j I'd prefer to walk.

How does the student introduce extra information? Complete the sentences. Listen again and check.

1 I like him .... he always makes our lessons interesting.
2 I'd like to visit different countries, ... the United States or maybe Australia.
3 There are lots of beautiful buildings .... are very famous.
4 I'd prefer to walk, ... it's too far for me.
5 We usually have a match every Saturday. ...., we didn't win last week.

7 **Practise answering the questions. Use a range of tenses, and add extra information.**

- What's your name?
- What's your surname?
- Where do you come from?
- Do you work, or are you a student?

- What did you do yesterday evening?
- Do you think that English will be useful to you in the future?
- Tell us about a place you would like to visit in the future.
- Can you describe your house or flat?

- What do you enjoy doing in your free time?
- Tell us about your English teacher.
- Would you like to live in a different country?
- Can you tell us about your home town?
- How do you usually travel to school or work?
- What did you do last weekend?

SPEAKING PART 2

1 Listen to Pablo describing a photo. What guesses does he make?

KEY LANGUAGE AND IDEAS FOR DESCRIBING A PHOTO

Say what you can see:

The picture shows …   I can see …   There's a …

There are some …   but you can't see …   She's got …   He has …

Describe where things are in the picture:

at the front   in the background   on the left   on the right   in the middle
behind   in front of   next to

Use the present continuous:

He's wearing…   She's running …

Talk about the people:

tall, long/short hair   young   old

Talk about the place:

indoors   outdoors   attractive   comfortable   safe

Talk about the weather:

sunny   cloudy   wet

When you don't know the word for something:

It's a kind of …   It looks like a …

Make guesses:

He looks like…   He seems to be …   I guess he's probably …   I think maybe …
It might be …

Look at the photo. Choose the correct words in *italics* to describe where the people are.

1 There are two young women *at the front / in the background* of the picture.
2 There's an old man with a beard on the *right / left*.
3 There's a young couple on the *left / right*, further back in the bus.
4 You can see someone's legs *behind / next to* the old man, but you can't see their face.
5 *In the background / At the front*, you can see a man standing up.

Look at the photo again. Complete the sentences with the correct present continuous form of the verbs in brackets. Listen and check.

1 The picture shows some people who .... (travel) by bus.
2 They .... (smile).
3 One woman .... (show) the other one something on her phone.
4 The older man on the right .... (look) forwards. Maybe he .... (think) about where to get off the bus.
5 In the background, there's a man who .... (stand) up. I think he .... (talk) to another passenger.

4 Look at the photo. Complete the sentences with words from the box.

guess   looks   might   probably   seem

1 I think the people are .... father and son.

2 They .... be watching TV.

3 They're eating something from a box. It .... like pizza.

4 They .... to be quite relaxed.

5 I .... they're probably having a relaxing evening at home.

5 Look at the photo again. Practise describing it. Then listen and compare your ideas.

Practise describing the photos below and on page 158.

Listen to two students doing the task below. Do they talk about all the options?
Which present do they agree on?

It is your friend's birthday soon, and you would like to buy her a present.

Here are some ideas.

Talk together about the different presents you could buy, and say which
would be the most suitable.

KEY LANGUAGE AND IDEAS FOR DISCUSSING OPTIONS

Making suggestions:
What about ... ?   *What do you think about ... ?*   *Would ... be a good idea?*

Responding to suggestions:
That's a great idea.   *Yes, good idea.*   *I'm not sure.*

Giving your opinion:
I think ...   *In my opinion, ...*

Asking someone's opinion:
What do you think?   *Do you agree?*

Agreeing:
That's true.   *I agree (with you).*   *Yes, I think you're right.*   *OK, so ...*

Disagreeing:
I don't agree with you because ...   *I'm not sure about that because ...*

Considering alternatives:
... might be a better choice. What if we ... ?

Reaching agreement:
It's time to decide.   *Are you OK with that?*   *We'll go for that one, then.*

2 Complete the discussion with words from the box. Then listen again and check.

agree   go   idea   OK   opinion   so   sure   think

A: What do you (**1**) .... about that idea?

B: I'm not (**2**) ....

It's difficult to choose a book for someone else.

A: I (**3**) .... with you. And I don't think flowers are a good idea, because they're a bit boring in my (**4**) ....

B: Would a T-shirt be a good (**5**) .... ? Most people wear T-shirts.

A: Well, I don't really like it when people buy me clothes, because I prefer to choose them myself.

A: OK, (**6**) .... not a T-shirt .

B: Maybe we should choose the cinema tickets. Are you (**7**) .... with that?

A: Yes, good idea. We'll (**8**) .... for that one, then.

3 Match the beginnings and endings of the sentences.

1	That's a	**a**	agree with you.
2	Do you	**b**	be a better choice.
3	I don't	**c**	to decide.
4	Flowers might	**d**	great idea.
5	It's time	**e**	you're right.
6	Yes, I think	**f**	agree?

4 Work in pairs. Do the task below. Then listen and compare your ideas.

Two friends are discussing how their class should celebrate the end of exams. Here are some ideas. Talk together about the different ideas and say which would be the most fun.

SPEAKING PART 4

1 **Listen to two students answering the questions. Which things in the box do they do?**

    1 Who do you most enjoy buying presents for?

    2 Which people in your family are the most difficult to choose presents for?

    3 Do you like receiving money instead of presents?

> give reasons for their answers
>
> interrupt each other
>
> ask for each other's opinions
>
> disagree with each other
>
> use an expression to allow time to think about the answer

KEY LANGUAGE AND IDEAS FOR DISCUSSING IDEAS

Talking about likes/dislikes/preferences:
I like/love + -ing   I prefer to …   I enjoy …

Talking about habits:
I sometimes/usually/always …

Giving your opinion:
I think …   In my opinion, …

Asking someone's opinion:
What do you think?   Do you agree?

Agreeing:
That's true.   I agree with you.   Yes, I think you're right.

Disagreeing
I don't agree with you because …
I'm not sure about that because …

Giving yourself time to think:
That's an interesting question.
That's a difficult question.   Let me see.

2 **Choose the correct words in *italics*.**

    1 I enjoy *to buy / buying* things for my nephew.

    2 It *sometimes is / is sometimes* nice to receive money.

    3 I *usually get / get usually* money from three or four relatives.

    4 I prefer *get / to get* money from people who don't know me very well.

    5 I love *get / getting* presents.

3 Complete the dialogues with phrases from the box.

| Do you agree | That's an interesting question |
| That's true | What do you think |

A: I think surprise presents are the best presents.
(**1**) ....?

B: Yes, I do. I love opening presents when I have no idea what they are!

A: I think money is sometimes the most useful present to get.

B: (**2**) .... Because then you can use it to buy something you really need.

A: In my opinion, men are the most difficult people to buy presents for.
(**3**) ....

B: Yes, I think you're right. I never know what to buy for my dad or my uncle.

A: Do you think that some people spend too much money on presents?

B: Hmm. (**4**) .... I think most people spend as much as they can afford.

4 Work in pairs. Discuss these questions together.

1 Would you like to have more social events with your class?
2 Do you think watching sports events can be more fun than taking part?
3 Do you prefer cooking a meal for friends or eating out in a restaurant?

5 Listen and compare your ideas.

Prepositions of place

Writing Part 2

capital letter	• the first letter of a sentence: *Football is very popular in Britain.*
	• for countries, nationalities, languages, names of people, places, trademarks, days, months, **P**ortugal, **R**ussian, **L**ego, **M**rs, etc.
	• for titles of books, films, etc.: **S**tar Wars, **S**hrek
	• for abbreviations: ***UNICEF, WWF, FIFA***
full stop UK/ period US comma	• the end of a sentence: *I'm going for a walk.*
	• between items in a list: *I need some peas, butter, sugar and eggs.*
	• to show a pause in a long sentence: *If I lost my phone, I'd go to the police station.*
	• when you want to add information: *The woman, who I'd met last week, waved as she went past.*
apostrophe	• for missing letters: *don't, I'll, it's*
	• for possessives: *Paul's bike*
hyphen	• to join two words: *good-looking, hard-working*

Extra resources

Unit 4

Comparative and superlative adjectives

a True. The population of Canada is approximately 37 million. The population of Tokyo is 9 million.

b False. The longest country is Chile. It's 4,270km long.

c True. There is about 83 cm of rain every year in Rome. There is about 62 cm of rain every year in Paris.

Unit 9

Starting off

Add up the points from your answers.

1	A=0	B=1	C=2
2	A=1	B=0	C=2
3	A=0	B=1	C=2
4	A=2	B=0	C=1
5	A=0	B=2	C=1
6	A=0	B=1	C=2

Your total score = ...

Your total score = 0–4

You're not keen on exercise, are you? By not getting a minimum 30 minutes of activity a day, you're missing a great way to feel less stressed, sleep better and get more energy. As it's all new to you, start with a little at first. Remember you can do parts of your half hour at different times, so why not walk to school, clean the house, go for a swim – anything that stops you sitting on the sofa, really. You don't have to run 40 kilometres to improve your fitness.

Your total score = 5–8

You're quite relaxed and, while taking it easy can be a good idea, it shouldn't take too much extra effort to do the recommended 30 minutes a day, five times a week. You enjoy spending time with your friends, so why not take up an activity together? It can be anything – from a street dance class to basketball. Or if you don't fancy organised classes go out dancing instead of sitting around doing nothing.

Your total score = 9 or more

Well done! You're fit and active. Half an hour of activity a day is a minimum for you. While keeping active now means you feel great, you can also look forward to a healthy future. You shouldn't have to worry if you stay active. As you enjoy being fit, make sure you do all the activities you can: from hill walks to rock climbing.

Unit 11

Starting off

Quiz answers

1 True, **2** True, **3** True, **4** False, **5** True, **6** False, **7** False, **8** False

The authors would like to thank Alison Bewsher, Helen Kuffel and Jane Coates personally for all their input, efficiency and good humour.

Emma would like to thank her colleagues and her students at Lacunza – IH San Sebastian for trialling some of the materials. She would also like to thank her family for their patience, support and understanding.

Peter would like to give special thanks to Tek for her patience, support and encouragement.

The authors and publishers would like to thank the following contributors:

Grammar reference: Simon Haines

Writing and Speaking bank: Sheila Dignen

The authors and publishers are grateful to the following for reviewing the material during the writing process:

Spain: Yolanda Bau, Sergio Gomez, John Haywood; Italy: Ellen Darling, Helen McKinty; Portugal: Diana England; Russia: Liubov Desiatova.

Key: U = Unit, GR = Grammar Reference, PVB = Phrasal verb builder, SB = Speaking Bank

Text

Cambridge University Press for the word references throughout the book from Cambridge Learner's Dictionary 3rd edition. Copyright © 2007 Cambridge University Press; **U1**: Cambridge ESOL for the PET content and overview. Reproduced with kind permission of Cambridge ESOL; **U9**: NHS Choices for the text 'How fit and active are you?' adapted from content on the NHS.UK website. Reproduced with kind permission.

Photography

All the images are sourced from Getty Images.

U1: Steve Prezant/Image Source; Image Source; Ryan McVay/Photodisc; Louis Turner/Cultura; Image Source; Hero Images; Cultura RM Exclusive/Nancy Honey; Lisa Stirling/DigitalVision; Paul Bradbury/OJO Images; Maskot; 3sbworld/iStock/Getty Images Plus; Caiaimage/Tom Merton; Jamie Grill/The Image Bank; Mario Gutiérrez/Moment; Adam Crowley/Blend Images; ViewStock; Gary John Norman/Iconica; Alistair Nicholls/ArcaidImages; Mike Daines/ArcaidImages; phototropic/E+; Hero Images; Sofie Delauw/Cultura; Carol Yepes/Moment; Erik Rank/The Image Bank; Bluexhand/iStock/Getty Images Plus; Kroeger/Gross/StockFood Creative; gerenme/E+; gerenme/iStock/Getty Images Plus; Grassetto/iStock/Getty Images Plus; fatihhoca/E+; shutswis/iStock/Getty Images Plus; dmitriymoroz/iStock/Getty Images Plus; talevr/iStock/Getty Images Plus; Tuul & Bruno Morandi/Photolibrary; duncan1890/DigitalVision Vectors; Nora Carol Photography/Moment; Mika Mika/Moment; the_burtons/Moment; Janos Somodi/Moment; **U2**: Guang Niu/Getty Images News; Jon Feingersh/Blend Images; Pawel Toczynski/Photolibrary; fitopardo.com/Moment Open; shomos uddin/Moment; Hero Images; BraunS/E+; MirageC/Moment; David Arky; pearleye/E+; Utamaru Kido/Moment; **U3**: skynesher/E+; gbh007/iStock/Getty Images Plus; Anthony Lee/OJO Images; J.W.Alker/imageBROKER; Bruce Laurance/The Image Bank; pmcdonald/iStock/Getty Images Plus; gbh007/iStock/Getty Images Plus; Tetra Images; Diana Mulvihill/The Image Bank; Jutta Klee/Canopy; Olivia Bell Photography/Moment; Johner Images; Jupiterimages/Stockbyte; Paulo Amorim/Moment; Dean Pictures/Corbis; Hero Images; GibsonPictures/E+; Dina Belenko Photography/Moment; enjoynz/DigitalVision Vectors; **U4**: Timothy Allen/Perspectives; Michael DeYoung/Blend Images; Alenmax/iStock Editorial/Getty Images Plus; Creatas/Getty Images Plus; Kate Mitchell/Fuse; shalamov/iStock/Getty Images Plus; webguzs/iStock/Getty Images Plus; joebelanger/iStock/Getty Images Plus; Marco_Piunti/iStock/Getty Images Plus; Shana Novak/DigitalVision; Nigel Killeen/Moment; Zhang Peng/LightRocket; Manuel Blondeau/Corbis Sport; Merten Snijders/Lonely Planet Images; Chris Jackson/Getty Images News; Sylvain Sonnet/Photographer's Choice; gaspr13/iStock/Getty Images Plus; anatoliy_gleb/iStock/Getty Images Plus; Massimo Borchi/Atlantide Phototravel/The Image Bank; Jose A. Bernat Bacete/Moment; **U5**: VisualCommunications/E+; Phonix_a/iStock/Getty Images Plus; Rubberball/Mike Kemp; aldomurillo/E+; Jason Hosking/Stone; Vanessa Davies/Dorling Kindersley; Martin BernettI/AFP; Tobias Titz; Arto Hakola/Moment Open; Kimberly Brotherman/Moment; Steve Debenport/E+; JulNichols/iStock/Getty Images Plus; **U6**: PAUL FAITH/AFP; Michael Cogliantry/The Image Bank; Ron Crabtree/DigitalVision; Jack Hollingsworth/Blend Images; Ariel Skelley/DigitalVision; Plume Creative/DigitalVision; PT Images; Juanmonino/E+; Rudy Sulgan/Corbis Documentary; Francesco Castaldo//Mondadori Portfolio; Andre Vogelaere/Moment; Neil Emmerson/robertharding; David Shvartsman/Moment; BJI; Alex Tihonovs/EyeEm; Yuri_Arcurs/DigitalVision; **U7**: Kaori Ando/Image Source; Australian Land, City, People Scape Photographer/Moment; Frank and Helena/Cultura; GregorBister/E+; Fabrizio Di Nucci/NurPhoto; NurPhoto; Issaurinko/iStock/Getty Images Plus; kali9/E+; monkeybusinessimages/iStock/Getty Images Plus; Ernst Wrba/Picture Press; DavorLovincic; Bob Langrish/Dorling Kindersley; Robb Reece/Corbis Documentary; Lee Woodgate/Ikon Images; Don Farrall/DigitalVision; **U8**: Print Collector/Hulton Archive; Paul Popper/Popperfoto; Shaun Botterill/Getty Images Sport; Christopher Polk/AMA2013/Getty Images Entertainment; Dominik Magdziak Photography/Getty Images Entertainment; Jim Craigmyle/

Acknowledgements

First Light; Siri Stafford/Stone; pressureUA/iStock Editorial/Getty Images Plus; DMEPhotography/iStock/Getty Images Plus; Ron Levine/DigitalVision; SensorSpot/E+; Emya Photography/Moment; Juanmonino/E+; R.Tsubin/Moment; **U9**: AP Dube/Hindustan Times; James Porcini/Cultura; SolStock/E+; mediaphotos/iStock/Getty Images Plus; SolStock/E+; Hybrid Images/Cultura; strickke/iStock/Getty Images Plus; jashlock/E+; eugenesergeev/iStock/Getty Images Plus; fstop123/E+; The Sydney Morning Herald/Fairfax Media; yulkapopkova/E+; monkeybusinessimages/iStock/Getty Images Plus; PeopleImages/DigitalVision; Larry Dale Gordon/The Image Bank; PeopleImages/DigitalVision; tommaso79/iStock/Getty Images Plus; Maximilian Stock Ltd/Photolibrary; milicad/iStock/Getty Images Plus; Vijay kumar/DigitalVision Vectors; MirageC/Moment; **U10**: Image Source; Dorling Kindersley; Maximilian Stock Ltd/Photolibrary; Davies and Starr/The Image Bank; alptraum/iStock/Getty Images Plus; monkeybusinessimages/iStock/Getty Images Plus; Jose Luis Pelaez Inc/Blend Images; Robert Daly/OJO Images; RedChopsticks; Education Images/Universal Images Group; Cecilia Puebla/CON; Carl D. Walsh/Portland Press Herald; Eye Ubiquitous/Universal Images Group; IndiaPictures/Universal Images Group; Stephen J. Boitano/Lonely Planet Images; Jean-Pierre Lescourret/Lonely Planet Images; Westend61; 22kay22/iStock Editorial/Getty Images Plus; Artur Widak/NurPhoto; Atlantide Phototravel/Corbis Documentary; Purestock; Rana Faure/The Image Bank; Nikada; Alexander Spatari/Moment; coldsnowstorm/E+; Digital Vision/Photodisc; **U11**: Gilbert Laroda/EyeEm; Aditya Singh/Moment Open; Raimund Linke/Oxford Scientific; Vicki Jauron, Babylon and Beyond Photography/Moment; Momatiuk - Eastcott/Corbis Documentary; Ian Cumming/Axiom Photographic Agency; Photocech/iStock/Getty Images Plus; Piotr Krzeslak/iStock/Getty Images Plus; Robert Pickett/Corbis Documentary; BernardBreton/iStock/Getty Images Plus; Joanne Hedger/Moment; Raimund Linke/Oxford Scientific; Blend Images - KidStock/Brand X Pictures; Wendy Stone/Corbis News; Anna Zieminski/AFP; Panoramic Images; bluecinema/iStock/Getty Images Plus; Guy Edwardes/VisitBritain; bgfoto/E+; **U12**: Vincent Besnault/Photographer's Choice; JGI/Jamie Grill/Blend Images; shanghaiface/Moment; Hero Images; Westend61; Jutta Klee/The Image Bank; Chris Moore - Exploring Light Photography/Moment; Vijay kumar/DigitalVision Vectors; Aşkın Dursun KAMBEROĞLU/DigitalVision Vectors; **GR**: kali9/iStock/Getty Images Plus; Yagi Studio/DigitalVision; Betsie Van Der Meer/Taxi; Tolga Tezcan/iStock/Getty Images Plus; Westend61; monkeybusinessimages/iStock/Getty Images Plus; Michael Dunning/Photographer's Choice; majorosl/iStock/Getty Images Plus; Jeff Greenberg/Universal Images Group; funky-data/iStock/Getty Images Plus; onurdongel/iStock/Getty Images Plus; Pekka SakkI/AFP; Pola Damonte/Moment; monkeybusinessimages/iStock/Getty Images Plus; Inti St Clair/Blend Images; Andy Cross/The Denver Post; Helena Schaeder Söderberg/Moment; Hero Images; Hoxton/Tom Merton; Sascha Steinbach/Getty Images Entertainment; Hill Street Studios/Blend Images; JaruekChairak/iStock/Getty Images Plus; Jupiterimages/PHOTOS.com/Getty Images Plus; Philippe TURPIN/Photononstop; darioracane/iStock/Getty Images Plus; Roger de la Harpe/Gallo Images; LeoPatrizi/E+; Lucidio Studio, Inc/Moment; **PVB**: Image Source; narvikk/E+; BJI/Blue Jean Images; Prasit photo/Moment Open; **SB**: Ronnie Kaufman/Larry Hirshowitz/Blend Images; Hero Images; Caiaimage/Chris Ryan; NoSystem images/E+; Hero Images; filadendron/E+; Henn Photography/Cultura; Juice Images; Joe Beynon/Perspectives.

The following photographs have been sourced from other library/sources.

U2: Courtesy of Ørestad Gymnasium; canbedone/Shutterstock; Matt Rourke/AP/Shutterstock; **U3**: Courtesy of Christopher Short; Courtesy of DS Projects, LLC; **U7**: Angela Hampton Picture Library/Alamy Stock Photo; **U8**: Courtesy of Hannah Alper.

Front cover photography by Tetra Images - Erik Isakson/Brand X Pictures/Getty Images; Xinzheng/Moment/Getty Images.

Illustrations

Amerigo Pinelli; Abel Ippolito.

Audio

Produced by Leon Chambers and recorded at The SoundHouse Studios, London

Page make up

Wild Apple Design Ltd